THE SHAPE OF
WARS TO COME

(Continued from front flap)

fiction) exist. It is now possible that a particle beam weapon, mounted on a space vehicle, will be able to destroy nuclear missiles as they are launched, thus enforcing peace. Yet an enhanced version of that device could destroy *all* life in the country against which it is used.

David Baker has an impressive array of qualifications to write on this subject, including a Ph.D. in earth and planetary sciences and a diploma in astronautics. He has worked with NASA both in Houston and at the Washington, DC headquarters. During the past five years he has been deeply involved in mission planning for the space shuttle system.

Jacket photo: National Aeronautics and Space Administratio
Jacket design: Bob McBroom
0-8128-2852-6

THE SHAPE OF
WARS
TO COME

DAVID BAKER

Foreword by General George Keegan

Chief, US Air Force Intelligence (Retd)

𝔰𝔡
STEIN AND DAY / *Publishers* / New York

First published in the United States of America in 1982
First published in Great Britain in 1981 by Patrick Stephens Limited
Copyright © 1981, 1982 by David Baker

Designed by Louis A. Ditizio

Printed in the United States of America

STEIN AND DAY/*Publishers*
Scarborough House
Briarcliff Manor, N.Y. 10510

Library of Congress Cataloging in Publication Data

Baker, David, 1944-
   The shape of wars to come.

   Includes index.
   1. Space warfare. I. Title.
UG1530.B34 1982   358'.8   81-48447
ISBN 0-8128-2852-6   AACR2

Picture credits
The author would like to thank the following for providing pictures
for this book: Maurice Allward, Aeronautic Ford Corporation, Associ-
ated ·Press, Bell Aerosystems Co, Boeing Aerospace, Vince Driver,
Flight International, Ford Aerospace, Fotokhronika Tass, General
Dynamics, Hughes Corporation, Lockheed, Martin Marietta Aero-
space, McDonnell Douglas, NASA, Novosti Press Agency, Philco
Corporation, RCA, Rockwell Int, Stephen Smyth, TRW, United Press
International UK Ltd, US Air Force, USIS, US Navy.

Frontispiece *Rockwell International's Navstar global positioning system satellite.*

Contents

Foreword   7

Introduction   11

Scenario   15

1. Lines of constraint   19

2. Orbital eyes   45

3. The Soviet ploy   71

4. The military mission in space   105

5. Sentinels and killersats   139

6. The big lift   169

7. The ultimate threat   205

8. Star Raker   241

Appendix   258

Index   259

(Photos between pages 70 and 71 and pages 168 and 169.)

Foreword

Space has become an extension of the Earth battlefield. Soon it will dominate that battlefield—as it now controls America's strategic peace-keeping potential.

The world of H.G. Wells and Buck Rogers is upon us. And science fiction is now edging on reality. Regrettably, but not irretrievably, the world's most threatening imperial force is seeking to control and dominate the "high ground" of near space, that it may more effectively impose its will upon the troubled Earth below.

America's utopian dream of "Space for Peace" has been rudely shattered. Just as the Columbus explorations of the New World opened the greatest flowering of Western Civilization, it also brought a level of depravity, death and destruction unprecedented in human history. Then, as now, the opportunity for enhancing the human condition was at hand. The opportunity remains with us. It shall be the measure of man's nobility of spirit that he will learn from his past, apply his free will, and make space the channel and vehicle for structuring a better and more peaceful way.

The free have less than a decade to decide.

Events depicted in this volume *are* the new reality! In fact, space is now the key to free world survival—or extinction. Unfortunately, only the Forces of Darkness are seeking to capture the high ground. The vision of a utopian peace has blinded America's diplomats, scientists and political leaders. And so the tragic events of the 1930s are to unfold upon us once again. On a scale that boggles the mind.

By mid-decade, the Soviet Union will probably have a deployed capability to destroy all of America's satellites, most of its retaliatory missile forces and, with Russia's existing civil defenses, she will be fully capable of withstanding and surviving any leakage of nuclear weapons fired in retaliation. High energy lasers and particle beam

7

weapons—both pioneered by the Soviets—are the revolutionary new tools of space warfare. They will neutralize America's strategic deterrent and invalidate most of the free world's conventional land, sea, air and logistic forces as currently structured and employed.

One "directed energy weapon" (laser or particle beam) based in space may be capable of destroying hundreds of satellites and re-entry vehicles or missiles per minute. The particle beam may also be capable of destroying thousands of important land- or sea-based targets with surgical precision and blast impacts ranging from sub- to multi-megaton. Within minutes! A high energy laser gun aboard an orbital vehicle could probably fire several thousand precisely aimed sub-kiloton non-nuclear bursts against key ground targets in but one orbit of the Earth. Not in recorded history have science, technology and imperial ambition combined to achieve so much destruction, over such a wide area, so quickly. Regrettably, few if any of these extraordinary possibilities have ever been made public or discussed with responsible members of the US Congress. Yet, while the West sleeps, a chilling body of evidence and basic scientific research data continues to be produced which the highly politicized CIA, along with its richly subsidized stable of Left-leaning pro-disarmament consultants, refuse to accept lest such acceptance put at risk their utopian hopes for SALT, detente and the diplomacy of appeasement.

Short-sightedness about space is not new. The Tsiolkovskys, Jules Vernes, Goddards, H.G. Wellses, Herman Oberths and Hollywood fantasisers have been closer to the mark. In the 1950s, the US Strategic Air Command was working on the blueprints for *Orion*, a nuclear-powered spaceship capable of keeping the peace in space throughout this century. About 25 years ago a space plane of limitless range was in design. A nuclear rocket engine was working. Ion propulsion engines were under active development. All were cancelled by utopian non-visionaries.

Later, the US foresaw the opportunity to improve the efficacy of both its arms-control diplomacy and military capabilities through the innovative use of non-offensive space technology. By the early '60s, cameras deployed in space monitoring Soviet compliance with arms treaties and accurate surveillance of strategic forces and deployments were under way. Soviet communications and electronic emissions were being monitored. Accurate global weather prediction, early warning of Soviet nuclear attack, global communication and command networks for the control and direction of military forces and precise navigation for ships and submarines at sea were all being provided through space. By the 1970s, US dependence upon space had reached such a point that it was no longer possible for the US to deploy or employ its military and transport capabilities except through use of its vulnerable space technology.

In the 1950s, the Soviets clearly foresaw the enormous potential for space technology, along with the possibilities for wresting a military advantage and exploiting the remarkable vulnerability of the US in space.

Thus, while the US was being seduced by its self-inflicted doctrine of "Space for Peace," SALT, detente, technology transfer and "tacit" understandings that the Soviets would do nothing to interfere with US space-borne "means of verification," the Soviets were experimenting with and deploying "orbital" weapons systems, depressed-trajectory intercontinental rockets designed to evade our warning radars, satellite killers, high energy lasers and the revolutionary particle beam weapons which are now being tested in operational prototype (pre-production) form.

But all is not lost. The Soviets can still be checkmated. The first step has been taken by the return to common sense and reality in our relations with the Soviet Union as characterized by the Thatcher and Reagan Governments. Secondly, there are some highly creative *young* US engineering groups who are prepared to reassert US technological creativity and recover the lost high ground. Thanks to the solitary persistence of US Air Force Intelligence—in the face of near total opposition by all relevant agencies of the Government, including the White House and the office of the Secretary of Defense (both commit-ted to SALT at any price), the US could now probably beat the Soviets at their own game by deploying the *first* generation of space-borne directed energy weapons. The implications—for being able to restore military balance or for not doing so—are simply staggering. The potential for near total defense against nuclear weapons *and* for the offensive destruction of prime military targets on land, at sea and in space surpasses all military weapons development in this or any other century.

There are other possibilities. The military balance—long since lost by the US and NATO—can now be restored quickly and at bargain basement investment costs. The present restoration of strategic deterrence as crudely perceived by the Reagan administration will require hundreds of billions of dollars, decades of time and involve challenging the Soviet military-industrial-technological base with its presently unmatchable momentum. Directed energy weapons provide an opportunity to revolutionize deterrence for virtually all levels of nuclear or conventional warfare at affordable costs, before we reach the maximum window of danger in 1985. Ironically, such a commitment now provides the only realistic basis, in my judgment, for meaningful and equitable arms control diplomacy obviating two decades of Soviet deception, cheating and violation.

The failure to mobilize free world technological potential now—on an urgent basis—is to invite the worst visions of H.G. Wells. The future is at hand as is the survival of freedom. Space is their handmaiden and the primary area for reversing the potential of Soviet science, technology and hegemonic ambitions.

This gripping and timely volume brings us to the edge of a much needed perception that space is the new battlefield. If the new imperialists are allowed to dominate that battlefield, little imagination is required to visualize the outcome. In control of the industrial democracies the high ground becomes a servant of the free and an instrument serving mankind's continuing quest for peace. The oldest lesson of history—least recalled—is that peace is preserved only through strength. All recorded efforts in history to substitute arms control diplomacy for the maintenance of adequate peace-time defenses has invariably led to or accelerated the onset of war. We cannot allow history to repeat itself.

George J. Keegan, Jr.

Major General George J. Keegan, Jr.
USAF (Retd), former Chief, US Air Force Intelligence.

Introduction

This book has been written because of the author's deep concern for the stability of international relations and the expanding commitment of the Soviet Union to achieve by military pressure, and perhaps force, what it is increasingly unable to obtain by persuasion and negotiation. More than twenty years ago an American President warned of the dangers inherent in a military-industrial complex unfettered from policial oversight. Left to run amok, the Soviet military machine is an example of a new totalitarianism, a force that has no room for controlled legislation evolved as an integral part of the "people's democracy" it purports to represent.

Added upon the unceasing application of common technologies to the works of war, Soviet research into hostile, space-based weapon systems has led to a universal search for directed-energy devices capable of transforming the equations of conflict and dramatically upsetting the balance of terror that for more than three decades has kept a fragile stability while the world moved toward universal coexistence. That coexistence will be shattered if either side gets the powerful capacity for insulating its populations from the effects of nuclear war. The tragedy of power-balance is that the disarmers are right when they say nuclear weapons are too terrible to use, for it is that belief that validates the concept of deterrence. But there is a subtle division between weapons of mass destruction that serve to keep a balanced peace and those that provide unequivocal advantage to the owner.

Directed energy weapons—lasers and particle beams—are in that category. There can be no balance where one side has superiority because the conditions that prevailed before Russia had the Bomb no longer apply. For nearly a decade after the war the United States alone had the power to incinerate the world. In that period more countries obtained freedom and independent rule than at any other time this century. A willingness to coexist prevailed. But the decades since have fostered a belligerent Soviet Union that would not receive again the same ingratiating concessions were the West to obtain superiority in lasers and particle beams. Moreover, because of superiority in conventional weapons, the Soviets would not refrain from using influence snatched through power, if they became the first to get the beam devices. Only in the ridiculous notion of mutual agreement to develop, at the same rate simultaneously, the weapons that unilaterally would invoke superiority for one side or the other could the balance be retained in the post-nuclear age of directed energy beams.

It is up to the reader to determine whether it is in the best interests of either side to develop these systems or whether the time has come to work for a universal ban on weapons in space. There exists a treaty preventing the orbiting of "weapons of mass destruction" but the language of this accord excludes the legal definition of lasers and particle beams, permitting either side to exploit the ambiguity. At present, but not for long, it would be feasible to construct an international resolve to preserve space as the Antarctica for tomorrow's world, free from weapons and territorial claim, as a research place for science and a new domain for commercial applications. Unconstrained, however, the search for balance and reciprocation will drag both superpowers into the abyss of a new arms race far more damaging than the search for nuclear superiority.

In a very short space of time the world has become dependent on space systems for communication and navigation, for the weather forecasts so glibly taken for granted and for the earth resource surveys that reveal new fossil fuel deposits. Yet, largely unpublicized, the environment of the soldier, the sailor and the airman has also become populated with satellites vital to the prosecution of war. Now, unimaginable weapons are nearing completion that seem difficult to accept as a part of life today. But they are here and the turning point has arrived.

In a very real sense, Man stands at the crossroads of his destiny. Either he uses space for the benefit of all, helping to solve global problems that face the entire species, or he travels down the road leading to self-destruction. It is vitally important that these serious issues are broadened to the larger platform of wide public debate, for they will not wait. It is time to stop and face reality and to decide now, today, whether this is our future or whether we are capable of taking the bolder decisions that promise a better world for all people everywhere. There is a stop-watch on decision, and when time runs out it will be too late, the post-nuclear age will have arrived.

Scenario

It is 1995. For several days technicians have worked around the clock to prepare the Block 774 payload for Space Division's Star Raker-1. Soon, the hardware will be in orbit and the President of the United States will have an ace of unprecedented magnitude in his hand; the Soviets have gone too far, the stakes are too big, something has to keep resources flowing west.

It is just after dawn, the big Sun only a few degrees atop the glassy horizon, when the massive delta-winged transport ship edges its way out to Canaveral's main runway. It looks so benign in that tranquility before the hectic preparations for flight; a few engineers walking alongside the big bogies, each supporting eight small wheels, technicians leaning on the ground support trucks, and somewhere further down the Cape a three-man crew don flight suits and headsets. Soon, the ground tug has Star Raker in position and a personnel van brings the men assigned to fly this all-important mission.

The events of the past year seem to have brought their own anti-climax and the reality of the moment is difficult to accept. The old Party ranks have broken from the Kremlin, replaced now by hard-line military officials dominating Soviet policies—how different the days of Brezhnev and Kosygin when super-powers jostled passively on the international scene. Deepening economic problems in America have seen disorder on a massive scale. The President has just introduced strict fuel rationing and only the tension of a worsening crisis in the Middle East seems to have stopped, temporarily, the onward rush of domestic anarchy.

Everywhere, people hold their breath and wait for the inevitable holocaust. Internationally bankrupt, due to diminishing oil resources, Soviet power leans toward the Indian Ocean for possession and control of vast oil fields in the Middle East. Threatened by a massive build-up on its border, Saudi Arabia calls for US protection while the junta leaders in India—shocked by the sudden turn of events—appeal to the Soviets for assurances of security.

If it comes to war the entire planet will be engulfed in conflict and both the Soviet Premier and US President know they would have to use their ultimate deterrent. Russia has just completed tests with her ground-based particle beam device designed to screen Soviet territory from incoming warheads; America is ready with an orbital device for the same purpose. Check-mate, if only Star Raker can reach orbit with its payload intact. For then America will have its anti-ballistic-missile defense in space and it will be another day before the super-powers again rattle their sabres in haste.

The Sun is high in the Florida sky as the ten massive turbofans along the trailing edge of Star Raker's delta wing send thunder claps across the Cape. Minutes later the flight control center gives its clearance for take-off, computers having checked every system, and the 2,300 ton freighter accelerates down the runway which only two years before carried the last Shuttle atronauts into space. Extended now to accommodate the Shuttle's replacement, it provides the necessary 3½ km path along which Star Raker now rolls before lifting cleanly into the bright sky.

For a while the transporter gains altitude lifting, under the forward thrust of the ten turbofans, to a height of 6 km before levelling out and starting the long cruise due south toward the Equator. En route, the crew turn to a full systems check while the onboard computers receive signals from orbiting navsats and steer Star Raker on the appropriate course for a rendezvous with airspace due north of Quito on the South American continent.

It takes nearly three hours, cruising just below the speed of sound at about 890 km/hr, to cross the Caribbean and reach that rendezvous point. All the while, satellites in space monitor air traffic within a 5 km corridor either side of Star Raker's flight path to watch for hostile Soviet intruders and wandering commercial aircraft. The world is not yet at war but in the next few hours, anything could release the trigger.

It is noon local time as Star Raker nears the equatorial rendezvous point and in the final 30 minutes the three crewmembers work down a comprehensive checklist ensuring the correct sequence of events to bring the expected results from myriad subsystems on board. It is time to change course and, as the coast of Ecuador comes into view far ahead and 6 km below, the massive space freighter slowly banks over to the left, holding that angle as the 94 m long Star Raker turns to a due east heading.

Quito is now off to the right and the flight systems engineer catches a fleeting glimpse of the sprawling South American city as a count-down begins on Star Raker's flight deck which would start the ascent into space. Already, Star Raker has accelerated past the speed of sound and at zero, three big rocket engines fuelled with hydrogen and oxygen stored in the fuselage, wings and tail, thunder into life and the freighter surges forward under the combined thrust of 13 propulsion units.

Minutes later, at a height of 32 km and a speed of 7,900 km/hr, the ten turbofans are shut down and massive ramp doors in front of the air intakes slide shut to protect the engines. On and up in a shallow climb, Star Raker accelerates at 2.7 g toward space, passing now across the Atlantic. At a height of 122 km the trajectory flattens out and the space freighter accelerates to a speed of nearly 26,700 km/hr. Seconds later the main rocket engines cut off and Star Raker is in orbit, drifting in an elliptical path which would carry it to an apogee of 556 km.

About 50 minutes later it reaches that high point and a set of small rocket motors fire briefly to circularize the path. Over the next several hours the freighter maneuvers toward a large cylindrical space tug placed in orbit several months before to ferry cargo up to stationary orbit and to return, if necessary, with redundant hardware. When the Star Raker crew bring the two vehicles to within a few meters, four large doors on top of the freighter slide back down inside the fuselage walls, exposing the cargo bay, 43 m long and 6.1 m in diameter. Inside, the large, elongated shape of Block 774 slowly raises itself out of the bay on telescope rods which now extend their full 15 m in length.

On a television screen somewhere inside Star Raker-1, a crewmember controls the space tug, maneuvering it in by radio signals from a hand controller at his side. Soon, the tug has coupled its circular docking collar to the attachment ring at one end of payload 774, now standing proud above the top of the open fuselage. Docked together, the tug and its payload move lazily to one side of the giant winged freighter; two small rocket motors burn briefly and Star Raker slides away, distance between the two increasing visibly.

Minutes later, again on command from the freighter's flight deck, the tug's engines pulse into life and begin the long haul up to a height of nearly 36,000 km while far below Star Raker-1 monitors the burn. Several hours later a second firing of the tug's motors pushes the massive Block 774 payload into a stationary path centered on the Equator just north of the Seychelles. Thus positioned over the Indian Ocean, the tug slips its shackles and moves back. It will return to Star Raker's lower orbit, leaving payload 774 in place.

For the next few hours, whenever the freighter comes within view of the stationary orbit satellite, a flurry of commands go up and reports are received from computers aboard payload 774. It is not too long before Star Raker's commander places a call to the White House via the global strategic communication satellite service: mission accomplished.

The President, too, reaches for a telephone, the one which links other satellites to Moscow. What he says tells the Soviet Premier that America has just placed in orbit the first operational US beam weapon capable of neutralizing Russian ICBMs as they ascend from their underground silos. Only months before, the Soviets had completed deployment of their own land-based system, essentially achieving the same objective. It is stalemate; nobody can strike the other with the holocaust of armageddon.

THE SHAPE OF
WARS TO COME

1. Lines of constraint

Principles and beginnings

It was, perhaps, to have been expected that when man first sent artificial satellites into space it would similarly be the dawn of a nuclear age where massive ballistic missiles provided world powers with unprecedented muscle. After all, one does depend upon the other. Yet for all that, the first quarter-century of space exploration has been remarkably free from the threats many people felt were an inevitable postscript to satellites and Moon flight. Only now, in the closing years of the 20th century, are the military muscles of East and West acquiring tremendous capacities in the form of unimaginable weapon systems which will relegate nuclear bombs to the museum of war.

Today, in the vanguard of research and development, scientists and engineers are desperately seeking answers to bold questions no-one before thought seriously to ask. Are there such things as laser weapons? Do particle-beam energies promise to bring unthinkable destructive potential? Can another generation fight World War 3 by proxy in space and spare the weeping billions on Earth who would otherwise be left groping for light on a radiation-drenched planet? Science is today at the crossroads of decision and no one knows for sure whether such things will be possible within the forseeable future, let alone a practical reality for ultimate application. Developments of the present seem to point convincingly at the theories which say such might is there to unlock, given the added knowledge a new generation of learning may bring. But for the moment, plans are available should those systems become a practical proposition.

As if marked out neatly in calendar time, the turn of the 1970s into a new decade has brought reality to military space plans for the '80s and a new range of technical resources available to the super-powers can open dramatic opportunities to pave the way for lasers, beam weapons, and proxy-war in the cold vacuum of orbital space lanes. It really only wanted a major world event to trigger the door on new and urgent fighting machines, and that event was handed to the military planners of the Western World when a cruel invasion of neutral Afghanistan sent a weak leader to swift execution and a new government to seats of power.

In the closing days of the old decade, while people around the globe celebrated the birth of Christ nearly 2,000 years ago, massed infantry divisions of the Soviet Red Army poured across the border to crush dissent among people outside the Russian orbit. Within two months the Soviet divisions had control of the capital, Kabul, established killing zones in mountains to the south and had shock armies on Soviet territory to east and west of the Caspian Sea ready to encircle Tehran in neighboring Iran. Thus cut off from their own forces, Iranians so recently elevated by riot and anarchy to the haughty ranks of political independence would wait helpless as the forces from Afghanistan raced for the Straits of Hormuz, blocking the Persian Gulf.

That final move did not come, but there hangs today across the veiled skies of the old Persian Empire a sword of Damocles, ready at an instant to threaten the entire middle East. If there was a single turning point in the affairs of states East and West, it was the military campaign in Afghanistan during December 1979. If there was ever a time when a US President resolved never again to placate the Communist threat with words and treaties, it was during the days following the invasion when Jimmy Carter understood with irony the threats so many had warned him to avoid.

From the very first day of 1980, the hope for sustained co-existence seemed never quite as close to reality as it had in preceding years. And so, at the close of the old decade and at the beginning of the new, both the mood and capability for war emerged simultaneously where the ability to develop and obtain new technology for hostile ends appeared at the same time as the political and military necessity for exploitation.

It had happened once before, when mood and capability met in 1961 and President John F. Kennedy used a Moon landing goal to placate concerned Americans about strident Soviet aggression. This time, the product was to be more diabolical than footprints on another world. The lessons from Afghanistan were to reverberate through every foreign policy initiative planned by the US State Department, for as Secretary of State Cyrus Vance said in March 1980, "We confront a serious and sustained Soviet challenge, which is both military and political. Their military build-up continues unabated. The Soviet Union has shown a greater willingness to employ that power directly, and through others. In that sense, Afghanistan is a manifestation of a larger problem."

And so the die was cast. Many Congressmen and Senators who before had shown reluctant agreement with nuclear weapons treaties favoring Soviet might, now openly opposed constraint; deeply offended by the brutal machinations of the puppet regime set up from the Kremlin, international morality forbade acquiescence. Flagrant contravention of international space treaties drawn up by United Nations in the 1960s had been shown by Soviet Russia in tests with systems desgined to destroy or cripple foreign satellites in Earth orbit. For more than ten years the Russians had flaunted their "killersats" before the West, throwing up targets only to demonstrate a chase vehicle dispatched to fly close on a mission of potential destruction. For more than ten years the United States watched and waited, reluctant to exploit this ostensibly scientific medium for the purposes of conflict. Endlessly, the Soviets refused to vacate the space lanes and consistently showed blatant disregard for UN pressure to outlaw the use of weapons above Earth's atmosphere. In the wake of political, military, and psychological pressure brought to bear on the West, President Carter authorized the development of a reciprocal system. And so began the journey toward space weapons which could transform the way nations wage war. It was not always this way. Seemingly very long ago, but actually only three decades, the prospect of space travel tentatively approached reality in technical studies carried out by leading aviation companies and industrial contractors. Even then, in 1950, it all seemed so unreal, and yet there were men who openly professed their belief in the imminent availability of space flight for the investigation of our own Earth from orbit, for the scientific study of other worlds by manned robots, and for the use of new technology for better management of our natural resources. Such talk had once been the prophecy of extremists and the writers of comic strip stories; now, the men who shaped Germany's nascent rocket program two decades before were planning the colonization of other worlds. Wernher von Braun, the effervescent spokesman for space travel, helped promote at meetings organized by *Collier's Magazine* a genuine feeling of hope that, with the tools soon to be available, man would reach out for the stars. In the Army, to which von Braun had been assigned on transfer from a defeated Germany, studies already in existence proved the feasibility of such claims.

While operating under the aegis of Nazism, the German rocket men had forged schemes for using the V-2 as a prototype for larger vehicles capable of placing an artificial satellite in orbit. Free now to exploit their theories, the engineers wrote technical papers on how this could be accomplished and supported research programs at US Government facilities. The Air Force, too, had its eye on space. In fact everyone was sure of the role for man in space but nobody was clear just who should manage such a program.

The importance of getting in on the act was highlighted by events in Soviet Russia. For a while after the end of World War 2 suspicion about the intent of opposing forces restrained cooperation between America and the Soviet Union until the different political systems moved to a grudging acceptance of peaceful co-existence. Throughout, however, the United States was fearful of the ascending might of Soviet military power and, when Russia refused to expose its true strength, rumor went wild on what the Soviets were planning and what they were building. World domination, an unyielding principle of Marxist thought, seemed to be an important part of Russian doctrine and it was in an aura of suspicion that military intelligence estimates of Soviet potential went far beyond the actual capabilities of Soviet forces and Russian scientists. On the surface it all looked very convincing. Just four years after America acquired the atomic bomb Russia, too, exploded a nuclear device, news of the Soviet test being given by a somber Harry Truman, then US President, in a radio broadcast during late September 1949.

By now, scientists in America were sure the atom bomb was merely a precursor weapon on the road to something much more horrific and, where many had throught Hiroshima to represent the ultimate in mass destruction, a few began to unlock the equations which would release thermo-nuclear power. For a while there had been frank debate on the morality, and the political desirability, of pressing ahead with large-scale development of the so-called hydrogen bomb. But when Soviet Russia was observed to have acquired a working atom bomb by diligent research, the decision to move on was inevitable. Truman authorized work to continue.

It had seemed a wise move when, in June 1950, just six months after Truman announced development of the hydrogen bomb, communist forces invaded South Korea and the United States moved a step closer to the precipice of global war with Russia. On November 1, 1952, the world's first hydrogen bomb was detonated with an explosive yield 350 times that of the atomic bomb dropped on Hiroshima more than seven years before. One year later the Russians dropped their own hydrogen bomb and the world was in the nuclear age with a vengeance. Nothing, it seemed to many Americans, could stop the onward rush of Soviet war-mongering. It was not just a political threat, more a crusade against mighty forces and all the drama of little England facing alone the forces of Nazi Germany was re-kindled with different players. So it was, by the early 1950s, that leading advisers to the Pentagon were strident in their conviction that what Soviet Russia threatened to develop or possess must be reciprocally acquired by the United States. The concept of Mutually Assured Destruction (MAD) staving off the day of violence was well and truly embedded in geopolitical doctrine. It was from this that military men finally prised open government coffers for money to build large rockets, the most effective way of quickly delivering the new weapons for nuclear war.

Intelligence reports consistently spoke of Soviet work on rocket projects and that did, after all, make very good sense for the Russians were without the large bomber fleet possessed by the United States, or bases close to the borders of their potential adversary. While technical and scientific studies realized the feasibility of nuclear weapons small enough to be contained within the nose cone of a single missile, command structures evolved to give the Air Force and the Army an administrative organization for the new projects. For many years the Army had assumed the right to act on behalf of defense interests by controlling research and development on missile projects; the Air Force had promoted several ballistic rocket designs but received little support from politicians except where rocket-propelled, air-launched projectiles were concerned. The Army had received the surrender of von Braun and his men in southern Germany during May 1945, and they had returned 120 German rocket engineers to Fort Bliss, Texas, before the end of the year. Almost exactly five years later the Army research facility moved lock, stock and barrel to Redstone Arsenal near Huntsville, Alabama, there to build the medium-range rockets deemed essential in the wake of Korean hostility.

Von Braun was technical director and his men moved several steps ahead of current plans in concepts formulated for the future use of rocket propulsion. In February 1956, with Redstone and Jupiter missiles developed and in production, the Army sought to strengthen its hold on the research and development field. Redstone Arsenal came under the control of the newly formed Army Ballistic Missile Agency (ABMA) with responsibility for design of future systems and management of the industrial contractors responsible for building elements of rocket vehicles.

The very nature of military thinking was conducive to Army control for long-range missile programs. Back in the 1930s, Major Walter Dornberger took control of the German Army's rocket plans, recruiting von Braun among others to concentrate on developing a projectile ultimately known as the V-2. Dornberger was an ex-artillery man who thought of rockets in terms of self-propelled shells rather than an extension of winged flight or, for that matter, a new form of transport and conveyance in themselves. When the German engineers, impregnated with this view, came to the United States, the politicians and strategists concurred with this view and the Army became convinced they alone should have command and control of what were even then being confidently termed intercontinental ballistic missiles, or ICBMs.

Yet, separate from Army research, and quite independent of anything developed by the von Braun team, the Convair company successfully convinced the Air Force of the value of a proposed ICBM which could fly half-way round the globe and deliver an atomic bomb wherever it was assigned. Eventually called Atlas, the project suffered nearly a full decade of stop-go policies until emerging ultimately in 1954 as a ballistic missile project using propulsion systems originally developed for an Air Force winged missile. In July of that year the Air Force set up its Western Development Division, an arm of the existing Air Research and Development Command, and began the chain of developments which would ultimately be responsible for all military interests in space. By the end of 1956 the WDD had a work load which included not only Atlas but a complementary ICBM called Titan and a missile of more modest capacity called Thor. The latter was intended as an Air Force equivalent to Army developments and would be deployed in Britain to counter Soviet threats along the European flank.

By now the Redstone rocket was at the end of its development and the Army Ballistic Missile Agency only had the Jupiter rocket for which it had temporarily received support from the Navy for application as a submarine-launched projectile, ultimately to emerge as Polaris. When the Navy dropped out of the combined Army-Navy project that left Jupiter with only one customer and, by the end of 1956, the missile had been taken from the ABMA and given to the Air Force. Lines of demarcation were now clear. The Air Force would be responsible for ballistic missile development, with the Army taking care of battlefield or tactical missiles only. However, the Army had built up the nation's most valuable asset for future applications in space. In acquiring the von Braun team the Army had tapped the most successful think-tank capable of transforming ideas into practicality. By 1956 the needs of future programs had already inspired grand concepts and the Huntsville Germans conceived the idea of clustered rockets, literally binding together as a single booster several Redstone or Jupiter rockets to form a mighty launch vehicle of immense size and power. Rather than build from the ground up a new and unique design based on untried technology, the think-tank short-circuited the problem, coming up with a plan which would, as time revealed, provide America with big boosters quicker than any other method then available.

By this time, dreams and ideas about space travel were slowly maturing into firm plans in Russia and America. But not only in the two super-powers. Britain too was forging important links in the development chain leading to space flight. Shortly after the cessation of hostilities in 1945, technical examination of the captured V-2 rockets inspired members of the British Interplanetary Society—still an active body for promoting advanced space technology, the oldest rocket society in continuous existence—to use this offensive weapon as the basis for a manned test-bed. It would be possible, said the BIS, to improve the performance of the V-2 and attach to its nose a capsule carrying a man on a specially adapted seat to withstand comparatively high forces of acceleration, or "g" loads. In this way, it should be possible, said the proponents, to propel a test pilot well above Earth's atmosphere and thereby sample for the first time the experience of weightlessness, thought by some to pose hazards for space travellers. It was hardly space *flight,* since the rocket case would be a ballistic shell not unlike an artillery projectile, but it would have provided early experiment results on the physiology of high-speed travel. The Ministry of Supply was not convinced and promptly shelved the idea. It would probably have received little publicity had not Chapman Pincher of the *Daily Express* boldly written about the possibilities for scientific study such a project would obtain. But post-war Britain was only just beginning to pull itself round to some semblance of normality; there were no funds for such an operation and many doubted public acceptance of a scheme so firmly based on German technology. Yet for all that, "Megaroc," as the project was called, would have provided quicker and cheaper access to ballistic high-altitude flight than any comparable scheme available at the time.

Elsewhere, another member of the illustrious British Interplanatary Society, science writer and fiction author Arthur C. Clarke, wrote in May 1945, that, "there is at least one purpose for which the [space] station is ideally suited and indeed has no practical alternative . . . ." He went on to say that a satellite, or station, placed above the Equator at a distance of about 36,000 km would appear to remain stationary above Earth and would, "greatly simplify the use of direction receivers installed on the Earth." Clarke proposed the use of artificial satellites placed in stationary orbit for communications between separate continents since nearly one-half of the planet would be in view to radio antennae placed on such a satellite. In beaming a signal from one point to the satellite and then retransmitting the signal to another point several thousand kilometers distant, vast areas of the globe would be covered for radio communication, linking people in remote areas or ships and aircraft over large seas and oceans. It was a novel proposition, not quite the first in the field since several lesser known prophets had suggested similar schemes two decades before. But coming at a time when rocket flight by V-2 was an established fact, it lent credence to what many had considered a ridiculous notion. Clarke was thinking with the uncluttered mind of a theoretician and, like so many in parallel fields, had little inkling of the ultimate use of such technology in space; driven by the expediency of political and military need, the stationary orbit would become invaluable for maintaining peace.

In America, the Navy Bureau of Aeronautics studied the question of space flight, recognizing the value orbiting vehicles would have for military control. The Navy wanted to develop a satellite vehicle, but the then Director for the Office of Scientific Research and Development, Dr Vannevar Bush, protested at talk of intercontinental ballistic rockets, saying, "such a thing is impossible for many years." Bush went on to affirm his belief that: "The people who have been writing these things that annoy me have been talking about a 4,800 km high-angle rocket shot from one continent to another, carrying an atomic bomb, and so directed as to be a precise weapon which would land on a certain target such as this city. I say technically I don't think anybody in the world knows how to do such a thing . . . we can leave that out of our thinking."

Dr Bush was addressing in particular the concept of ICBMs but his opposition extended to all debate on Earth-circling satellites. The Air Force, meanwhile, working on their own studies, commissioned the Rand Corporation to prepare a report on an Experimental World-Circling Spaceship. Ready by May 1946, the report proposed a four-stage rocket weighing 106 tons at launch for placing a payload of 277 kg in a 480 km high orbit. Nowhere in the report was there a breath of condemnation for the basic idea; technically, the project was sound and could begin immediately, if approved, for culmination by 1951. It was not approved simply because the politicians, and several theoretical scientists, refused to believe such a venture to be in the best interests of US defense policy, failing to foresee the day when such programs would be an essential part of military needs. But it took two years for the Navy and Air Force proposals to die down, strenuous efforts by many personnel playing important parts kept the project in the pending tray.

The Navy was not to be diverted and pressed hard to pursue its own High Altitude Test Vehicle. With a more modest weight of 46 tons, HATV would be propelled into orbit on the thrust of nine separate rocket motors, reaching a circular path 241 km above the Earth's surface. Yet by 1948 depleted funds from Washington starved the project of the sustenance essential for getting it off the drawing boards and into metal. Meanwhile, the Air Force received strident criticism from Press reports deeply concerned with the apparent waste of public money on such needless effort. Taking its case to the Rand Corporation, the Air Force received, in 1949, affirmation that satellites had a vital role to play in the defense of the United States and that the observation and surveillance of potentially hostile countries from space was the only sensible way to conduct such activity. The argument was convincing, but with heavy responsibilities for developing a nuclear capability, defense chiefs were too busy with other programs to set up yet another major technology venture. Apart from that, ambitious calls for sateillite surveillance seemed a long way off compared to existing research, only then beginning to embrace the comparatively small Redstone rocket.

So it was that in the early 1950s, all talk of space travel and Earth-orbiting satellites was relegated to private debate or discussion groups set up to invite public participation. It was in the open forum of a meeting run by *Collier's Magazine* during October 1951 that the American public first heard serious proposals for the colonization of space. For von Braun was not thinking alone in terms of stationary orbit satellites or spy-vehicles from space. His vision was one which embraced convoys of manned spaceships descending to the dusty lunar plains before assembling the first assault on Mars.

In books which appeared with precise technical details for the missions then envisaged, design layouts and systems' plans were carefully revealed to endorse the viability of such seemingly ambitious schemes. And on careful examination of the facts it certainly appeared plausible, for Air Force and Navy experiments with rocket-powered aircraft were already pointing toward space, preparing the public mind for the most radical concepts in transportation.

When von Braun publicly discussed plans for Moon flight, the Navy's Skyrocket research aircraft had already flown to a height of more than 24 km and nearly twice the speed of sound. The Air Force's X-1, used to propel a man through the speed of sound for the first time in 1947, had thoroughly researched the supersonic and transonic flight regimes, and development of the X-2 was in hand with a promised performance carrying manned flight through Mach 2. But still, in late 1951, the prospect of building giant rockets for space seemed difficult for the public to accept. The Redstone rocket, only recently commissioned, weighed 28 tons and provided a thrust of 34 tons from its single engine; Jupiter was still several years away from inception. Yet von Braun was far ahead of even the Atlas concept which would emerge late in that decade with a weight of more than 100 tons. To build the prototype space station in Earth orbit, the German rocket engineer proposed a spaceship standing 81 m tall with a weight of 7,000 tons. Carrying 36 tons of cargo it would lift off under the combined thrust of 51 rocket motors at the base with a total thrust of 14,000 tons. The second stage would take over at a height of 40 km, igniting its 34 rocket motors for a combined thrust of 1,750 tons. That stage would burn out and separate at a height of 64 km, falling like its predecessor back to the Earth's surface. The third and final stage was to comprise a winged cargo-carrying transporter with a crew in the nose and five rocket motors in the tail delivering a thrust of 220 tons. It would fire its engines to put itself in an elliptical path 102 km above Earth at the low point, 1,730 km distant at the high point.

After 30 years a winged space transporter would stand ready at the Cape Canaveral launch site with a cargo-carrying capacity almost identical to that of the contraption proposed by von Braun in 1951. Such would have been the progress in technology and materials research that the total launch weight would be less than one-third the original estimate from the German rocket designer. Called the Space Shuttle, it would use only seven rocket motors to reach orbit compared with a total 90 motors for the 1951 model! But the winged Earth-orbiting transport of 1951 was to be only the first step toward a major space endeavor culminating in a large wheeled space station built from the cargo of many such transports and a manned Moon ship assembled in Earth orbit. The Moon vehicle would weigh 4,370 tons and be assembled with equipment brought up in 120 ferry flights of the transporter. For the lunar expedition, three such Moon ships would be assembled to support the needs of a total 50 people en route to the Moon and back. In all, 13,110 tons of hardware.

Less than two decades after the von Braun plan was first mooted, three men comprised the first manned Moon flight with two spacecraft weighing a total 44 tons. Suffice it to say that the first serious space flight plans publicly displayed as a definitive design were hardly likely to gather much support. It was all very much in the style of Buck Rogers, and the pressmen said as much in comment across the United States.

However, there were those working in scientific research facilities at the National Advisory Committee for Aeronautics who believed in the prediction that space travel was merely a matter of waiting for the right time and the necessary motivation. NACA had been formed in 1915 to equip America with halls of aeronautical research when Alexander Graham Bell stressed the importance of keeping up with European countries surging ahead on the lessons of World War I. NACA was empowered to research aeronautical developments, a government body unconcerned with commercial or political exploitation. They were in a good position to do what the military men had been prevented from attempting.

One year after von Braun so eloquently campaigned for expensive space projects, the NACA wrote up a specification for rocket-propelled aircraft to replace the X-1, X-2 and Skyrocket designs. It was to be a vehicle capable of exploring the trans-atmospheric region at high Mach numbers. In other words, a winged aircraft designed from the outset to reach heights of more than 60 km and speeds in excess of 6,500 km/hr; existing records were less than half those target levels. It was a start, an official acceptance that man would very soon push his technical challenges beyond the atmosphere. This project would emerge before the end of the 1950s as the X-15, a research aircraft funded by the NACA, the Air Force and the Navy with a rocket engine marginally more powerful than that used to propel the V-2 rocket. It still holds speed and altitude records for winged vehicles not built to fly into space.

The recognition by NACA teams that severe gaps existed between theory and practical test served to highlight the considerable work then necessary to achieve space travel. At Huntsville, von Braun was concerned to get a satellite into orbit first before practical development of manned systems. Scientific opinion endorsed this view in conclusions reached separately to the effect that the United States should use the International Geophysical Year, being 1957, to launch a small sphere into orbit. President Eisenhower was concerned about the global image should America employ military missiles for this feat. He had already soft-pedalled on the development of big military missiles like Atlas and Titan, using cuts in research and development projects to balance the federal budget books. It would not look good if the United States used Redstone or Jupiter to achieve such a prominently scientific goal. Apart from which, Redstone was only marginally capable of lifting a satellite into orbit, and then only if it was fitted with small solid propellant rockets as an additional stage.

Accordingly, Vanguard was brought into being as a civilian venture using new rocket stages derived from the Navy Viking, itself a research tool not built for hostile purposes. Despite major developments in Soviet technology, and the possession of atomic and hydrogen bomb weapons, nobody seriously considered the possibility of Russia also launching satellites into space. The general mood of public opinion in the mid-1950s believed America to be in the lead with all but unimportant areas of research. Yet no one should really have been all that surprised that Russian scientists were actively working on their own project, for Krushchev had ordered top priority for the first Soviet ICBM. There were few other ways to prove to the world that Russia was a real force to be reckoned with than for it to demonstrate sheer power by the ability to place large weights in orbit. Military missiles were always something claimed, but not really seen, to have specific powers; the man in the street could not easily equate scale or size since range or throw-weight were parameters observed only by the most privileged personnel. Satellites, however, were another matter. For then everybody would have a yardstick by which to measure the capability of placing warheads at any desired target on Earth.

Von Braun had talked to a lot of people about the possibility of putting small rockets on the top of Redstone and pushing a satellite into orbit. Many farsighted military men discussed with this German expert matters that even then prompted thoughts about the necessity for control of space. Called Project Orbiter, the Redstone-based plan lay dormant for several years while the civilian Vanguard project slowly moved ahead toward a satellite flight in 1957. In one ironic development during a scheduled rocket test, von Braun had to put sand in the nose cone of his Jupiter C, a derivative of Redstone, to prevent its going into orbit and beating Vanguard to the prized achievement! The irony was that when Vanguard collapsed in a flaming heap weeks after Russia proudly boosted Sputnik I into orbit, von Braun's team were pressed into service to get the Jupiter C ready; two months later it successfully put Explorer 1 in orbit, partially to restore American pride.

The shock waves which reverberated through Congress moved politicians to restore money drawn back by the Eisenhower administration for the big missile projects, and it re-emphasized the need for a serious look at space projects so recently ignored as irrelevant. Suddenly, time and speed were of the essence.

In theoretical concepts worked up by von Braun and his associates, and in design studies completed by the National Advisory Committee for Aeronautics, the road to space travel was assumed, correctly, to depend upon some form of lifting surface by which to recover the terminal stage of the rocket. It was little use adopting military missiles for permanent space applications for they were designed like artillery shells to be used once and thrown away; in fact the idea of physically separating the warhead from the main body of the missile before re-entering Earth's atmoshere was quite a radical concept brought about by the need carefully to shape the nose cone for survival through the air prior to reaching the target.

So winged lifting vehicles formed an integral part of the early proposals and design studies as well as funded projects like the X-15. Given logical sequences of evolutionary development, space vehicles would have matured from designs like this NACA/Air Force/Navy research aircraft. But in the exposed position of having been beaten into orbit, developments could no longer wait for logical patterns of development and expendable, albeit expensive, systems were conceived. Within a few months of Sputnik 1 and Explorer 1 reaching respective space lanes, plans were laid by the armed services for a manned space project. Nobody had a mandate from Congress to pursue such a goal. It merely seemed the right thing to do in the light of Soviet objectives. But man in space was only one goal among many which suddenly became important in that spring of 1958 when the world woke up to the idea that it was, after all, now firmly in the Space Age. Plans which had been quietly maturing in Air Force and Army think-tanks would now stand a real chance of success.

Under the designation Weapon System 117L the Air Force conceived as early as 1954 the workhorse for military space applications, a rocket stage to be lifted into space on the back of Thor or Atlas missiles to which would be attached payloads separated into unique functions. Much of the theory associated with just what was desirable to do in space depended on the forward projections of the propulsion men, for it was no easy thing to place a satellite in orbit and what was to be accomplished, or what was sensible to conceive as a job to be done in space, relied almost exclusively on what the engineer could provide in the form of a rocket stage. So a reliable rocket engine, carried along as a space "bus" with payloads on its back, was the best form of assured access to different orbits.

Lockheed was selected in October 1956 to build the stage which matured from WS-117L. Called the Agena A, it was to provide payload capacity for any one of three specific roles then envisaged: reconnaissance; development of advanced photograhic techniques from orbit; and early warning of missile launches. These projects will be dealt with in later chapters but suffice it to say here that, had it not been for studies already in existence when the sudden need arose to finance major space programs, little that was to be achieved over the following decade would have had any chance of success.

As it was, fully two years before America got its first satellite into orbit, the Air Force was well advanced with its design concepts for Agena A, a comparatively small rocket stage only 6 m in length. With a Thor rocket as the first stage, combinations of Thor-Agena launch vehicles would each lift a payload of up to 200 kg. Developed versions would raise this to 700 kg and by replacing Agena with more advanced upper stages and adopting several modifications to the basic Thor, payload capacity would reach 1,200 kg witin six years of Explorer 1. But back in 1958 there were more problems than lifting capacity to daunt the prospective space powers.

Orbital flight is not, as some believed in those early days, merely an extension of flight through the atmosphere. To get a satellite into space requires precise guidance in a three-dimensional frame, a very accurate positioning and a means of achieving the necessary speed with a high degree of accuracy. The reasons are no all that complex. Planets orbit the Sun according to principles first put to paper by Johannes Kepler in the 17th century according to the gravitational constant calculated by Galileo. Yet it is perhaps the Newtonian principle, that a body remains at rest or moves in a straight line unless acted upon by some force, which is the most important law for orbital flight.

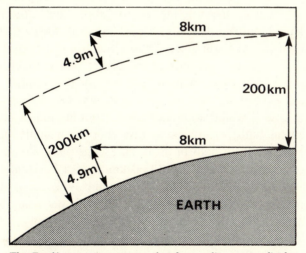

The Earth's curvature means that from a line perpendicular with the planet's centre the surface will be, on average, 4.9 m lower along a distance of 8 km. Outside the atmosphere, at 200 km, say, a satellite will continually 'fall' around the Earth's curvature.

There are only four known forces in the universe: two are associated with nuclear activity in the atom, one is electromagnetic radiation, the fourth is gravity. It is the force of gravity which keeps a satellite in orbit, or a planet revolving around the Sun. To take the case of a satellite orbiting Earth, the force of gravity continually acting upon it exerts an influence which draws the satellite down. But since the force attracting the satellite is a product of the Earth's mass (gravity is proportional to the value of the mass), it does so at a rate which is unique to the Earth; because the Moon has less mass than Earth it attracts bodies with less force but, because the Sun has more mass than the Earth, it exerts a stronger pull. Accordingly, with the given mass of planet Earth, an object close to its surface will be drawn down at a rate of 9.8 m/sec^2, that is, in the first second it will fall Earthward a distance of 4.9 m. Now it so happens that the curvature of the Earth falls 4.9 m in a distance of nearly 8 km. It follows, therefore, that if an object can be propelled at a speed of 8 km per second, or about 28,000 km/hr, it will perpetually orbit the Earth since in each second it will be drawn toward the surface at the precise height the Earth falls away across the distance of 8 km. A body moving at nearly 8 km/sec will fall back to Earth at the rate at which the Earth's surface seems to recede. It will never reach the surface and continue to orbit the planet, provided, of course, the satellite is just above the atmosphere and devoid of any significant drag which could slow it down. If it did slow down it would fall to Earth since the satellite would not gain sufficient ground on the receding curvature of the planet. Alternatively, if it was speeded up it would more than compensate for the force of attraction (gravity) and exceed the rate needed to match the distance of curvature. In that case it would accelerate away from the planet into either a highly elliptical path, or, if going fast enough, actually beyond the capacity of the Earth to hold on to it: an escape path. Consequently, a vehicle propelled to a speed of 28,000 km/hr in a horizontal direction will reach orbit. Speed is essential to get the object into the correct relationship with the receding curvature; height is necessary to free the object from drag in the atmosphere. Because Newton's first law of motion allows a body to continue at the rate imparted to it, if the satellite is not further affected by other forces it will remain in the same orbit. Theoretically. In practice this requires a perfectly symmetrical Earth with homogeneous distribution of mass inside. The Earth is not a perfect sphere, neither is the material it contains evenly layered. The polar radius is marginally less than the equatorial radius, since the magnitude of the Earth's spin causes it to bulge slightly at the middle, and the gravitational value will change accordingly. Moreover, centrifugal force (or, to be precise, inverse centripetal force) exerts influence on the inertia of a body at the Equator so that the acceleration at the poles is actually 9.832 m/sec^2 while at the Equator it is only 9.78 m/sec^2 due to the tendency of a body to resist the force of gravity close to the Equator.

Also, inconsistencies in the Earth's make-up introduce local variations in the mass directly beneath the satellite at any one point in its orbit compared to another. Because the force of attraction—gravity—is an unyielding product of the mass, the gravitational force will fluctuate as the mass changes. The net effect of this during a single revolution of the Earth may be quite small but magnified over several orbits the summed product can be quite important. Satellites, therefore, will drift away from their predicted positions unless calculations are made to adjust for this. Now, because the force of gravity decreases on the inverse square law, orbits further from the Earth will call for less speed to counter the force of attraction. For example, a satellite at 1,600 km will circle the planet at about 25,400 km/hr, while a satellite in a circular path at 4,000 km will be required to travel at less than 22,400 km/hr. The same criteria for under- or over-speed conditions apply here as they do at extremely low altitudes: slow the satellite down and it will start to fall; speed it up and the satellite moves further out, making an ellipse. Because the precise dynamics of the orbit will be known before such a path is reached it will be possible to calculate the period of the orbit, defined as the time it takes the satellite to make one 360 degree revolution about the Earth. For the time being it is necessary to ignore the fact that the Earth itself is spinning, where a point on the surface will appear to move with time when aligned with an apparently fixed point in space.

Since the circumference of a circle is $2\pi R$, where R is the radius of the circle, the exact distance the satellite will have to travel will be obtained by knowing the precise height it is from the center of the Earth: the radius of the orbital circle. And because the exact speed of the vehicle will be calculated from the known force of gravity at that height, the period of the satellite will be determined by dividing the speed into the circumference. For instance, at 5.26 km/sec, in a path 8,045 km in radius, the satellite will take 9,610 seconds to travel

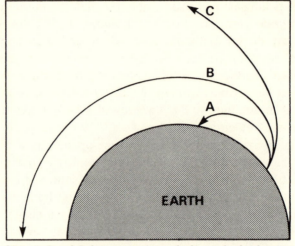

Lines A, B and C show respective paths for a suborbital trajec-tory, an orbital path about the Earth and escape from Earth's gravity.

around the circumference of its orbit. This is because the satellite has to travel 50,548 km to make one revolution of the Earth and that distance divided by 5.26 km equals 9,610. In this way a specific orbit can provide either one of two separate requirements: a particular height, according to speed and position, or a specific period of revolu-tion, dependent upon the altitude or the orbit.

A requirement to pass over certain areas at assigned times can be met by planning an appropriate orbit or, alternatively, a particular height required for technical reasons can be matched as necessary. Only a little sophistication is required to appreciate that the characteris-tics of an orbit can be changed at will if the satellite is equipped with a rocket motor to speed up or slow down the orbital velocity. Given that too severe an alteration in speed will result in the satellite either falling to Earth or leaving the planet for ever, careful and precise changes in the order of just a few meters per second will produce the desired result.

There is one pitfall ready to snare the practitioner who believes that because a satellite orbiting further out is required to travel less quickly, a less powerful rocket can do the job. It is true to say that the kinetic energy required to achieve orbit is less, but untrue to believe the *potential* energy is also less. It is, in fact, greater because more work must be applied to resist the force of gravity while the satellite is lifted a greater distance from the Earth's surface. The total quantity of energy required to put a satellite in high orbit is shown to be the square of the characteristic velocity, this latter value being the specific velocity applied to the given orbit. For example, the speed necessary to remain in an approximately circular orbit at 1,600 km is 25,400 km/hr. The actual expenditure of energy to reach this altitude is equal to the square of the velocity. From this it will be seen that the situation gets markedly worse the higher the orbit. There is, however, an advantage to be obtained by placing a satellite in orbit parallel with the plane of the Earth's Equator.

When the satellite is in space the value of its speed is not affected by the rotation of the planet below. But when it is launched the Earth's spin is of vital importance, for the Earth is moving on its axis at an equatorial rate of 1,670 km/hr, or 0.47 km/sec. Thus, if a satellite were to be launched on the Equator and fly due east it would have a flying start and the rocket propelling it to orbit would need to have a characteristic velocity of only 7.44 km/sec. This effect decreases, of course, at higher latitude; at Cape Canaveral for example, the speed of rotation is about 0.42 km/sec so the rocket must travel that much faster than it would if launched on the Equator.

If launched into polar orbit, one where the satellite's ground track passes over both North and South Poles, the characteristic velocity of the launcher will be unaided by Earth's rotation and must make up the full amount necessary to achieve orbit. If launched due west, into what is known as a retrograde orbit, the launcher will be required to provide the 7.91 km/sec for orbital speed *plus* the 0.47 km/sec necessary to compensate for the Earth's rotation in the opposite direction, a total velocity increment of 8.38 km/sec. It transpires that the situation gets progressively less accommodating for increments of increasing latitude, so the effect is a gradual one based upon the precise angle of inclination to the Equator.

The first two orbital parameters necessary to fix a path around Earth are the low and the high points of the orbit respectively. Because no orbit can, theoretically, be a perfect circle the exact dimensions describe a path around the Earth with the center of the planet located at the focus of an ellipse. The low point of the ellipse is known as the perigee and the high point is called the apogee. The third parameter, the orbital period, is a product of these orbital characteristics while the fourth, the inclination to the Equator, describes the angle between the plane of the orbit and the plane of the Equator.

Thus defined, an inclination of, say, 50 degrees means that the satellite will travel around the Earth with the groundtrack—the point directly below the satellite—covering all latitudes between 50 degrees north and 50 degrees south of the Equator; this path would carry a satellite as far north as the southern coast of Britain and as far south as the Falkland Islands. There is, sometimes, a need to use a further frame of reference to describe the characteristics of an orbit.

The Earth orbits the Sun with a polar tilt of 23.45 degrees. The polar axis remains at a fixed inclination so that sometimes the South Pole is biased in the direction of the Sun while, six months later, the North Pole will favor the Sun's direction. The line where the plane of the Earth's path around the Sun crosses the plane of the Earth's Equator is known as the first point of Aries. The Earth crosses this line twice a year, at the vernal (spring) and autumnal (autumn) equinoxes. The plane of a satellite's orbit about the Earth can be defined with reference to this intersection. But to what purpose? It is necessary to remember that, because the Earth maintains a fixed polar tilt with respect to the Sun, the plane of a satellite's orbit fixed with respect to the Aries line will also state the angle of the Sun to the satellite's position.

Now from this it will be seen that only one more parameter is necessary precisely to locate the orbit within its frames of reference. That is the angle between the major axis of the orbital ellipse and the line of intersection between the Earth's orbital plane and the Equator. This angle is known as the argument of perigee. Because an orbit is free to point its major axis in any direction the argument of perigee fixes it precisely within the co-ordinate system.

To summarize, the regions over which a satellite will fly are dictated by one parameter—the orbital inclination; the height at which the satellite will pass over any given point is determined by the perigee and apogee—the low and the high points of the orbit respectively, always on opposite sides of the Earth; and the energy necessary to reach higher orbits increases with altitude although the speed at orbital injection will decrease with height.

Because the orbital period gets progressively longer with increasing orbital distance from the Earth, it follows that, at a certain distance

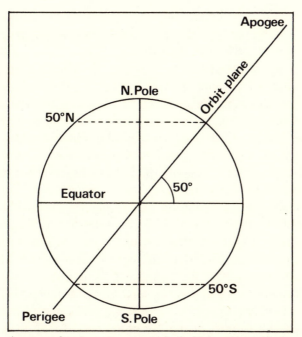

Apogee and perigee are respectively the high and low altitudes of an orbit around Earth while the plane of the orbit is the inclination to the planet's Equator, also defined as the highest latitude over which the ground track passes. From the above illustration it can be seen that although the path remains the same, by increasing apogee an observer can see more of the northern hemisphere than he can of the southern hemisphere at perigee.

from the planet's surface, this period will exactly equal the period of the Earth's rotation. Such a path is known as a stationary orbit when the orbital plane lies in the plane of the Equator. When it does not, the orbit is said to be synchronous (because the period is the same as the period of the Earth's rotation) but the satellite will wander along a figure-of-eight, moving as far north and south of the Equator as the orbital inclination.

The advantages of stationary orbit are such that an object placed over one point on the Earth's surface will seem to remain there indefinitely, seemingly suspended in space for continuous access 24 hours a day. The only problem here is that the very great distance required to match the rotation period of the Earth (35,880 km) similarly requires a very great deal of energy from the launching rocket since, as we saw earlier, the potential energy is the product of the *square* of the characteristic velocity.

So, once again, it all comes down to what rockets are available. There are plenty of orbital slots for many varied and unique tasks: a low orbit provides close examination of surface features at high speed; high orbits allow a more casual observation but with decreased resolution; higher orbits still prolong the period a given satellite is within a range of ground site; low orbital inclinations restrict the groundtrack latitudes but intensify successive periods of observation; high orbital inclinations overfly increasing areas of the planet.

Much of the precise definition required to get the first satellite into orbit prompted military personnel to consider the opportunities which they now had. When von Braun spoke in the mid-1950s to military specialists he was unwittingly recruiting a supporting cast which would soon begin to put together the framework for military space projects. It was an ideal environment. International law was unclear on the use of space for surveying foreign countries. Logically there seemed no restrictions present to prevent the use of satellites for many useful tasks impossible to achieve by other means. One of the first projects to reach maturity was the Agena stage to be used with Thor and Atlas rockets. But that would only suffice for an initial period until the advantages of orbital flight were made fully apparent by use and experimentation. Yet large rocket programs were expensive and satellites would probably have to make do for a long time with what was available from existing inventories. Atlas and Titan were prime candidates for development as space rockets because they were the most powerful systems then available. But here too the requirements were just a little daunting, for it took a lot of rocket to lift a little satellite.

In 1957, during the period immediately before Sputnik 1, America's Vanguard satellite launcher had a capacity to lift 23 kg to orbit. Plans already under way in the Air Force put the Agena stage, then on the drawing board, on top of a Thor ballistic missile to provide a launch capability of 200 kg. The big Atlas ICBM was still several years away from development but combined with an Agena similar to that used with Thor, the assembly was thought capable of lifting weights in excess of 1 ton to high Earth orbit. But not yet, for much development had to take place.

Titan was another candidate for application to the space program but this was even further from operational readiness and no significant role was foreseen before the mid-1960s. When it came, on October 4, 1957, the launch of Sputnik 1 was significant not only for the achievement of actually placing a satellite in orbit but also because it demonstrated the enormous lifting power available to Soviet engineers. The first satellite weighed 83 kg—four times the projected Vanguard capability. Several weeks later Sputnik 2 went into orbit carrying a dog called Laika. That satellite weighed 508 kg. Within seven months Sputnik 3 was bleeping its way around the globe with an announced weight of more than 1,300 kg. All three satellites used essentially the same rocket vehicle design, a configuration known subsequently by the NATO code-name of Sapwood, or the SS-6. It had first been launched only two months before lifting Sputnik 1, the proud possession of the bombastic Nikita Krushchev, designed from the outset as the long-promised Soviet ICBM with one prime function: to carry a thermonuclear warhead to the United States. As an effective deterrent it was a non-starter. With liquid oxygen and kerosene propellants it would require several hours of preparation for launch, exposed all the while on a concrete launch pad. But as a booster for space probes and satellites it was admirably suited for brandishing Soviet capability and launching useful payloads into orbit. Inherent in its design was a cluster concept developed concurrently in the United States by Wernher von Braun. The Russians chose to place groups of four comparatively small rocket motors, each with a thrust less than that of a Redstone missile, on four boosters and a single sustainer. The sustainer formed the central core with the four boosters strapped to its sides. They would be jettisoned on the way up but the total lift-off thrust, at more than 500 tons, was greater than the proposed thrust from three Atlas missiles. And Atlas had yet to fly!

Over the next few years the Soviets experimented with several additional rocket stages placed on top of the basic configuration, gradually expanding its capability. In the United States, meanwhile, hot debate raged about the responsibility for America's nascent space endeavor. Clearly, went the argument, the Russians were making an all-out bid to achieve supremacy in weight-lifting capacity and, mindful of the prestige they had already gained with Sputnik, would probably go ahead with plans for putting men in orbit. All the old arguments about the military advantage of gaining the high ground were rolled out by Air Force and Army proponents. Having lost control of large ICBM programs, the latter were in no mood to relinquish their coveted role in space. The Air Force was busy planning reconnaissance and early warning projects based on Agena while the Army had the considerable resource of the Redstone facility at Huntsville. During 1957 serious study began on the specification for a very large rocket motor capable, as a single unit, of thrust exceeding 600 tons. As an interim measure, the von Braun team developed a candidate design which would cluster together rocket motors previously developed for the Jupiter and Thor missiles. By clustering also the propellant tanks necessary to supply propellant to these motors, the United States could, claimed von Braun, gain the advantage of a heavy satellite launcher in good time to catch up with the Russians. This design concept, originally called Juno V but later re-named Saturn, was to provide civilian research activity with a much needed capacity for lifting heavy weights into space.

Within a few weeks of sending Explorer 1 into orbit, the United States Congress debated the issue of future responsibility for the nation's space program. Eisenhower was reluctant to respond in haste to gains seemingly acquired by the Soviet Union. He preferred to play down the whole issue and cynically referred to the "little ball in the sky" about which he had small concern. Privately, advisers warned of imminent uses for satellite technology which could quickly threaten the security of the United States. In the shock of Sputnik, anything seemed possible and projections of orbital war which had filled magazines only a few years earlier were now resurrected by technically-qualified students of future developments. Accordingly, in the background to public debate, serious concern was evolving and became linked to a determination to pull back the apparent lead gained by the Russians. That left a very difficult issue. Eisenhower was convinced of the need to work for peace in the new medium and was impressed by argument that suggested some form of civilian administration set up to control the national space effort.

Lyndon Johnson, then the ranking majority leader in the Senate, pressed Eisenhower for White House authority and, by the end of 1958, the National Aeronautics and Space Administration (NASA) had been brought into existence. The NASA charter required the complete and unexpurgated publication of all civilian space activities, making it the show-case for national achievement and scientific research. There was certainly an eye toward the propaganda value such an organization would have, for surveys conducted in the United States and abroad convinced the White House that prestige among foreign countries would be modulated by a demonstration of technical prowess.

The Soviets had sought a means by which to advertise the capacity they knew they possessed but which they could only demonstrate globally by putting a satellite in orbit. That gauntlet was effectively picked up by the new civilian space agency, whose first job was to be the development of a manned space project.

In the furor over that first Russian satellite, military think-tanks suggested the use of large rockets—the type proposed by von Braun—for all manner of doubtful schemes. Big rocket transports, it was said, could be used to propel large numbers of troops across intercontinental distances, and large orbiting space stations could be employed to survey the Earth and keep watch on potentially hostile countries. In addition, in several serious in-depth reports never released to the public, Pentagon projections even included major bases on the Moon controlled and administered by the Army. Both forces were fighting for a role in space, and only the Air Force seemed to have a reason to be there.

While NASA went about its own public relations exercise, the real business of satellite activity would be conducted by the Air Force. Or so the junior service believed. It too wanted men in space and immediately set up proposals for development of the manned project assumed by NASA to be its responsibility. The Air Force failed to get control of that endeavor, and quietly went about the business of planning a successor to what NASA called the Mercury project. The Air Force was interested in getting a vehicle in and out of orbit rather than merely achieving the goal of lifting an astronaut into space. While NASA chose a space capsule shaped rather like the re-entry cone of a ballistic missile, the Air Force designed a glider-like vehicle capable of flying back and forth several times. It was soon dubbed Dyna-Soar because of its projected "dynamic soaring" capability. A launch vehicle for Dyna-Soar was needed and the Air Force looked to derivatives of the big Titan ICBM, even then being considered for several major modifications. But the Army still fought to utilize the large clustered rocket concept developed by von Braun at Huntsville, proposing ambitious schemes for Moon bases and orbital platforms. Clearly, Saturn rockets would only be applicable to a major effort in space, for each clustered rocket would be capable of lifting 10 tons into orbit.

In 1959, the battle was lost and Eisenhower agreed that the ABMA Development Operations Division—the group comprising the von Braun team—should be moved to NASA from the Department of Defense. No clear role existed for such large rockets under Army auspices and the civilian space agency was more in need of heavy lifting power than any projected military application. NASA had consumed many of the national research facilities, indeed it had been formed out of the old National Advisory Committee for Aeronautics originally responsible for writing up the specification for rocket-powered X-15 aircraft. Now it would have the big booster research.

The lines of demarcation and constraint had been defined and the Air Force Ballistic Missile Division was to administer the needs of military men in space. NASA would soon gain new and bold commitments when John F. Kennedy forged a Moon landing goal. The Air Force, meanwhile, had a job to do convincing Pentagon and Defense Department officials that their military responsibilities in space were as profound as other more peaceful goals assigned to NASA. If there was one single event which swung the decision it was an occurrence in 1960. During the summer, on a reconnaissance flight over Soviet territory, special agent Francis Gary Powers was shot down and publicly tried for spying. The message was clear. Reconnaissance would have to take place from outside Earth's atmosphere.

2. Orbital eyes

Reconnaissance from space

Far from the prying eyes of local inhabitants, such as there were on this barren desert, a strange looking aircraft slowly circled Watertown Strip, Nevada, and gracefully swept in to land, its central wheel assembly sharing support for the airframe with two wing-tip skids. It was early 1956. The first U-2 had arrived for special training sessions with selected CIA agents. Less than a year before, the Lockheed Corporation had successfully flown for the first time the aircraft which would remain veiled from the text books until a major international incident revealed American intelligence plans. But now, at the secure base in Nevada, missions would be rehearsed for deep penetration over Soviet Russia.

There were no markings on the U-2 and nothing externally to suggest its nationality. Only a pilot, a single seat, and equipment for photographing the surface. The U-2 was not a large aircraft, barely 15 m in length, but its enormous high-aspect ratio wing, spanning more than 24 m, provided the high lift necessary for flight at extreme altitude. Several U-2 variants evolved, and the performance improved, while flight after flight probed communist countries by intrusion through air space believed safe from surface-to-air missiles.

During the remainder of the decade intelligence sources brought word of activity at the rocket testing station called Kapustin Yar, close to the River Volga near the city of Volgograd. A radio listening post, with facilities for tracking Russian missiles on test, was quickly set up close by the Turkish Black Sea coast. Many flights were observed and tracked as rockets and warheads flew south-east to a firing ground by the Aral Sea. But there were other facilities, deep inside Kazakhstan, which held the more important hardware.

This was the time for final preparations leading to tests with the Sapwood missile, the big ICBM urged on by Premier Krushchev, and

45

US intelligence got word of a rocket site 350 km south-west of the railhead at Tyuratam. Deep in the remote desert region of the southern Soviet Republic, engineers were constructing buildings, concrete launch pads, assembly sheds, and tracking equipment in anticipation of major development work. It was imperative to United States' interests that information on this project be obtained, and quickly! Because the site was too far inside Soviet territory, and too remote from accessible ground sites, a U-2B was prepared for very long distance flight at an altitude above 26 km. This version of the U-2 had a range exceeding 6,000 km, more than enough to fly the planned route from Peshawar in Pakistan to Bodo in Norway. The mission was to carry CIA special agent Gary Powers north-west on a reconnaissance flight lasting several hours. It was May 1, 1960 when he made that journey, the first of several planned one-way trips across Russia. In full knowledge of the fate which would probably await him were he to crash in Soviet territory, Powers carried a suicide needle just 7 cm long and equipment for survival were he to come down in a deserted area. Only three years before, an earlier U-2 had photographed the Tyuratam launch site, now a more detailed survey was to be obtained of this and other zones. The big Sapwood rocket had by this time launched several heavy satellites into space and fears grew that the missile would, in its ICBM role, present a severe threat to the United States and other NATO countries. It was important to get details of the scale of this rocket's deployment, for intelligence estimates by the CIA and military analysts believed more than 100 such missiles to have been set up already. As time would tell, this was a ridiculously inflated estimate, leading to dramatic overkill for American ICBM deployment plans. In fact, in 1960, Russia had only a handful of intercontinental missiles. In May of that year, however, there was pressing need for good photographic details of Soviet military equipment. But Gary Powers never did reach Bodo, his high-flying U-2 being hit by a surface-to-air missile launched from a site near Sverdlovsk. Powers was unable to continue flying the aircraft and elected to parachute to the ground where he was taken prisoner and eventually charged with espionage. The incident damaged US-Soviet relations and wrecked a summit conference being held in Paris.

Several months later the Russians put Powers through a show trial where they spoke of a wide-angle camera found in the wreckage of the U-2 with sufficient film for 4,000 pictures, a special tape recorder with stored signals picked up as the aircraft flew over secret radio installations, and an explosive device to destroy the aircraft at will. Powers was found guilty and sent to a Soviet prison.* It was the end of plans for long U-2 overflights of Soviet territory but it was also the turning point in the development of space reconnaissance.

Four important areas of information were essential for Western defense and responsibility for collecting this data would now fall almost exclusively on the shoulders of military personnel preparing the new generation of reconsats, the spacecraft built specially to replace the manned high-flying U-2 machines. It was vital to obtain technical information about the operation and performance of the Sapwood missile; it was vital to obtain sound figures for deployment of this and other long-range rockets; it was desirable to find the anti-aircraft radar stations and locate ground-to-air missile sites; and it was very important simply to map the Soviet Union, for Russian maps were deliberately confusing and cities were found to be several kilometers from their stated locations! The last piece of intelligence was significant for targeting US missiles.

When Gary Powers flew over Soviet territory his mission coincided with preparations for the launch of Sputnik 4, a precursor development flight of the Vostok spacecraft, one of which would place Yuri Gagarin in orbit less than a year later. It was a significant development, for Sputnik 4 weighed 4½ tons, nearly six times the weight of the heaviest American satellite launched so far. The missile gap was widening; intelligence was now more important than ever. But the Air Force was already well advanced with development of the first generation reconsats based on the Discoverer program set up in March 1958.

Discoverer evolved from the WS-117L specification based on the Agena A rocket stage. Following presentation of satellite system requirements in March 1955, design studies were examined in a nine-month period starting June that year. By October 1956, Lockheed had been signed up to do the job. Close by the contractor's manufacturing and test facility, in Sunnyvale, California, the US Air Force's 6594th Test Wing set up the Satellite Test Center to support WS-117L and other defense-oriented space work. The Central Intelligence Agency played an important role in pressing military satellite duties on the new Air Force organization and reconnaissance was an early objective.

Within two months of the launch of Sputnik 1, funds for WS-117L

---

* In February 1962 Powers was released in exchange for Soviet agent, Colonel Rudolf Abel.

were increased four-fold and by January 1958 a complete re-examination of the program's objectives resulted in the three-phase assignment of mission tasks: Discoverer, a recoverable capsule project for expanding basic technology; Sentry, for operational photographic reconnaissance duties; and Midas, an early warning system designed to watch for pre-emptive Soviet missile strikes. Up to 24 satellites were envisaged for the Sentry and Midas programs, following several score Discoverer missions to evolve systems technology. All were to be placed in polar or near-polar orbits from launch sites at Vandenberg Air Force Base, California. Discoverer class satellites were to begin flights late in 1958, followed by a network of Sentry and Midas vehicles fully operational by the mid-1960s.

Very soon the Sentry codename was changed to the now familiar Samos designation, an acronym of Satellite and Missile Observation System. But before Samos and Midas could be fully developed, Discoverer would pave the technical and conceptual way. Accordingly, the system would utilize the Agena A as a purpose-built "bus" for several unique scientific and technical experiments in addition to the recovered capsule, an integral part of the structure until separated in space. The mission plan for Discoverer pioneered the use of polar orbit. And that was why they had to fly from Vandenberg on the west coast of North America, in fact, Discoverer 1—launched February 28, 1959—became the first satellite to reach orbit from this site. Vandenberg was no second-runner to Cape Canaveral, fast becoming the prime missile test center in the USA, for missions destined for orbital inclinations higher than about 50 degrees were prohibited from launch at the Florida site. This was because jettisoned rocket stages would fall over inhabited areas and an early stipulation restricted launch trajectories to flight across open sea only. At least until the vehicle reached orbit. Consequently, Vandenberg was as important a launch site as Cape Canaveral for without the capacity to head south over the Pacific, flights to polar orbit would have taken place over land. Vandenberg was the home of the 1st Missile Division, then equipped with Atlas rockets for test and operational checkout. Satellite launches were an added responsibility, as they had been at the Eastern Test Range, Cape Canaveral.

The Discoverer satellite would comprise an integral package of instruments with the Agena A. The stage itself weighed 3,850 kg when full of propellant. In orbit it would weigh less than 780 kg,

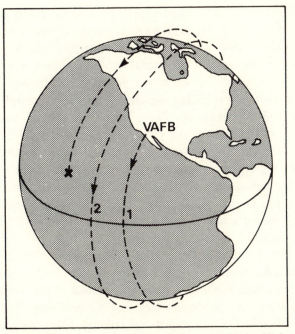

Discoverer capsules returned to Earth on the third orbit by which time the path had 'migrated' west to a point near Hawaii, actually displaced by the rotation of the Earth in a counter-clockwise direction when viewed from the north pole.

having boosted itself to orbital velocity. Agena would take over from the Thor first stage at a height of about 120 km and, while the stage fell back to Earth, Agena would fire itself to an elliptical path. After shutting down its main engine, the Agena would turn through 180 degrees so that its forward section would point back along the line of flight. Small gas jets, or thrusters, would turn the satellite and maintain its attitude through the use of special sensors. During the flight from Vandenberg into orbit, performance would be monitored by two ships downrange of the launch site, located in the Pacific Ocean, 2,600 km south. Passing down and across the Antarctic continent, Discoverer would move back up across the Indian Ocean and Asia, passing over the North Pole before coming within range of the Kodiak, Alaska, tracking station, the first point of communication with the satellite after reaching orbit.

Because the Earth spins from west to east, one full revolution of the globe in a single 90-minute orbit will cause the groundtrack to migrate west; the satellite's path is fixed with respect to the center of gravity—the Earth's core—and planetary rotation plays no part in the satellite's orbit. Because of this, a second receiving station was set up in New Hampshire on the eastern seaboard. A third station was located at Kaena Point, Hawaii, to monitor recovery operations and receive telemetry from the descending capsule. A recovery control center was situated at nearby Hickam Air Force Base. It was from here the C-119 recovery aircraft would fly out physically to retrieve the data capsule. When the time came to return the capsule to Earth, the Agena would pitch down 60 degrees. After separating from the main body of the satellite, the capsule would fire its own small rocket motor reducing speed by 1,400 km/hr. Thus slowed, the capsule would begin its long fall through the atmosphere. Re-entry activity would have been ordered by radio command sent from the ground.

Shaped like a truncated bullet, the Discoverer re-entry capsule made the best of information generated during tests to find optimum shapes for ballistic missile warheads. Until an engineer at the Ames Aeronautical Laboratory came upon the idea that the best shape for a warhead was not a sharply pointed object but rather a blunt body designed to create drag, no one could effectively design a re-entry body for survival. The temperatures generated by dissipation of kinetic energy into thermal energy would simply melt any known substance. By shaping the body for maximum resistance the shock wave was made to stand proud of the structure and so inhibit thermal conduction through the intervening space, lowering surface temperature to an acceptable 1,700 degrees C. This was the temperature experienced by a returning Discoverer capsule, protected by an ablative shield designed to char and partially burn away, carrying thermal energy with it. At a height of about 15 km the parachute would deploy, simultaneously jettisoning the heat shield, so that the capsule could slowly fall at the end of an extended line. Tracking the capsule on radar, an airborne recovery aircraft would fly directly above it and snag the line on a trapeze device. The capsule and its collapsed parachute would then be winched aboard the aircraft for return to Hickam AFB. In 1961, C-130 aircraft replaced the C-119s used for the first two years. At a time when basic satellite technology was hard enough to perfect, the complex mission sequence of a Discoverer vehicle was bold initiative indeed. The widely publicized activities of the civilian NASA organization frequently eclipse creditable technical achievements from the Defense Department.

In 1958, when the sequence of mission needs was first completed, it was a forward-looking program indeed. But just what should Discoverer carry into space? It was, after all, a research and development tool from which Samos and Midas photo-reconnaissance and early-warning satellites were expected to mature. Clearly, photographic equipment would play a vital role in developing the necessary hardware.

There were three possible ways of obtaining a picture from space. The most obvious means of sending an image back to Earth involved a television camera sending information directly to a ground station, an operation known as "real-time" transmission, or storing that image on a tape recorder until the satellite passed over an appropriate point on the surface. That was considered the best operational mode, but detail from space of objects on the ground seen through a TV image was considered too poor for useful application. An alternative concept involved the use of a film emulsion exposed over the target for recovery at a later time. That would depend exclusively on safely retrieving the capsule, an activity not expected for the majority of attempts!

A hybrid system was selected whereby the satellite carried a conventional camera and film spool which would be scanned, following exposure and development, by a light beam capable of returning the data to Earth on telemetry. The concept was proposed and developed by Eastman-Kodak. It was the best of all three choices and represented the first operational satellite reconnaissance technique. In fact the process was so successful it became the adopted system for NASA's Lunar Orbiter series of five spacecraft sent to photograph the surface of the Moon in 1966 and 1967. That system adopted the Kodak "Bimat" process and is typical of the equipment designed for Samos and tested by Discoverer. Divided into camera, processor, and readout sections, the system provided a spool of film presented to one long and one short focal length lens. After exposure the film passed on to a loop buffer designed to hold it between the camera and the processor. For processing, the film was drawn across a drum and on to a Bimat web, or processing film layer, with the gelatin soaked in a combined developer-fixer solution. The Bimat acquired a positive image because silver halide would quickly be reduced to silver and undeveloped silver ions move by diffusion transfer to the web. After this, the two surfaces were separated and the negative film drawn between two pads to remove moisture before drying in front of a small heater. The positive image acquired by the web was not used. The negative image retained by the film was stored on a take-up reel, ready for the readout process.

Developed by CBS Laboratories, a special Line Scan Tube was incorporated to move an electron beam across the surface of a phosphor-covered drum which would, in so doing, present a thin spot of light, focused on to the film by a scanning lens. The lens moved the light spot across the film in a regular pattern, covering a 6.1 cm wide strip of film with 17,000 horizontal scans 0.25 cm in length. After completing one horizontal scan of the full width of film, the film would be advanced 0.25 cm for another complete scan. And so it would go on until the picture was complete. As the spot of light passed through the film it was modulated by the density of the negative image, the light level being sensed by a photomultiplier tube. This generated an electrical signal proportional to the intensity of the modulated light. Finally, each signal was amplified and sent to the satellite communications system for transmission to Earth. The complete assembly weighed less than 70 kg. The finished product was not as good photographically as an image obtained without going through the readout process, but in the absence of assured recovery from separate capsules, it was an acceptable beginning and thus became the prime payload for satellites of the Samos class.

Selecting a suitable orbit for the Discoverer development missions was handicapped by certain needs which could not be avoided. Satellites would have to use polar orbits, inclined 90 degrees to the Equator, to pass effectively over the targets of interest in Asia and the Far East and to travel down across the Pacific so that the capsule could be recovered, for if the aircraft failed to snag the descending parachute line the object would fall safely to the water for recovery by surface ship; no such contingency would be present should the capsule fall on land.

The Air Force wanted to recover the capsule during a specific period each day and that too restrained the orbital altitude because the period of revolution would have to provide daily passes over the eastern Pacific. There were, also, considerations about the performance of the camera system, for the higher the satellite travelled the less resolution would be available in the photographs. But more about that later. As it turned out, a path providing orbital periods of about 92 minutes was the best for all requirements.

The first flight went well to begin with but, soon after reaching orbit on February 28, 1959, the satellite began tumbling uncontrollably. No capsule was carried on this initial development mission but a capsule was carried by the second, Discoverer 2, launched less than two months later. That flight went well until human error caused the re-entry sequence to begin too early and the capsule fell somewhere to the north of Norway. It was seen to be falling gently to the ground but extensive searches were to no avail and the object was never found. During June, two more Discoverer flights lifted off the launch pad at Vandenberg, both failing to reach orbit, until the fifth seemed to be going as planned before a mis-aligned Agena propelled its capsule deeper into space rather than back to Earth!

Partial success was again achieved on August 19 when Discoverer 6 got through all the pre-planned procedures; only the capsule's radio beacon failed to work, causing the object to fall to the Pacific undetected. But this disappointing record was a mere prelude to a further spate of ironies which plagued the next six attempts. Discoverer 7 gyrated wildly in orbit and could not be controlled; Discoverer 8 shot into the wrong kind of orbit due to problems with the Thor launch vehicle; Discoverer 9 and its successor never did make it into orbit, again because of the launcher; Discoverer 11 lost a capsule during re-entry; and Discoverer 12, sent up in June 1960, succumbed to yet another Thor failure.

The Air Force had been flying Discoverer for 18 months without a single perfect flight. As yet, no capsule had been recovered from orbit—indeed at this time no object had *ever* been safely returned intact from space by either the United States or Russia—and hopes for an early operational date for the follow-on successor, Samos, paled in the wake of so many technical problems. And then success came. Air Force engineers considered flight 13 a shakedown mission designed to carry into space a special package of instruments to troubleshoot the satellite. Even the capsule, technically referred to as the satellite recovery vehicle, or simply the SRV, was fully instrumented to report its own performance and in so doing, it was hoped, to provide data for succeeding flights.

It was afternoon, Wednesday, August 10, 1960. A historic day for the Air Force and satellite flight in general. As the Thor rocket blazed its fiery path to space, tracking stations monitored the performance of the launch vehicle; Discoverer went through its most severe test a minute or so into flight, for here the vibrations were extreme and the shocks magnified. On and up the assembly rode a path into an almost perfect orbit, 258 km high at the low point (perigee) and 683 km out at the high point (apogee). Discoverer 13 slipped into space just as planned and in the next several hours engineers cautiously watched its telemetry signal beaming vital information to the ground. Next day, at about 4:15 P.M. Pacific time, engineers sent the all-important signal to begin the re-entry sequence. Agena pitched down, facing backwards, the capsule separated, the solid propellant motor ignited and down came the SRV. Through the atmosphere the small object slithered and buffeted its way in the searing temperature of re-entry and, shortly after the parachute popped out, a circling C-119 from the Air Force tried, in vain, to pick up and track the radio beacon. The aircraft eventually sighted the capsule but was unable to get a bearing before it hit the ocean. From the USS *Haiti Victory* a helicopter reached the scene and a Navy frogman jumped into the water and swam to the capsule, bobbing in the heavy waves. Attaching a line to the capsule the frogman waited as the helicopter slowly winched up the very first man-made object ever successfully to return from orbit. Exactly one week later, following careful scrutiny of the Discoverer 13 capsule and telemetry from the orbiting satellite, preparations reached completion for the next in line. Launched from Vandenberg on August 18, Discoverer 14 returned its capsule a day later following ejection over Alaska. Several C-119 aircraft were in the recovery area downrange across the Pacific and this time a grim determination to upstage the Navy found one of these aircraft directly under the parachute at an altitude of 2,600 m. Safely hooked aboard the recovery plane, Discoverer 14 was retrieved as planned. It was a boost to morale for all personnel on the program. During the rest of 1960 the Discoverer flights gained mottled success and in five missions only two capsules were returned; one flight did not carry any capsule at all but tested infrared sensors for the Midas early warning program.

Discoverer 16, however, had introduced a new Agena B stage, longer than the "A" model and capable of lifting heavier weights into orbit. Operating techniques explored by the Discoverer satellites called for recovery of the protected capsule after one, two or three days in space on the 17th, 33rd or 65th orbits, respectively. The first two-day satellite had been put up as Discoverer 17 in November 1960, and just three weeks later Discoverer 18 satisfactorily tested the three-day duration. The program was doing just what it was supposed to and, in both this type of technical activity and in the host of several different experiment packages attached to the satellite and its capsule, engineers learned how to control complex space missions and scientists tried out new concepts.

The following year saw a flurry of activity with 17 Discoverer launches of which only seven were a complete success. Yet the limited reliability of hardware in those early days of the space program brought little success to any of the many nascent projects undertaken by military or civilian agencies. In 1962, Discoverers 37 and 38 completed the program, which had begun more than three years before as the Defense Department's first satellite research and development program. In selecting a basic "bus" for fundamental research into techniques, operations and equipment hitherto untried, considerable time, money and effort were saved.

The operational successors to Discoverer flights set up the world's first active military satellites: Samos and Midas. Long before Discoverer was terminated, Air Force preparation for the first fully operational reconsat led to several highly successful missions. This was the time when fears about Soviet supremacy in space technology were the tip of a much larger and deeper concern for the intentions of what was believed to be a burgeoning defense capability. America was intent upon the early retrieval of data acquired in space, to see just what the missile deployment levels really were and to confirm, or otherwise, the belief held around intelligence circles that the US would have to go all out for production of large numbers of land-based missiles.

In late 1960, in the publicity wake after Powers' abortive attempt to photograph Soviet installations, a race was on for the White House which had seen John F. Kennedy and Richard M. Nixon, the principal contenders for the Presidency, wholly endorse announced plans for the Samos reconnaissance satellite. But what of the legal implications? Surely, if the Russians objected strongly to spying eyes from space it would be tantamount to calling for a ban on satellite flight, for anything placed in any type of orbit is inevitably made to fly over *somebody's* territory.

There was almost no legal precedent for complaint. Only the 1944 Chicago Convention, to which Russia had not been a signatory, established authoritatively that although "complete and exclusive jurisdiction over the air space above its territory" would inhibit foreign flights by aircraft, there was nothing to define the void beyond the atmosphere. Accordingly, a mood of "suck it and see" prevailed when, in late 1960, the Air Force prepared Samos 1 for launch by Atlas Agena A. This configuration put the same stage used for early Discoverer flights on top of the much more powerful Atlas rocket, with the payload forming an integral part of the upper stage. Where a typical

Discoverer vehicle, Agena stage included, could weigh up to 1,150 kg, the Samos vehicle would orbit the Earth with a mass of 1,900 kg. A large part of the weight, in both cases, was taken up by the Agena. Hence, the larger Atlas required to provide the initial boost. In space, Samos would not look unlike Discoverer, but early models employed the radio transmission of pictures scanned by the method described earlier rather than hard-copy photographs returned by capsule. There were distinct advantages in both concepts: the radio technique provided information very soon after it had been obtained, little time being lost in retrieving pictures from retrieved capsules; the capsule descent method provided better resolution of surface detail, no loss of quality penalizing the intelligence value of the finished product. It was the comparative unreliability of the capsule recovery method which pushed Air Force planners toward the radio transmission concept. Yet the two were to be operated concurrently for many years and the transmitted pictures were employed for "area survey" scans while hard-copy photographs originated from "close look" satellites.

So the world's first truly operational reconsat program emerged in late 1960 with much hanging over the observed Soviet response. Many suspected that the Russians would protest vehemently over the apparent intrusion brought about by the spy in the sky. Some were convinced, however, that Russia would see in the ability to observe each other a means by which verification of arms stocks and weapons capabilities could become reality. This was, to be sure, one of the engaging aspects of military satellite development, for without such "national technical means" neither America nor Russia would have found it possible to agree to limitations put up by negotiating teams.

Yet, for all that, there was a hostile purpose to reconsats which others thought would negate any advantages. General James M. Gavin wrote in a book published during 1958, the year America first put a satellite in orbit, that effective use of "an ICBM will require accurate and timely intelligence and this can only be secured through the use of a reconnaissance satellite." The argument, it could be said, had the complexion of a chameleon, about to change its color according to the background. One thing was certain, there was full and mounting support for the military role in space and opinion was polarized by the new President John F. Kennedy little more than a year after he assumed office at the White House: "Only if the United States occupies a position of preeminence can we help decide whether this new ocean will be a sea of peace, or a terrifying theater of war." And so, on the premise that to be preeminent the United States must know as much as possible about its potential adversary, Samos emerged as the orbital watchdog for the West. It was not a distinguished beginning. The first attempt failed to get the satellite very far off the launch pad for, although the Atlas performed well, Agena failed to propel the assembly into orbit. The second attempt, on January 31, 1961, safely achieved orbit, a path inclined 97.4 degrees to the Equator. It was an incredible success and over the next few weeks returned to Earth a considerable amount of information which significantly altered Pentagon projections about the size and scope of Soviet defense forces. The Russians were furious. Not only because their carefully orchestrated plans to hoodwink the West could be exposed for the bombastic bluff they would later be seen as, but also because it would directly open access to activities the Russians had no intention of telling anybody about. Bluster and furor became the order of international business at the conference table for a decade. The Russians were clearly smarting behind the curtain which now seemed to be made not so much of iron as transparent paper.

"A host of all kinds of fabulous stories is now in vogue in the United States," said the Soviet newspaper *Pravda*, "that it has the most 'all-seeing' spy satellites, the 'greatest number of rockets,' the 'most invulnerable submarines' and so forth and so on . . . This does not agree with the facts, since the authors of such stories rely on those simpletons who have never considered what rockets, sputniks, submarines, and other technical equipment the Soviet Union has."

The fact of the matter was that the Russians had much fewer strategic weapons which they could use to repel a United States' attack than they wanted the world to believe, and the price the Soviets paid for secrecy in the early years brought a dramatic imbalance. During the years of Kennedy's administration tension escalated almost to the point of conflict when the Russians attempted to place on Cuba's land a number of missiles capable of reaching the continental United States. Kennedy placed a blockade on Cuba and threatened to go to war unless the Russians turned back the ships bringing the missiles. At the time, Russia had less than 80 ICBMs capable of reaching America, while the United States had more than 400 land-based ICBMs and submarine-based SLBMs, plus several hundred strategic bombers each capable of deep penetration and nuclear attack. The President knew the balance and acted accordingly, seeming to bring the world to the edge of conflict but in reality gambling with figures he could never make public, for that would reveal too much of the West's ace hand: the rapidly expanding global intelligence network.

The Russians resolved there and then, never again to be dictated to in this way. So began the build-up which would eventually equal and then surpass the strategic capability of the West. It was a lesson on strategy for worldwide domination the Russians would never forget. The impact of that one Samos flight in early 1961 reverberated through plans for more effective means of using space for military ends. But times were changing. The initial thrusts into space had shown both sides the folly of too much publicity concerning reconnaissance or early warning duties. A major propaganda campaign surrounded Soviet rhetoric about American "imperialism," while Russia's plans embraced similar capabilities with the same type of spacecraft as that employed to put the first cosmonauts in orbit.

Called Vostok, the 4½-ton satellite emerged publicly in April 1961 when Yuri Gagarin became the first man to circumnavigate the globe in space. But the spacecraft which could satisfactorily return through the atmosphere with a human cargo was equally applicable to the task of carrying photographic equipment for spy purposes. International agreement, endorsed by both super-powers, required each country publicly to acknowledge ownership of satellites and space probes by announcing the launch. Hostility in the United Nations about attempts from America for satellites on military tasks to ascend without announcement called forth protest from countries who were interested in having the host country make recompense for damage caused by descending fragments.

However, there was nothing illegal about preserving intact the secret nature of military missions. Accordingly, on November 22, 1961, the Air Force launched an Atlas-Agena B without disclosing the name or the nature of the flight. From then on, almost all military operations would disappear beneath a cloak of secrecy designed to placate concerned public opinion that the two major super-powers were engaged in a dangerous race for supremacy. Four months later, on March 16, 1962, Russia launched Cosmos 1, announcing that the program would embrace scientific research, technical tests, and general research in space. In fact, it has been used from that day to the present as a cover for both civilian and military satellites and space probes.

Under the Cosmos designation, Russia began its own clandestine reconnaissance from orbit. Cosmos 4, sent into space on April 26, was the first of these. It was the 4½-ton Vostok design originally revealed as a man-carrying satellite one year earlier. Both countries were now engaged in large-scale programs aimed at improving their knowledge of each other's military operation. By the end of 1961 the first E-6 data capsules arrived with the Air Force, design and fabrication having been completed in record time at the General Electric plant, and the last Atlas-Agena B launch of the Samos-class satellites propelled its payload into orbit on December 22. The gap between this and the first successful Samos vehicle had been filled with two failed launch attempts. From 1962, however, all satellites of this type were launched by Thor-Agena launch vehicles, first with the "B" series second stage and then, via a transition period during the second half of 1962, with the Agena D. This had a still larger performance capability and carried a restartable main engine capable of changing the orbit of the satellite in space. The payload would remain attached to the Agena throughout. For the remainder of 1962 the program moved ahead successfully without a single failure in 18 attempts. In the meantime, the first generation "close-look" satellites were placed in orbit with the new General Electric data recovery capsules; confidence in this system had been generated by the successful recovery of Discoverer 13's capsule in August 1960. These satellites would employ the Atlas-Agena B and fly missions lasting a few days at most. In 1962, their first year of use, six flights were attempted of which only one was a suspected failure, reaching an unusually high orbit of the type used later for ferret missions. The last of these first generation close-look satellites ascended on November 11, 1962, for a one-day flight prior to recovery of the data capsule. The year had similarly seen completion of flights with the first generation area-survey satellites, transmitting pictures by radio signal to receivers on the ground. But also in 1962, the Air Force introduced the first generation ferret satellites, electronic ears designed to pick up and collect radio transmissions over foreign countries, military communications between stations, and details of radar installations employed for early warning or ground-to-air missile control. More on these later.

By early 1963, plans were moving ahead with development of the second generation area-survey and close-look satellites, employing more powerful rockets and modified versions of existing hardware. By attaching to the Thor first stage three solid-propellant "strap-on" rockets to supplement the lift-off thrust, more payload could be lifted into orbit. Two unsuccessful launch attempts early in the new year preceded the first orbital flight with the second generation area satellite during May 1963. This type would continue in operation for the next four years, gradually replaced during 1967 with a larger machine possessing expanded capability and a new role.

Throughout 1963, '64 and '65, however, 45 satellites of the second generation type were launched at intervals thoroughly to map the world, provide detailed information on the location and distribution of geographic features in remote or concealed areas, and satisfactorily to lay the geoid across the physical features of the planet. This latter application found increasing relevance as the accuracy of major strategic and tactical weapon systems improved. President Kennedy had been primarily responsible, through Defense Secretary Robert McNamara, for the build-up of US strategic missile systems.

Development of exposed Atlas and Titan 1 missiles, capable of sending heavy warheads across intercontinental distances, turned toward the use of storable propellants in Titan 2 type rockets, concealed within protective silos until seconds before launch at which time the massive concrete doors would open and the missiles emerge. But the belief that Russia was achieving, in the late-1950s and early-1960s, an ICBM production capability equal to America's motor industry, drove the incumbent President to order full-scale deployment of solid-propellant Minuteman missiles similarly housed in protected silos.

The plan was to have at least 1,000 such projectiles buried throughout the mid-Western United States with an assured reaction time of less than 60 seconds. Because each missile was much smaller than the earlier "city-buster" rockets, accuracy was a vital ingredient of maximum efficiency at the target. Consequently, it became very much more important to know exactly where the targets lay with respect to the launch site. Conventional maps were no good—the old, deliberately confusing, Soviet maps had been replaced by the first few pictures brought back from reconsats—for the level of accuracy was simply not good enough for a missile which could, in a majority of attempts, put its warhead in a circle 400 m in radius. During the first half of the 1960s, this mapping job was done to perfection, providing missile men with the information needed to refine and update the guidance equations used for trajectory analysis. But while the second generation area satellites were mapping, looking for major geographic changes indicating extensive surface (or more local subsurface) alterations connected with defense programs, the close-look satellites using Atlas-Agena D launchers kept up a continuous support role. Lifetimes were invariably less than one week and orbits dipped as low as 120 km.

Over the first half dozen years or so in which space activity built up in civilian and military programs, considerable knowledge was gained on the nature of near-Earth space. Hitherto, while recognizing that the outer atmosphere had been sparsely probed, scientists believed it to extend much further from the surface than appeared to be the case from observation of satellite decay. As each molecule of air impinged upon the outer surface of a satellite, it was slowed by a very small amount. Careful observation of the rate of this orbital decay provided vaulable information on the actual makeup of the outer regions.

Where orbit planners once thought conservatively that reconsats would never remain in space at altitudes below 300 km, confounding the technical projections about the view from space, engineers now regularly commanded the reconsats to fly below half this altitude for high-resolution pictures of selected targets. Already, by the time second generation area and quick-look satellites emerged, reports from America's first orbiting astronauts had told of detail seen from orbit beyond the wildest expectations of scientists trying to calculate the visible resolution. But by this time, the Russians, too, were well into operational use of a second generation, high-resolution, system.

Based on the Vostok manned spacecraft, the first generation system was used for military reconnaissance beginning in early 1962, as discussed earlier in this chapter. By late 1963 a new version, probably still based on Vostok, had appeared. Called Cosmos 22, this vanguard flight sent a 5.5-ton satellite into orbit for a mission lasting six days. At 5 m it was slightly longer than the earlier version but retained the same 2.4 m diameter. It was the first of many high-resolution satellites launched under the Cosmos veil. Unlike American reconsats, the Soviet equivalents were sent into orbits at inclinations of 51, 65 or 73 degrees. All were launched from the Tyuratam site until 1966 when reconsats were also sent up from Plesetsk.

A new round of US reconsats emerged during 1966 and '67, designed to utilize new launchers. The third generation area satellite was based on the Agena D stage and would be launched into orbit for flights lasting, on average, about three weeks, by a lengthened version of the thrust-augmented Thor. A trial shot was launched on August 9, 1966, but not until May 1967 did this third generation variant completely replace the earlier model. It was a new version indeed, for now pictures would be taken at night using specially designed infra-red scanners and it possessed a data return capability greatly in excess of that used hitherto. The added volume of data was sent via a new, 1.5 m diameter, antenna, folded for launch and unfurled in space, sending high-bit rate material faster than before. This was a much better system in that it needed few launches to accomplish the same objectives. Area satellite launch rates had been falling steadily as performance improved. In 1963, 17 had been launched, 14 had been sent aloft in 1964, 14 in 1965 and nine in 1966. With the introduction of the day and night variant, only nine would be sent into space during 1967, followed by eight in 1968 and six in 1969, four in 1970, three in 1971 and two in 1972, the last year the third generation reconsat flew.

Meanwhile, the close-look satellites had gone through a similar design change. It will be recalled that the second generation type was introduced in 1963 with Atlas-Agena D launchers. The replacement for this system emerged atop a much more powerful Titan 3B-Agena D in July 1966. Their purpose was to employ multi-spectral cameras capable of photographing objects on the ground across several wavebands of the visible spectrum. By this time the intensive application of reconnaissance satellites to intelligence gathering had created a family of countermeasures designed to evade the prying eyes. To counter the concealment methods, discrimination between radiated bands of color was thought capable of displaying objects and areas where the camouflage was used. This multi-spectral camera was built by the Itek Corporation, carrying with it large quantities of film significantly to improve its usefulness.

In orbit, this third generation close-look vehicle weighed about 3 tons and was operated in a slightly more elliptical path than its predecessors. Swooping low across the top of the atmosphere, the Agena engine was relied upon frequently to boost the path back up to an acceptable altitude for survival. Without such propulsion capability the satellite would quickly have decayed to a fiery re-entry. In the period between 1967 and '72, when the area satellites had their heyday and finally were replaced by a radical new concept in reconnaissance, the close-look vehicles more than doubled their average useful lives from less than two weeks to about 30 days. This effectively reduced the launch frequency, annual totals of this type going from ten in 1967 to eight in 1968, six in 1969, five in 1970, four in 1971 and five in 1972. Further improvements would be made with the basic system, which was retained for close-look duties throughout the decade. By 1976, orbital lifetimes had almost doubled again, providing useful operations for nearly two months. But it was the area survey satellites which displayed the greatest change when a fourth generation design emerged operationally in 1972 effectively to replace the existing vehicles launched by the much modified, and thrust-augmented, Thor-Agena D.

During the mid-1960s considerable thought had been given to the next round of reconnaissance hardware and, even before the third generation emerged, plans for the distant future envisaged manned observation from space stations launched atop the biggest rocket to find a place in the military launch inventory. Called the Titan 3C, the rocket employed two large solid propellant boosters strapped alongside the first stage, itself an adapted variant of the Titan 2 ICBM. By increasing the length of the solids, converting it to a 3M variant, the big Titan would lift into low Earth orbit a laboratory more than 12 m long and 3 m in diameter weighing 9 tons. On top would be a 3-ton capsule of the type used in NASA's manned Gemini program, capable of returning to Earth with two astronauts, launched with the station for manned operations lasting about four weeks.

The laboratory itself would contain a pressurized atmosphere of oxygen and helium. McDonnell Douglas was contracted to build the Manned Orbital Laboratory (MOL), and to provide facilities inside for living, working, eating and sleeping. MOL was a massive undertaking calling for a major industrial effort over several years. The project formally began on August 25, 1965, at the hand of an enthusiastic Lyndon Johnson, then President. Only eight months earlier the Air Force's Dyna-Soar manned space glider had been cancelled in preference to a more permanent kind of space station launched on an expendable rocket. Plans for MOL envisaged a test flight with mock-ups of the hardware and this was successfully carried out on November 3, 1966. But the schedule for manned activity slipped when minor problems beset development and hopes for an orbital flight with astronauts in 1968 evaporated.

By 1967 the first manned launch was still a projected three years away, although the Air Force had already picked 16 candidates for crew selection. Increasingly, MOL came under criticism from those who questioned the wisdom of pursuing a military platform in orbit. The basic requirement evolved primarily from the outstanding success gained by the civilian space agency with astronauts performing observation of the planet for purely civilian objectives. A wide range of defense orientated needs could, said the Air Force, be met with a single facility containing a large selection of sensors and equipment. But at this time NASA was going all out to convince Congress that it, too, wanted to pursue development of a series of manned space stations based on redundant Apollo hardware. That effort would eventually materialize in the form of Skylab, actually only one station launched in 1973 for three visits lasting one, two and three months, respectively. During the fight on Capitol Hill for approval to go ahead with this project, NASA effectively squeezed the Air Force out. When Richard Nixon successfully made a second bid for the presidency, reaching the White House early in 1969, MOL was in for a shake up. Budget cuts had already sent cold ripples through the program but during the coming months an in-depth evaluation of just where the program stood exposed an Achilles heel which provided an opportunity for cancellation. Surely, said the new administration, it would be folly to proceed with two separate space station projects, one run by NASA and the other by the Pentagon. MOL's program director General Bernard A. Schriever fought hard to keep the schedule intact but it was a fight between further Moon landing flights—the first was still several months away—and continued work on the Air Force laboratory.

With unexpected suddenness the Pentagon announced on June 10, 1969, that MOL was cancelled and all further work would be terminated. Secrecy surrounded much which contributed toward the MOL program and its veiled public image belied the effort applied to this project in the preceding five years. But the work was not entirely lost. For some time, secret development of Project 612 had been pursued as a back-up to the Manned Orbital Laboratory. Two years before MOL was cancelled, the Air Force notified its Titan contractors that a 3D version would be required. This basically transformed the three-stage 3C into a two-stage launcher optimized for placing weights of about 13 tons in low Earth orbit; Titan 3C had been developed for putting satellites in stationary orbit nearly 36,000 km above Earth. Project 612 was a design concept taking all the more important features of MOL and putting them into the most ambitious Agena-based satellite mooted so far. It was a massive, 15 m long satellite designed to carry two camera systems. One, developed by Perkin-Elmer, was a high-resolution system for photographing in detail small objects or surface features. The second, built by Eastman Kodak, was the area survey system. Several other sensor packages could be attached to the satellite as and when requirements dictated a need, and special side-looking radars were designed for use on some flights. A large, 6 m diameter, antenna was kept folded for launch and released in orbit for communications with the ground stations and the transmission of telemetry. In addition, six recoverable capsules, working on the same principle adopted by the Discoverer test satellites and close-look satellites, were carried for periodic return to Earth with film in several canisters packed before launch.

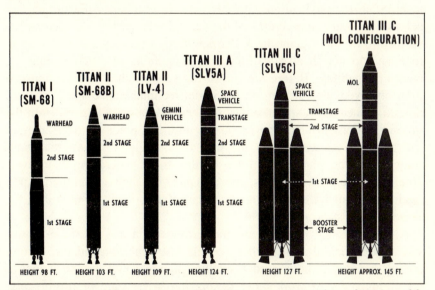

Built to match the rapidly expanding needs of military man in space, these adaptations of the basic Titan 1 ICBM evolved between 1960 and 1965.

In 1968, one year prior to the MOL cancellation, the satellite's code was changed to Project 467, which it retains to this day. In the light of developments with this major program, Pentagon acceptance of the MOL cancellation was better understood. Project 467, however, was an even tighter security problem than the manned contemporary. It had been hoped to get the first satellite into space during 1970 but continued teething troubles with the camera system and certain detectors held the schedule up for nearly a year. This was the fourth generation area-survey satellite built to replace the Thor-Agena D model and as such was sorely needed by the defense intelligence agencies. Dubbed "Big Bird" unofficially, Project 467 got its first launch on June 15, 1971. It was late in the morning when the Titan 3D thundered from the Vandenberg launch pad and climbed slowly into the sky. Big Bird was indeed a large satellite, four times heavier than any previous military reconnaissance vehicle. It was the beginning of a new era in space observation. But the Russians, too, made significant changes by providing a third generation satellite with the launch of Cosmos 208 in March 1968.

Weighing 5.9 tons, 400 kg more than the second generation type used first in 1963, the new variant retained the basic Vostok shell but included in the payload an ejectable capsule returned to Earth one day before the main spacecraft. Moreover, where earlier models had a useful life of about eight days, the new design remained in space up to four days longer. It all added up to the beginning of a major improvement in capability. Before the end of the year another modification had been observed. For the first time, Soviet reconnaissance satellites were able to maneuver in space, adjusting their orbits on command from the ground stations to place the orbital groundtrack precisely over areas of interest, without waiting for the path of the satellite to migrate naturally round the planet. Satellites of this third generation, maneuverable, type weighed 6.3 tons, more than twice their contemporary US equivalents but little more than half that of Big Bird, albeit still in the development stage during 1968.

Added technical requirements had provided, in this latest US recon-sat, capabilities denied earlier models. Several unavoidable factors would dictate just how good a satellite picture could be and it took a lot of ingenuity to work these factors into a package of instruments. Basically, resolution in photographic terms means the minimum distance between two points of light by which the two spots can be visually separated. In optical terms this is calculated with black and white lines but, in space reconnaissance, the term implies the smallest distance across which the line resolution applies. Many criteria impede easy calculation of the theoretical resolution inherent in any given system. The shape, obliquity, color and chemistry of the camera lens, added to composition and temperature of the film, confound predictions on just how good a system will be in practice. Where satellites are concerned, attitude stability is all-important, for the induced error caused by drifting off a precise alignment with the target will, if greater than the resolution limit of the camera system, create its own limitation on the picture quality. The satellite must have a stability in excess of the camera system's ground resolution. The resolution of a ground target is equal to the sum of the camera's altitude in kilometers divided by the focal length in millimeters, multiplied by the size of the image on the lens. The latter is the value in lines per millimeter of the combined resolution of the camera and the film. Image resolution is in large part restricted by the type of film employed. Early films available during the initial Samos experiments were restricted to line resolution of approximately 40/mm; that is, discrimination between 40 black and white lines laid across a 1 mm span. With a focal length of about 102 cm the system probably had a resolution of about 2.5 m at the operating altitude employed for this type of satellite. With modern film and camera systems a line resolution of at least 150/mm is quite possible and given a focal length of about 2.5 m, ground resolution should be equal to approximately 60 cm. With even longer focal lengths this figure could, in theory at least, be cut to about 15 cm. There is, however, a limit, due to Earth's atmosphere, below which no camera system would be able to go. That value is 10 cm, given a standard atmosphere. It is fair to say that by the time Big Bird commenced operational tests in 1971, the defense intelligence network was accepting images capable of resolving objects little more than 0.5 m in size. It was possible to pick up individual human beings, measure the size of vehicle wheels, determine the length of a tank gun, or gauge the jet intake size on a modern combat aircraft. The applications for this kind of capability are legion. Yet the intricacies of visual acuity are such that the resolution itself can be further enhanced by the shape of the object concerned. The scale resolution of 0.5 m for the high-resolution Big Bird camera applies to a square test patch 50 cm on each side. Discrimination of lines on the ground is effective even where the width, or diameter, is only 5 per cent of the calculated line resolution. This meant that a cable only 2.5 cm wide would be easily recognized on the developed film. In this kind of situation it would be possible to pick out the steel hawser used by, for instance, one tank to pull another. It would be easy to see a cluster of overhead power cables, or to follow the ruts made by a small wheeled vehicle in muddy ground.

As the plan evolved within the framework of a cancelled MOL program, Big Bird was used for high- and low-resolution area survey work from an orbit slightly higher than that used for close-look satellites retained to back up the system. This was because the close-look vehicles were short lived and were not designed, like Big Bird, for operations lasting five months. Big Bird predecessors had rarely been operated for longer than about three weeks. But like all previous satellites for this purpose, the new Lockheed satellite would employ the same kind of Sun-synchronous orbit around Earth, especially set up to observe a given area of the Earth at least once a day during daylight and at the same solar elevation. This is important for measuring the relative height of objects on the ground, and permits easy computerized comparisons between many pictures taken over a fixed period. A Sun-synchronous orbit is one in which the precession of the path about the planet is made to keep pace with the movement of the Earth around the Sun. Placed in a path which contains the plane of the Earth and the Sun, such a satellite, inclined in its orbit almost 90 degrees to the Equator, will repeatedly visit the same area on a regular time schedule. Several options emerge as a result of this geometrical ploy. If an object's size and shape cannot be determined from single pictures taken at fixed Sun angles, the use of other satellites to view the target at different times of the day provides a catalogue of photographs where the shadows will move around the object. Simple calculation will reveal the contours of the object in question, using the changing pattern of the shadows to build a three-dimensional view. Orbital maneuvering, too, can help by bunching up the ground-tracks for prolonged survey of a particular country or geographic region, a capacity well received by Russian intelligence experts when Cosmos 251 first used this device in 1968. The United States acquired the technique with the advent of Agena D stages in 1962.

Precision in placing Big Bird in a Sun-synchronous path was necessary due to the prolonged life of the satellite, operating durations getting longer as the program evolved. The first launch was followed by the second in January 1972, and a third nearly six months later. Several times the orbital characteristics were changed, sometimes the perigee was lowered and at other times the apogee was extended. Always, the period of robital revolution remained the same to preserve the geometry of the Sun-synchronous path.

As related earlier, the last of the Thor-Agena D, third generation area-survey satellites, was launched in May 1972. The time had come to complete the transfer to a new mode of operation. From this time on, Big Bird would do the plodding work of continuous blanket reconnaissance while the smaller close-look vehicles, dipping low for better resolution, pursued new and interesting targets of opportunity. From 1972, two or three close-look satellites would be launched each year, with a similar number of Big Bird vehicles gradually achieving greater operational lifetimes. Limited at first to operations over two or three months, satellites from late 1973 worked continuously for up to five months before being ordered down to destruction in the Earth's atmosphere over a 'pre-determined area. The final development involving this type of reconnaissance emerged in December 1976, not actually a fifth generation design, more an adanced and re-worked Big Bird vehicle introduced to speed the movement of information from the satellite to the user. Throughout the operational use of reconnaissance satellites, the CIA had been concerned that timely application of the data was a vital ingredient and a full measure of its value. The defense agencies agreed that film recovery pods released from Big Bird arrived for analysis via a route not designed for maximum speed! When the pod separated from the physical structure of the Lockheed satellite its own small propulsion engine reduced speed sufficient to cause it to fall back into the atmosphere. Recovered in mid-air by C-130 aircraft operated by the 6594th Test Wing from Hawaii, the capsule was returned for opening, then a special aircraft flew the film to Andrews Air Force Base, Washington, DC. From there it was taken to the National Reconnaissance Office where the National Photographic Interpretation Center got to work on the developed product.

Dramatic improvements in the digital transmission of information from satellites allowed development of a special instrument with a capacity to send pictures directly to the ground. In the early 1970s, soon after Big Bird emerged in its initial version, design engineers began to prepare the second generation variant which could send pictures by this method. Known as the KH-11 satellite, it stemmed from work contracted to TRW under the designation Project 1010. But direct digital transmission was to be only one of several modifications made possible by new technology and not merely improvements to existing concepts. KH-11 has been developed as the final stop-gap between the old, one-shot, satellite designs and the new era of reusable satellites where the complete assembly will be launched and retrieved by Space Shuttles from the mid-1980s. The first KH-11 lifted away from Vandenberg on December 19, 1976, into an orbit almost twice as high at apogee as the early Big Bird models. From the outset, KH-11 was to operate in space for one full year rather than the five months of its predecessors but would supplement, rather than replace, the Lockheed film-return type satellite.

Two Big Birds of conventional design were sent aloft in June 1977 and March 1978 before the second KH-11 was launched on June 14, 1978. Two more Big Birds ascended, in March and May 1979, before the third KH-11 on February 7, 1980. And all the while, as Big Bird and its derivative were swapping duties, the close-look satellites continued to fly in support of special targets and ground sites. Introduction of the KH-11 brought a new immediacy to satellite reconnaissance, providing information rapidly and on time for distribution to the relevant agency. By the end of the 1970s there were fewer satellites being launched each year in support of the continuous monitoring role, but each was a major system on its own with sustained responsibility for many additional tasks. Big Bird carried several different sensory packages on each flight as well as piggy-back satellites designed to fly away on their own clandestine duties. The 13-ton lifting capacity of the big Titan 3D provided adequate margin for flexible payloads.

Reconnaissance had come a long way since the first hesitant attempts to recover a small satellite from space in 1959. It had cost a lot of money and ballooned into a major national asset. Without the comprehensive coverage provided by these satellites, however, several important initiatives would never have taken place. Without them also, nobody would probably have been any wiser about one terrible miscalculation which set the world on an arms race unlike anything ever seen before.

Thor, the Air Force's first operational long-range missile, is seen here supporting an Agena rocket stage for use as a satellite launcher.

German V-2 rockets were taken to the United States for extensive tests after World War 2.

Early interest in the problems of space flight inspired tests like these, carried out by the Air Force to study the effects of weightlessness by simulating zero-g for several seconds in parabolic aircraft flight.

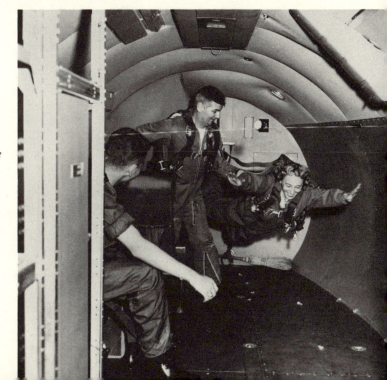

America's first operational ICBM, Atlas, was to provide the first stage for several multi-stage satellite launchers.

A flight readiness firing is performed with an Atlas-Agena at the US Air Force Vandenberg Air Force Base.

The X-15 rocket research aircraft, carried aloft by the B-52, helped push back the performance barrier leading to hypersonic flight.

Later variants employed high-energy upper stages like the Centaur, shown here atop an Atlas first stage.

Discoverer 1 on top of a Thor-Agena launcher.

Star Raker space transporters proposed by Rockwell promise significantly to lower the cost of placing cargo in orbit and put space travel firmly on an airline type basis.

The degree of lift and manoeuvreability in the atmosphere would be greatly improved over the Shuttle and, by using Star Raker's jet engines, the big transporter would fly to selected landing sites.

Unlike Atlas and Thor liquid propellant rockets, solid propellant boosters offered power and reliability, facilities for the type being assigned a special area at the Cape.

Huge steel gantries and solid concrete blockhouses shape the main firing line as activity builds up at Cape Canaveral during the early '60s.

Dyna-Soar was to be launched by a Titan rocket and propelled into orbit on a mission from which it would have returned like a glider to a landing on skids. It never got off the ground and was to be cancelled in favor of a manned laboratory.

Bizarre projects like this gas turbine-powered jet flying belt prompted suggestions for a rocket version to be used for lifting personnel to the battlefield.

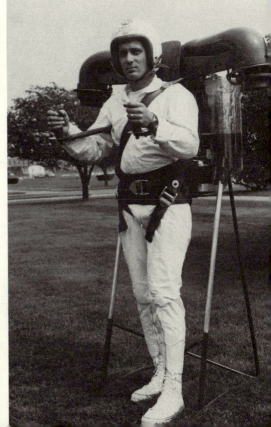

Dyna-Soar was a radical departure from the ballistic re-entry cones of the civilian space agency's Mercury project and carried wings with which to generate lift for a conventional landing.

Orbital work-horse for initial US Air Force space projects, this Agena rocket stage was built to lift spy and early-warning satellites into space on top of Thor or Atlas rockets.

Discoverer 1, seen here on top of a Thor-Agena launcher, was successfully launched on February 28, 1959, but failed in orbit.

Discoverer satellites were sent into space from the Pacific, Vandenberg Air Force Base, site in California. Note the service mast alongside this view of the seventh satellite in the series.

The Discoverer 13 instrument package arrives at Andrews Air Force Base on its way to the White House. General Schriever (left), General White, and Colonel Mathieson (right) examine the capsule.

The Discoverer 13 capsule is shown to President Eisenhower at the White House, August 1960.

Ready for the return of Discoverer nose cone, this C-130 prepares to leave Honolulu. Aircraft of this type were used to snare descending capsules.

January 31, 1961, just three years after the first American satellite was launched, Samos 2 on top of its Atlas-Agena launch vehicle stands ready for flight at Vandenberg.

Discoverer 14's descending capsule is snagged by a recovery aircraft flying over the Pacific.

It took careful aim by the pilot to have the snare catch the Discoverer capsule in mid-flight.

Launched on a developed version of Russia's first ICBM, the manned Vostok spacecraft was four times the weight of America's Mercury capsule. The combined Vostok spacecraft and launcher is seen here at the Paris Air Show.

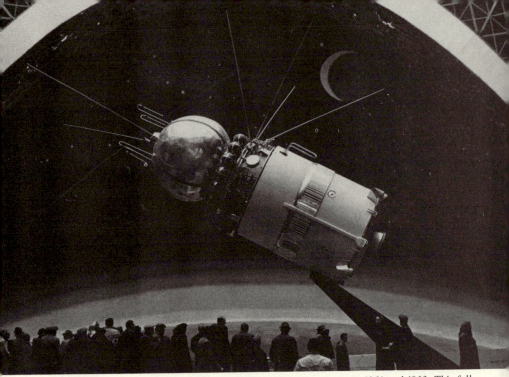

Vostok was employed to lift Soviet cosmonauts into space between 1961 and 1963. This full size replica shows off the spherical cabin and the cylindrical second stage of the launch vehicle which remained with the spacecraft until shortly before re-entry.

Seen reclining on its ejection seat, a dummy pilot gives scale to the spherical Vostok re-entry capsule covered with ablative material to protect it from the heat generated by atmospheric friction during descent.

The world's first space man, Yuri Gagarin, proudly shows off a replica of Vostok at the Paris Air Show in 1965, the first public disclosure of the spacecraft.

Development of the Air Force Manned Orbital Laboratory was based on the timely existence of the Titan 3 launcher, seen here in model form with two solid propellant boosters.

Lengthened Titan 3 solid propellant boosters and a laboratory module topped by a Gemini spacecraft characterized the shape of the Air Force's Manned Orbital Laboratory shown here in model form.

No military reconnaissance photos have ever been released for publication but this view from NASA's Landsat spacecraft of the Cape Canaveral area graphically illustrates the detail visible from space.

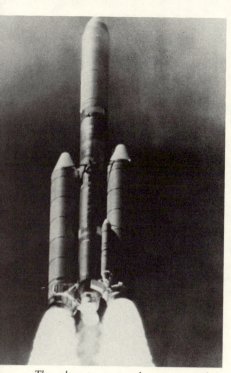

Observing the performance of the launch vehicle is frequently just as important as watching the way the satellite behaves. Here, Vandenberg technicians check telemetry receivers during the early 1960s when several new systems were being flexed.

The closest anyone has got to photographing a Big Bird military reconnaissance satellite for public release is the Air Force cameraman who shot this view of a mighty Titan 3D launch. Inside the shroud at top, one of the largest and most sophisticated satellites built, bristling with sensors and camera equipment.

When the Dyna-Soar was cancelled in favor of the Manned Orbital Laboratory, it was the end of reusable winged space vehicles for at least the next decade.

The Hughes Leasat communications satellite is the first totally Shuttle oriented hardware to reach the customer, designed to make good use of the orbiter's wide cargo bay.

*From stationary orbit the Hughes
Leasat will serve military users
for strategic and tactical communications.*

Photographs from space can be made to tell more about the surface below than would otherwise be possible with the naked eye.

Above *Clouds move across the right side of this satellite view of Minsk, with surface detail partially obscured. Elsewhere, routes of communication are easily visible.*

Below left *Satellite photographs can usefully provide detail of geographical phenomena of use to occupation forces. Here, the subtle terrain folds around Lake Baykal in Russia reveal contours and elevations with great accuracy. Note the stretch of land that has come away from the north-west edge of the lake and slid into Lake Baykal, an event which killed 1,300 people in 1861.*

Below right *From space, Leningrad is almost completely ice-locked in this spring view. Information about river blockage and ice distribution can be useful for troop disposition and for learning details of ship movements. Here, Lake Ladoga is at the top, with the Baltic and Gulf of Finland, left of center, frozen over.*

Above left *Dissected by roads and railways, the wasteland around Lake Balkhash provides conclusive proof of anti-ballistic missile tests west of Sary Shagan, a town on the lake shore at the center of the picture.*
Above right *The Baltic port of Riga is observed by satellite to be partially locked in with ice, but note how the image captures precise definition of the shape of ice packs and flow patterns.*
Below left *Precise outlines of communal farms reveal the agricultural function of this stretch flanking the Volga north-east of Volgograd. Multi-spectral pictures like this expose different surface activities, sometimes revealing industrial or military research.*
Below right *This multi-spectral view of Washington, DC, shows Chesapeake Bay and the Potomac River, with healthy crops areas, suburban areas, and barren land in various shades of black and grey.*

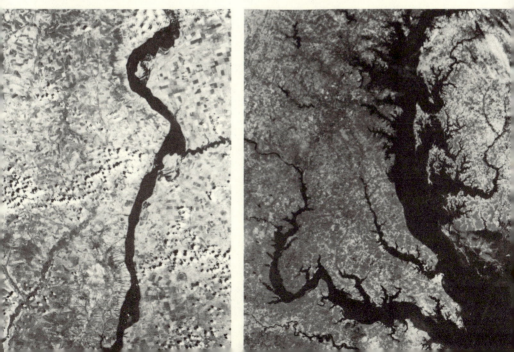

While major strides were being made with sophisticated unmanned satellites, Air Force "lifting-body" research vehicles were studying the needs of manned recoverable vehicles like the Shuttle which emerged in the early '70s.

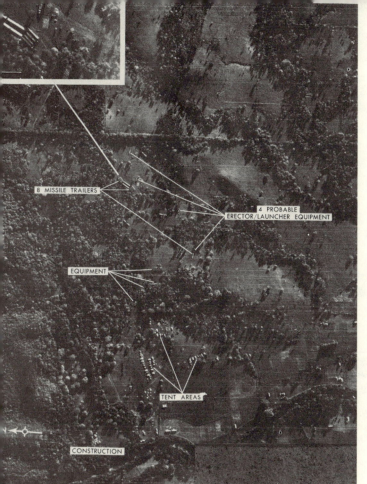

8 MISSILE TRAILERS

4 PROBABLE
ERECTOR/LAUNCHER EQUIPMENT

EQUIPMENT

TENT AREAS

CONSTRUCTION

Photographs like this, taken from a U-2 spy-plane, revealed in 1962 the preparation of Soviet missile fields on the island of Cuba, directly threatening the United States and adding momentum to the search for a global strategic reconnaissance apparatus.

MISSILE TRANSPORTERS

12 PROB GUIDELINE MISSILES

HEAVY EQUIPMENT

5 MISSILE DOLLIES

20 LONG CYLINDRICAL TANKS

MISSILE TRANSPORTERS

OPEN STORAGE

In this shot of Soviet missile fields in Cuba, the camera clearly picks out transporters and Guideline surface-to-air missiles for defense.

Above left *By the early 1970s, Soyuz spacecraft comprised the mainstay of Soviet manned space plans, a vehicle that would find application in the unmanned role as a military reconnaissance satellite from 1979.*

Above right *Retaining the basic launch vehicle employed for major space missions since Sputnik 1, the Soyuz launcher has adopted a much more powerful second stage than the Vostok which preceded it. Note the escape rocket on top to remove the spacecraft to safety in the event of a malfunction, and gantry arms either side being lowered prior to launch.*

Below *Salyut space stations have been used since 1971 to test equipment designed for both civil and military functions in orbit. Seen here is the Salyut 3 type which set the design for the later versions.*

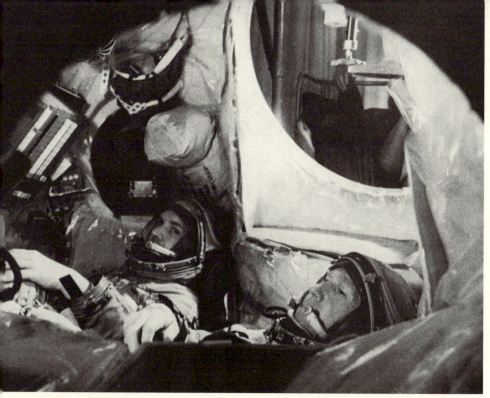

Above *When three Soviet cosmonauts lost their lives in a Soyuz accident during 1971, the spacecraft was re-designed as a two-man ship allowing the use of pressure suits for which there had been no room in the earlier version.*

Below *Cosmonaut Kubasov gives scale to the comparatively spacious Soyuz interior.*

The Apollo-Soyuz Test Project flown in 1975 brought an Apollo spacecraft to dock with a Soviet Soyuz for two days of tests. Note the US-built docking module between the two ships, and the difference in size between the two.

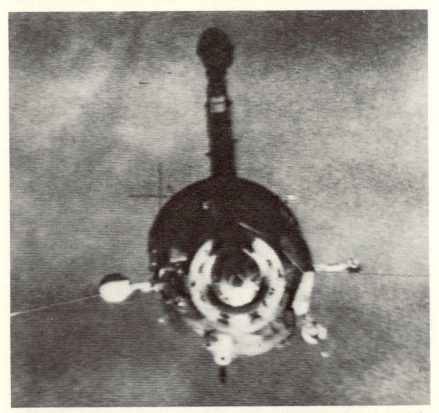

A TV camera on board Salyut 6 observes the nose of Soyuz 26 approaching to dock with the space station in 1977.

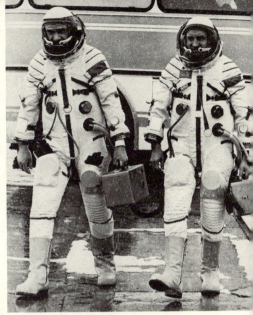

Regular use of space stations like Salyut for developing equipment for civil and military operational requirements calls for an all-weather capability as seen in this snow-bound view of Soyuz 27 cosmonauts Dzhanibekov and Makarov in 1978.

Docking equipment specially developed for the joint US-Soviet mission in 1975, seen here in a simulator, formed the basis for later units for Salyut.

Plush new control equipment introduced for the joint US-Soviet docking flight was retained for use with Salyut operations.

Two separate two-man crews from Soyuz 26 and 27 visit aboard the Salyut 6 in 1978.

Long duration flights were made possible by the spacious interior of the Salyut space station, here revealing the several instrument panels used to monitor and control on-board systems.

New space suits developed for Soyuz/Salyut flights included a hinged hood.

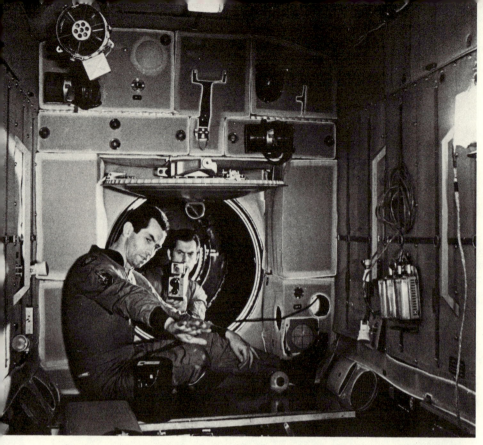

Cosmonaut training includes the use of Salyut simulators at the Gagarin Training Center, here seen occupied by Kovalyonok and Ivanchenkov who would fly later in Soyuz 29.

The size of the Salyut mock-up is given scale by cosmonauts Kovalyonok and Ivanchenkov. Note the solar array wing, at right, attached to the wall of the space station.

ОГОНЁК

ИЗДАТЕЛЬСТВО
«ПРАВДА» МОСКВА

№ 4 ЯНВАРЬ 19

Land recovery has been standard for all Soviet manned space vehicles because the geographical position of Russia makes it more probable that any return would be over land. Here, dust is blown high by retro-rockets on the spacecraft as the Soyuz lands back on Earth.

Pictured on the cover of a Soviet magazine, two Soyuz spacecraft are seen docked to either end of a Salyut station in this artist's illustration, with the three Salyut solar cell arrays fully deployed.

Water landing tests like the one shown here involving a Soyuz mock-up carried out in the late 1960s may have been authorized to support circumlunar flight preparations. There would be a greater probability of splashdown when coming back from the vicinity of the Moon than from Earth orbit because of the angle of entry.

Effectively serving as a political tool for pro-Communist enticement, the Salyut space station has been used to support several flights involving non-Russian cosmonauts. Hermaszewski (Poland), at left, trains with Soviet cosmonaut Klimuk before the Soyuz 30 flight in 1978.

Salyut stations are regularly used to gather large volumes of Earth science data, much of which is used by the military forces to catalogue activity in foreign countries, a function for which America's Manned Orbital Laboratory was conceived.

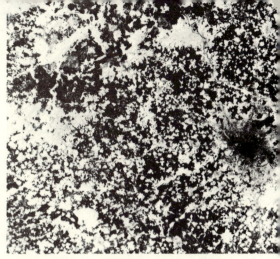

This picture of the Soviet launch sites located between the cities of Tyuratam and Baykonur reveals in part what can be seen from space. Note the roads connecting launch pads and laboratory complexes. Industrial development (top) is the main administration area, with Tyuratam directly below, connected by a main arterial route. Northwest of the complex is a new research facility, while just to the southwest is the rectangular smudge of a propellant storage site. The river at bottom is the Syr Dar Ya running through Tyuratam.

This satellite view of Moscow shows how natural phenomena changed by the presence of human activity can build a comprehensive picture of events down at the surface. Notice how the city, right of center, has generated heat to melt the snow prominent in surrounding areas. The dark patches are clumps of evergreens. Note also the Moscow Canal running north and the Moscow River flowing east through the city.

Ground and air-borne Navstar users will be fully integrated with a system essential to defense and, in time of war, satellites like these must be protected from hostile acts.

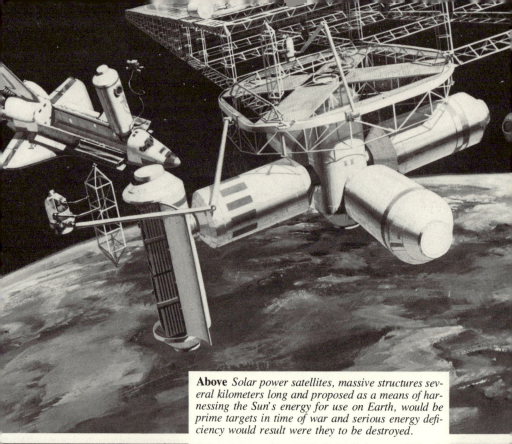

Above *Solar power satellites, massive structures several kilometers long and proposed as a means of harnessing the Sun's energy for use on Earth, would be prime targets in time of war and serious energy deficiency would result were they to be destroyed.*

Below *Large structures built up from several Shuttle loads will appear toward the mid-1980s, offering to transfer into orbit functions now carried out by computer and data transfer equipment on Earth.*

3. The Soviet ploy

Reconnaissance information and foreign policy

"I wouldn't want to be quoted on this, but we spent 35-40 billion [dollars] on the space program and, if nothing else has come of it except knowledge that we've gained from space photography, it would be worth ten times what the whole program has cost because tonight we know how many missiles the enemy has and it turns out that our [earlier] guesses were way off."

President Johnson was speaking publicly in the only forthright comment about military reconnaissance satellites prior to President Carter's public acknowledgement that they do actually exist.

"We were doing things we didn't need to do," he continued, "we were building things we didn't need to build, we were harboring fears we didn't need to harbor."

The truth that Lyndon Johnson knew was an echo of the situation expressed several years earlier by John F. Kennedy in private. America had set in motion a machine which could not now be stopped, orchestrated a massive undertaking in which major industrial contractors put tens of thousands of people to work for the government, and prepared an arsenal for World War 3 which might conceivably have been prevented. The only real point about reconnaissance is that it tells you what you do not already know about people and activities over which you have very little control. It had been assumed, quite widely, that Soviet assertions on the nuclear weapons issue were correct, or that at least a semblance of authority remained in confident statements concerning Russia's might. But such was not really the case. There was very little bite to back Krushchev's bark. Nevertheless when President Kennedy set re-armament as the first goal of his administration, seeking completely to outpace the already energetic efforts of the Eisenhower era, he was unaware of the true picture regarding Soviet capability. Very soon, the satellite pictures exposed the bluff for what

71

it was. But it was too late. Set up at least two years before the first full inventory of Soviet weapons had been acquired via the eyes of the area-survey and close-look reconsats, preparations for a major program of expansion had already been committed beyond the point of no return. Major developments in guided missile technology, briefly discussed in the last chapter, provided America with the capacity for large arsenals of intercontinental ballistic missiles.

Non-storable liquid propellants were replaced by storable fluids capable of remaining in the tanks of large missiles for many weeks. Moreover, the introduction of protective structures, hardened emplacements replaced by underground silos, allowed each missile to provide insurance against a pre-emptive first strike—an attack coming unexpectedly and without warning—which would surely have disabled the complete ballistic missile fleet long before it could get off the ground. With quick-fire capability from propellants already stored inside the tanks, and protection from covert attack, the United States' land-based ICBM force was an efficient and creditable back-up to the large bomber fleet then held as the prime mode of attack. During the early 1960s, that situation changed dramatically. From highly secret work aimed at miniaturizing the basic elements of a missile, plus advanced technology on reducing the size of nuclear warheads, scientists were able to develop a missile fired from vertical tubes in the hull of a submarine. The Polaris program involved the design and fabrication of a new fleet of boats filling a uniquely different role from any other underwater task force. For the first time, submarine-launched ballistic missiles—SLBMs—would serve in the front line of nuclear deterrence by forming the third leg of the defense triad. Land-based ICBMs would pack the heavy punch, Polaris SLBMs would fly from discrete locations to selected targets on the Soviet mainland, and massed bombers from Strategic Air Command would fly with several nuclear weapons in each aircraft, to penetrate the Soviet Union in large numbers. From a breakthrough in missile technology which made Polaris a feasible proposition for development, land-based deterrence was improved dramatically with the introduction of Minuteman. Under Kennedy, the plan evolved to give the United States a major stake in strategic warfare capability and the highly efficient production techniques acquired first by the motor industry and then by the war effort during World War 2 provided the overkill which sent shivers of concern through the stone walls of the Kremlin.

In the single-minded belief that Soviet Russia was engaged in an all-out effort to prepare massed armies for global conflict, President Kennedy set in motion the machine which would threaten the stability of the entire world. For instead of pausing, in the absence of adequately reliable intelligence, the President authorized an unnecessary response. Contractors had their targets, weapons development laboratories worked flat-out to produce the warheads, and the Air Force and the Navy built up facilities for the new hardware. Soon, missiles were slipping into silos with chilling frequency, while new and devastatingly lethal submarines rolled down the slipways. Within two years from go-ahead, where not a single missile stood ready, the United States had acquired, by the time Krushchev set up medium-range missiles on Cuba during 1962, the capability to launch more than 400 rockets, each carrying a nuclear warhead. And as discussed in the previous chapter, Russia had less than 80. It was just the beginning, for although intelligence reports from the CIA and from the Air Force defense agencies now warned of dramatic overestimating in previous years, it was too late to do much to halt the production lines. One year later, the United States had more than 650 land- and sea-based missiles capable of striking the Soviet Union, while Russia's late start kept its own force at less than 200.

The targets set by the Kennedy administration were much higher than this, though, and by 1968, just six years after the Cuba crisis, the American strategic aresenal included 1,710 missiles of the ICBM and SLBM class. Russia had just half as many. In the certain knowledge that the imbalance was likely to attract Soviet reciprocation, the United States halted missile emplacement in that year. After 1968, not one additional strategic missile was added to the total. But the Russians, bruised by the memory of Cuba when Kennedy used a massive superiority in strategic weapons to subjugate their foreign policy, continued to build. By 1969 their strategic missiles numbered more than 1,000, and by 1971 they had met and exceeded the total stocks held by the United States. For more than a decade America had the upper hand in the tools of global conflict and the new situation did not appeal to the Pentagon. Throughout the 1970s, in the background to public awareness, military concern was pressed upon the politicians who refused to be rushed into new initiatives for which the armed services were pleading. There was good reason to believe that if earlier decisions about the massive missile build-up had been properly tempered with caution, the dramatic imbalance observed by the Russians would not have given reason for such a major build-up. Behind the scenes, developments were proving successful with a radical new concept for strategic missiles.

Up to the late 1960s, each missile carried a single warhead designed to separate from the main body of the rocket in flight and continue on its way to the target. But further miniaturization of nuclear warheads provided the opportunity to place more than one atop each missile. In a cluster called MRV, or Multiple Reentry Vehicle, Polaris or Minuteman missiles could be equipped with up to three separate nuclear charges, released on the way down to spread a lethal trio of detonations over and around a larger target, or to provide concussive effect on a hardened structure.

In its wake, MRV was followed rapidly by an even more sophisticated concept. Called MIRV, or Multiple Independently-targeted Reentry Vehicle, the concept relied on a so-called "post boost control system," built by Bell Aerosystems, to support and control the release of three separate nuclear charges. After the main boost phase, in which the three stages of a Minuteman missile would blast the warhead on its way to the target, the boost control system would maneuver before releasing each charge sequentially, thus delivering each to a specific trajectory independent of the other. This effectively tripled the strike capacity of each missile, turning a single delivery vehicle into a very fast equivalent of a manned bomber, selecting separate targets in turn. In one stroke, by fitting Polaris and Minuteman with MRV and MIRV warheads, the United States had a ready means of significantly increasing the value of the strategic deterrent. Each warhead would be less powerful than the single charge carried hitherto, but careful application of less powerful heads to less demanding targets would get round that problem. The real intent in America's strategic force was not to send the population of the Soviet Union to Hades, but rather to hit and completely disable the means by which Russia could continue to fight a major conflict. This effectively shifted the missiles from targets aimed at terrorizing the pubic, and causing widespread loss of civilian life, to their opposite launch sites in Russia. Only by knocking out the hardened emplacements and the silos containing Soviet ICBMs could the war be contained. Or so went the argument. It was, therefore, logical to expand rapidly the number of warheads which could, with the greater precision and accuracy traditionally held by the US missiles, silence the opposing threat. By 1971 the Polaris was being fitted with MRVs and plans were well in hand to fit the more flexible MIRVs on a new variant of Minuteman.

Beyond a mere numbers game, the race to wield the biggest threat had broken through to a new level of escalation. For if single warheads had been retained on each missile, the United States would have been limited to 1,710 rounds in the ground and at sea since 1968. Yet because multiple warheads could be introduced without buying additional missiles, or risking a public debate, the potential number of targets available to the strategic missile force increased to more than 7,000 by the late 1970s. Faced with this further escalation in capability, the Soviets felt compelled to develop their own multiple warhead device. It was a dangerous game of supremacy, with neither side wishing to be left behind in the race. It began because the reconsats came two years too late and it would lead to major new initiatives for using space to win a global war. But first, there was the SALT negotiation.

Strategic Arms Limitation Talks had been an important element in the foreign policy laid down by President Nixon. Long regarded by the Russians as an anti-communist war-horse, Soviet leaders had a measure of respect for the hard line taken by this ex-lawyer turned President. With deep concern to reduce the level of conflict in the stagnant campaign in Vietnam, Nixon brought new policies to the White House and was seen by many foreign countries as a welcome change from the outdated nature of earlier administrations. It became possible for Soviet and American negotiators to sit down and discuss arms control. Without the extensive, and by now accepted, use of reconnaissance satellites, neither side would have been in a position to accept conditions calling for specific quantities of arms. Each side felt confident that the other would be incapable of concealing major weapons systems and so the general background to SALT was framed by awareness that agreements could be verified. Not in the deliberate and stated intentions of spying on each other from space, for the existence of such satellites had never been publicly admitted, but rather by the use of "national technical means" which everybody knew was the hardware no one referred to! Back in 1955, President Eisenhower impressed upon the Russians a need for free access to each others' air space so that photographs could reveal the force strength of each side. That was flatly rejected by the Soviets but it was a prediction of the only means through which East and West could get round a negotiating table. When satellites were exploited for reconnaissance, and when the initial trauma caused by their use had dissipated, conditions were right for international agreements. For anything decided at the conference table need not explicitly rely on trust; the means were available for detailed surveillance. Yet the very presence of the reconnaissance satellites was to turn the tables on the Russians and cause discontent in America about the real intentions of the Soviet armed forces.

In May 1972 the two super-powers signed an agreement limiting the number of strategic delivery systems to a total 2,400 launchers. This left open to both sides the application of MRV and MIRV warheads, and did nothing to restrict the size of any future missiles either side might wish to produce. But the intent was clear enough: if not a physical de-scaling of strategic power, then at least a genuine attempt to halt unrestrained growth in fire-power and offensive weapons. SALT-1 was a start, seen by the United States as a first step in getting agreement to dismantle the missile arsenal. Some even nurtured the hope that it was a beginning on the road to disarmament. But it was a false hope, for others saw it as a clever ploy by the Russians to tie America down with an ageing missile force while they developed new and better systems, and these people were to be proved correct in the years ahead. It was the reconnaissance satellites of the Big Bird and close-look categories which provided the evidence to expose the Soviet violations. But there was one other type of satellite, very heavily involved with photographic reconnaissance programs, which helped unfold the evidence. From the outset, Discoverer-type payloads were considered by the Air Force as a replacement in real terms for all the activities and intelligence gathering exercises employed by airborne methods before the satellite era. As discussed already, U-2 aircraft were equipped with instruments for picking up and recording electronic information about defense radars and other installations propagating electromagnetic radiation of one type or another. Even the communication frequencies could be determined and conversations "bugged" with these techniques. What the ground-based radars listening across the Turkish border could not detect, the high-flying aircraft did.

So it was that when satellites took over the role of spying from on high, it was equally important to retrieve as much electronic information as possible. This is frequently the forgotten arm of reconnaissance, for it is certainly less attractive than a collection of photographs showing actual hardware. To the intelligence analyst, however, the type, shape and intensity of electromagnetic activity generated by a photographic smudge can make all the difference between a puzzling blob and complete identification. The electronic ear is, therefore, the third dimension in an otherwise flat projection, adding a purpose to what could be a disused building or an apparently concealed command post. The history of electronic "ferret" satellites is a mirror of reconsat developments. Two types evolved in the Air Force program, one involving satellites based on the Agena B and D stages and a second riding piggy-back on satellites launced for photographic surveillance. The former weighed between 1,000 and 2,000 kg depending on the type of launcher employed, the latter were much smaller and weighed only a few tens of kilograms. Unlike the elliptical path of a reconsat, ferrets prefer the stable orbit of a nearly circular path for longer time across the target and longer mission life. The first flight with the heavy satellites launched by their own boosters came in May 1962, at the start of a regular series flown over the next ten years. The last flight of the launch-dedicated satellites came on December 14, 1971 when a payload comprising several such satellites was pushed into a comparatively high orbit. Most ferrets were put into paths between 400 km and 550 km. A few were placed in orbits 900 km above Earth and the last was one of those. In all, about 33 ferrets of this type were launched, all designed to study the geometry of radars.

The second type, those launched as sub-satellites and carried into space attached to a much larger satellite, began life in June 1963. From January 1972 the piggy-back ferrets were lifted into space by Big Bird satellites on the massive Titan 3D launcher, taking over the job carried out by the single satellites, but not all Big Birds carried ferrets although some carried at least two. One of these, separated from the seventh Big Bird in a path between 159 km and 275 km, lifted itself into a circular orbit almost 1,460 km above Earth. It was a process followed by others. Ferrets of both types were, however, used to cover the full gamut of electronic intelligence gathering, which included evesdropping on radio communications, listening in to operational tests, mapping the ground-to-air radar installations, observing antenna characteristics and determining radar screens, far from national borders where ground interrogation can occasionally supplement the satellites.

Plans for massed intrusion of hostile airspace rely on continuous updating to keep pace with the location of defense installations and, increasingly over the past decade, the Russians have concentrated on protecting their territorial borders from bombers and other intruders. In an age when cruise missiles will gradually take over the deep intrusion role hitherto assigned the manned bomber force, electronic maps are the only sure means of making that weapon an effective deterrent. The moment the enemy believes he can really stop the threat, that weapon is no longer a deterrent.

Back in the early 1970s, however, the combined intelligence gathering resources of the photographic reconnaissance satellites and the electronic ferrets played a vital part in warning the West of deeply troublesome violations in the SALT-1 treaty. As would be discerned later, the agreement to limit strategic nuclear capability was, in effect, a move by the Soviet Union to tie down US developments, legalize an expanding Russian defense program, and set up channels through which the Soviets could employ new and unannounced technologies. The evidence is the greatest vindication yet for reconsats employed as monitoring platforms and for the use of ferrets to check radar and radio deployments. No sooner had the Treaty been signed in May 1972, than the Russians moved ahead with several unexpected improvements to a force posture the Americans believed was still many years away. The Russians had done nothing to clarify developments which could, in theory, work against the intent of SALT and, with legalities concluded, they began to replace major missile units with larger and more powerful weapons.

Two techniques were also brought in effectively to upgrade the strategic capability. The US Titan and Minuteman ICBMs (54 of the former; 1,000 of the latter deployed from 1967) adopt what is called a "hot-launch" technique whereby the rocket is ignited with the missile still inside the silo; in the case of Titan, the exhaust plume is channelled into two separate ducts and then allowed to vent itself through openings on the surface either side of the silo. This means that sufficient space between the body of the missile and the wall of the tubular silo must be designed into the facility for release of gases and other exhaust products and so limit the surface temperature of the projectile before it ascends. All missiles were known to have this method of launch, allowing the round to lift itself up from the base of the vertical launch tube. But developments from Polaris technology, where submarine-launched missiles would first have to reach the surface before starting their ascent, allowed unique changes in the way big land-based missiles were launched. The language of the SALT-1 agreement stipulated that the number of existing silos observed by military reconnaissance satellites on Soviet territory must not be increased in size beyond certain modifications unrelated to the size of the missile inside. This was the subject of lengthy debate. The intent of the clause was clear and unambiguous, indeed it could have only one meaning: by agreeing not significantly to alter the diameter of the silos, each side would be prohibited from deploying bigger missiles.

There was no agreement as such on limiting larger ICBMs, but in successfully getting the Soviets to agree to make the silos no larger the end result would be the same. However, soon after the signatures were secured, reconnaissance satellites observed major alterations being made to the existing hot-launch silos to convert them to a method of launch similar to that used for Polaris and its Poseidon successor. Known as a "cold-launch" or "pop-up" technique, it required the use of a special liner placed inside the silo so that a very much bigger missile could take advantage of the full width of the existing tube without having to leave room for rocket exhaust. The cold-launch method pumped pressurized gas into the space between the missile and the silo, very much less than with the early method, physically to eject the projectile like a cork from a bottle. Once free of the surface, the rocket's motor would ignite for the projectile to ascend as normal. Polaris and Poseidon, and their Soviet equivalents, employ this method, the motors only igniting when the rocket pops up above the water. It was a simple ploy to remain within the language of the treaty yet install much larger rockets in existing silos. But there was more to it than that. For with a cold-launch technique the silo suffers almost no damage and can be used many times over. It is conceivable that a vacated silo could be made ready within a matter of an hour or two, reloaded with another ICBM of the same type, and used to send another clutch of warheads on their way. From the beginning of strategic satellite reconnaissance it has been known that the Russians were very interested in using launch pads more than once. They have even developed re-fire techniques and this had been recognized by the former Chief of Staff, Intelligence, US Air Force Headquarters, 1972-7, General George J. Keegan, Jr:

"A couple of us acquired some hard, incontrovertible evidence that each SS-7 missile on a launch pad had four missiles in nearby hardened storage for re-fire purposes . . . The fact of the matter was that each ICBM had at least four additional ICBMs for refire capability, which under their nuclear war doctrine makes great sense . . . Today there are two types of their silo-based, cold-launch, missiles in which the main engine ignition occurs outside the silo and does no damage to the silo. They can lower another missile in a canister in that silo and re-fire it, if not in minutes, in just a very few hours. Now the silos are too hard for us to destroy, so a great many more are going to survive."

In this way, Soviet rocket forces acquired a growth capability far beyond the intentions of the SALT negotiators, even though they legally remained within the written language of the accord. No sooner had the treaty been signed than the Russians began a flurry of launch tests with a complete new generation of missiles, two of them heavier than anything built before. Just one year after the agreement had been signed, the SS-16 appeared as a land-mobile ballistic missile with intercontinental range. The Russians had said nothing about this during protracted talks leading up to the protocol, but reconnaissance satellites picked up equipment associated with the project and a suspicion emerged that the Soviets had employed a clever trick to acquire an even greater strategic capacity. For the SS-16 had more than twice the throw-weight—the effective mass of the warhead—than the rocket it was supposedly designed to replace. However, careful counting by reconsats revealed the surprise that Russia had not produced more than 60 silos for the SS-16 and that, although it could be used from a mobile platform, it had not been deployed in any great numbers.

However, effectively to evade the introduction of more strategic weapons than allowed for under the 2,400 ceiling of SALT-1, the top stage of the SS-16 was removed and the missile relegated to intermediate-range outside the scope of the treaty. In this configuration, known as the SS-20, it represents a completely new category of weapon capable of sending anywhere in Europe a war load equal to America's Minuteman. With a range observed by satellites to be in excess of 7,000 km when carrying a very light nuclear charge, or 5,000 km with a single large or triple MRV head, the rocket poses serious threat to the entire NATO region. Estimates vary on projected SS-20 deployment plans but conservative estimates predict a total 400 launchers for this mobile missile. Used from a forest clearing or the outskirts of a town, each launcher could probably release three missiles, two being re-loaded in sequence after the first had been fired. In this way, the

European theater is threatened by up to 1,200 SS-20 missiles, each with an explosive yield equal to the Minuteman ICBM. Yet because it is deployed as a two-stage intermediate weapon, the missile is outside the scope of SALT. If the third stage is added, the resulting SS-16 configuration rapidly converts it into a missile of strategic proportions, able to fly more than 9,000 km with a nuclear warhead. In this way, the Soviets can quickly upgrade their strategic force by converting in the field, and this is a very difficult activity to predict even with reconnaissance photographs and electronic intelligence.

There was nothing the United States could do about the adoption of a cold-launch technique, or the deployment of the SS-20. Neither was there anything which could be done about three new ICBMs designed to use the cold-launch method and dramatically improve on rockets they were designed to replace. The older rounds had been in use when SALT-1 reached the negotiating tables but in a rapid sequence of tests and operational deployment, the Soviet Strategic Rocket Forces emplaced large numbers of a completely new generation far beyond the performance of missiles considered during the talks. First, there was the SS-17 and SS-19, observed on tests in 1974 and designed to replace an earlier missile called Sego. With a range of 10,000 km and a throw-weight of 700 kg, Sego had been the mainstay of the Soviet rocket force. But when SS-17 appeared it was immediately seen to have three times the throw-weight of its predecessor and to adopt the new launch method. The SS-19 was even more powerful, with a throw-weight more than four times as great, capable of delivering across intercontinental distances six nuclear warheads each equal in size to the single charge carried by each Minuteman Mk2. It was a staggering capability and served to expose the real reason why the Russians had refused to write in limitations on the size and weight of future missiles. Yet they were legally deployed.

More threatening, however, was detection by satellite of tests of the SS-18, a heavyweight rocket in three different versions: Mod 1, with a single warhead theoretically capable of packing a punch equal to 50 Minuteman 2s; Mod 2, with up to ten nuclear charges capable of devastating a large number of US silos; Mod 3, with much greater range and improved accuracy capable of lifting various combinations of weaponry. The SS-18 was quite simply the biggest and most powerful missile ever built, and it was being deployed in increasing numbers. By the time tests were fully under way in 1974, early rounds were already going into silos across the USSR. At the end of the decade, about 250 had been deployed. In its most powerful version each missile could pack a punch equal to 2,500 atomic bombs the size of that dropped on Hiroshima. In terms of destruction, it was the most effective nuclear delivery vehicle ever. All three—SS-17, SS-18 and SS-19—are very much more potent than anything available in the West and the Soviets have now prepared a total of more than 600 rounds deployed in underground silos. All three were unknown prior to the SALT-1 signing ceremony, although US intelligence knew the Russians were working on a new generation of strategic weapons. Very soon the Russians were also observed by satellites to be working hard to perfect multiple re-entry vehicles, the MRVs and MIRVs developed in the US and thought many years ahead of Soviet equivalence. But that was not so, for by the middle of the decade most ICBMs were being tested with this system. Since the Russians had been allowed, under the agreement, to possess the bigger missiles under a common number applicable to both sides, the possession of multiple warheads could effectively give the Soviets a larger number of possible targets. For, within a given number of missiles, each rocket would carry many more charges than its US counterpart. It was a miscalculation of extreme proportions and one resulting in dissatisfaction among intelligence experts in America. Many saw the administration's attempt to get agreements with Russia as a dangerous game of politicizing the issue of arms control. Richard Nixon openly expressed concern over his role in America's history, admitting his belief that the future would remember the actions of his people in setting up major agreements with the Soviet Union. Some saw in SALT-1 a pursuit of ideological goals to secure at any cost agreements which would crack the long-standing bitterness between the super-powers. Admiral Elmo R. Zumwalt, Jr, Chief of Naval Operations, openly explained the cover-up among associates of Dr. Henry Kissinger, arch-architect of SALT-1:

"In a briefing to 100 Congressmen at the White House, Kissinger was asked whether the agreement effectively constrained the Soviet numbers of heavy missiles; for if it did not, as Senator Jackson pointed out, it would be a dangerous and destablizing agreement. Kissinger sought to allay Jackson's concern by replying that the agreement contained 'a number of safeguards.' We believe that we have 'an adequate safeguard against substantial substitution of heavy missiles for light ones,' Kissinger assured the Congressmen. This flat assertion was backed up by testimony from the Director of CIA [Richard Helms] that the USSR had been told that 'any missile over 70 cu m in volume would be considered significantly greater in size.' Well, the Russians proceeded to do precisely what Senator Jackson was concerned they would do . . . They deployed a new missile, the SS-19, which was significantly larger . . . 50 per cent larger than the 70 cu m we had told the Soviets we would accept."

When this was detected by US reconnaissance satellites, several intelligence people at the Pentagon invited State Department participation in broaching this with the Russians. Kissinger, recalls Zumwalt, was generating resistance "even to raising the issue with the Russians," and only when the full weight of the Defense Department was put behind the effort did the Secretary of State acquiesce. Even at that time, however, Kissinger adopted a completely different stance on the interpretation of the agreement than that given to the Congressmen. Indeed, recounts Admiral Zumwalt, the State Department team "told the Russians that we noted their deployment of the SS-19 missile was an action we had said in 1972 would be a violation of the agreement . . . [and] then went on to condone it by telling the Russians that if they proceeded to deploy any new missiles that were *larger* than the SS-19, we would be 'seriously concerned'."

When asked about this matter shortly after Soviet violations became a widely discussed issue at the State Department, Kissinger said that in his view it was "open to question whether the United States can hold the Soviet Union responsible for its own [ie, US] statements when the Soviet Union has asserted that it does not accept that interpretation."

What the Secretary of State was saying was that it was not right to oppose an interpretation the Russians chose to put on something if it affected an action they wished to pursue. Or, as the *Washington Post* caustically remarked: "One wonders when defense of Mr. Kissinger's record becomes a pleading of the Soviet case." The entire issue was boiling when defense officials learned the full extent of Soviet abrogations. Admiral Zumwalt was clinical in his assessment of the entire issue:

"There are a number of lessons to be learned from this whole unhappy experience with SALT-1 . . . Henry Kissinger was confronted with the dilemma of admitting that he negotiated a very bad set of agreements in SALT-1, or of acknowledging that the Russians had seriously violated those agreements, or both. None of these alternatives was palatable to Kissinger; nor was any consistent with his overblown representations of detente. The only way out of this was to pursue a dual set of untruths: maintaining that the SALT-1 agreements were basically sound and that the Soviets have been in complete compliance with them. This sort of misrepresentation . . . has totally undercut the efforts of other US officials to turn the Russians away from their misbehavior, and at the same time, by condoning the Soviet violations, it actually encourages even more flagrant transgressions by the Russians in the future."

It was a bitter indictment of an issue revealed only by the wide intelligence gathering capacities of the spaceborne satellite net, but it was only the tip of a much larger iceberg of Soviet violations. In 1973, one year after the SALT-1 signing, satellites picked up views of several new silos built to carry missiles. Prohibited from constructing *any* new silos, the matter was referred to the Standing Consultative Commission (SCC) set up to monitor SALT protocol. The Soviets, when confronted with this intelligence, declined to admit they were anything other than new launch control facilities and insisted that they were not silos at all. Nevertheless, satellite reconnaissance continued to pick out nearly 100 such constructions all along the Trans-Siberian railway missile site. Four years later, after considerable discussion, the United States agreed to interpret these facilities as launch control centers.

In 1974, a year after the first pictures of silo work, reconnaissance satellites brought back views which showed dramatic new efforts to conceal activity associated with strategic weapons. The intent of the SALT agreement was that no one country should contravene the visual access allowed for inspection, but again lengthy discussion ensued, during which the Russians agreed not to *increase* their methods of concealing what they were doing. In 1977, a large net was seen over a specially adapted test silo in which several new developments were being put through their paces. It was not removed, the Russians merely assuring the West of its *incidental* use.

Then electronic inspection of radar installations picked up clandestine development of Anti-Ballistic Missile equipment. The ABM treaty, related to SALT, prohibited the use of such techniques. There was, and remains, a wide fear that if one country develops the capacity effectively to screen its airspace from incoming warheads the value of nuclear weapons will be transferred from deterrence to aggression; only as long as respective States remain exposed to the fury and

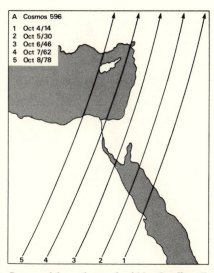

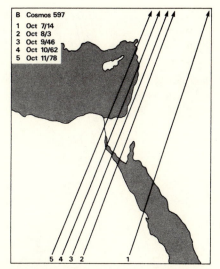

Prepared from the work of Mr. Geoffrey E. Perry, maps A-G show the reconnaissance operations of Soviet Cosmos satellites launched for Middle East monitoring duties during the Yom Kippur war in 1973. Here, the ground tracks for revs 14, 30, 46, 62 and 78 between October 4 and 8.

From right to left, revs 14, 30, 46, 62 and 78 for Cosmos 597.

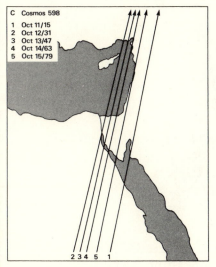

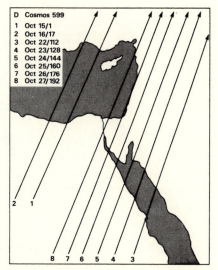

Numbers 1, 2, 3, 4 and 5 mark Cosmos 598 revs 15, 31, 47, 63 and 79.

Numbers 1, 2, 3, 4, 5, 6, 7 and 8 correspond to Cosmos 599 revs 1, 17, 112, 128, 144, 160, 176 and 192 respectively.

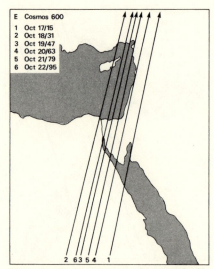

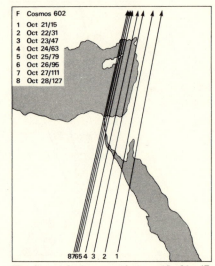

Groundtracks of revolutions 15, 31, 47, 63, 79 and 95, denoted by numbers 1-6 inclusive show passes across the Sinai on succeeding days from October 17.

Numbers 1-8 show revolutions 15, 31, 47, 63, 79, 95, 111 and 127 respectively. Note daily migration virtually halted on October 25 to keep satellite over Cairo each day.

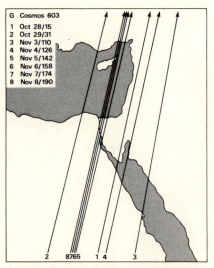

Stabilized over the battle zone on November 5, Cosmos 603 passes on revs 15, 31, 110, 126, 142, 158, 174 and 190 are shown in daily order by numbers 1-8.

force of a ballistic missile assault can nuclear weapons protect the peace.

Under the terms of SALT-1, the Russians were allowed to retain only 64 ABM weapons, a missile called Galosh which had been deployed from 1970. For its part, the United States had dismantled plans for Sprint and Spartan ABM sites. Nobody really wanted such an umbrella, for the costs of deploying such a system were enormous, and an effective counter to the strategic assault threatened by either side would only start up a massive escalation in other weapon systems. Yet the Soviets were interested in completing tests already begun and tenaciously held on to a research program. Russian use of outdated hardware displays fascinating ingenuity, for once deployed the Soviets rarely throw anything away.

Nevertheless, ferrets picked up a new ABM radar installation at the Kamchatka Peninsula in addition to an existing radar at Sary Shagan. When approached about this the Russians agreed not to put up any more facilities. The Kamchatka site remained. Also, other electronic ferrets observed trials with an air defense system which could have found application as an ABM radar. Satellites picked up antennae tracking ballistic missiles in flight: an indication that research was going ahead under cover of air-defense functions. The Soviets were again approached but denied any application to ABM roles, citing the system as a part of their anti-aircraft program. Shortly thereafter, the tests stopped.

For an intense five-year period after the SALT-1 agreement of 1972, the Soviets exploited every conceivable element of the treaty which carried language in any way ambiguous or open to a different interpretation. It was all part of the ploy to pin down US operations and incite development of reciprocal weapon systems across a wide range of applications. Wherever they could, the Russians pushed through a void in the treaty and exploited it to the full. Had it not been for effective cover from the family of area and close-look reconsats, backed up by the ferrets scurrying around for intelligence signals, almost all the violations would have gone undetected. Absent too, would have been deep concern over the partisan ethics involving Kissinger's negotiators. But open and bitter resentment over the satisfaction of a political goal to get the Russians to sign a treaty, seemingly at any cost, cut deep divisions between the State Department and the Pentagon. Admiral Zumwalt:

"The Soviets are lying to us about their cheating and Secretary Kissinger has not informed the Congress or the public about Soviet cheating. I believe there is a political commitment on the part of Secretary Kissinger to the success of detente that has made him, in effect, apologize to himself and for the Russians for these deals . . ."

Former Secretary of Defense James R. Schlesinger also agreed with the accusations of political backscratching when he concurred that there were many incidents "some would regard as cheating," on the intent of the SALT accord. Schlesinger also noted that in the years since the first SALT treaty there had been "some hardening" on the part of the Russians who, having got what they wanted from America, were less inclined to go along with further limitations.

During the 1970s, the Russians made notable improvements in their satellite activity, broadening the reconnaissance base and adopting new, longer-lived satellites capable of operating up to one month. Also, by 1978, the Russians had commenced replacement of the original hardware based on Vostok with spacecraft of the Soyuz type, also developed initially as a manned vehicle. It was a matter of necessity, a vital component of strategic defense, for each side to scrutinize the activities of the other and, while America introduced the second generation Big Bird satellites and upgraded the capabilities of electronic ferrets, the Russians continued to test new and better sensors on their production line space station called Salyut. This had first been launched in April 1971, at the start of an expanding role for men in space. By the end of the decade, six Salyut stations had been placed in orbit and, while some were intentionally brought out of orbit to destruction in the atmosphere at the end of their mission, all were involved with testing new equipment and conducting research into scientific and engineering applications. Salyut employed the largest rocket in the Soviet inventory of space launchers. Capable of lifting weights of about 22 tons, the Salyut space station was not much short of this in mass, with a length in orbit of about 22 m and a maximum diameter of 4.15 m. From the outset, combined roles of scientific, biomedical and military surveillance activity were central to the Salyut design. Unhampered by separate agencies controlling civilian and military operations, Russia's Strategic Rocket Forces was responsible for the entire launch operation. But payloads and packages carried aboard the station for research in space were divided between the two categories. Some Salyut stations were undoubtedly military in function while others pursued an essentially civilian role. Camera systems and new telephoto lenses were tried out by cosmonauts sent up to Salyuts. Some of these later found their way on to reconnaissance satellites.

Soyuz, the manned successor to the Vostok design, weighed almost 7 tons at lift-off and was about 7 m long with a maximum diameter of 2.7 m. Essentially an assembly of three modules, Soyuz came in several versions. Earliest in availability were two configurations: one for solo flights lasting several weeks, or a short-duration type employed for delivering cosmonauts to the Salyut station.

The space station taxi vehicle used batteries to provide electrical energy for a total three days' autonomous flight, after which time the cosmonauts had to return to Earth or run out of electrical energy to power their systems. Soyuz spacecraft of this type docked with their stations in space or quickly returned to Earth if unable to link up. The solo Soyuz, however, had solar cell wings spanning 8 m, and attached either side of the main structure, and supplies for several weeks. They were further developed as reconnaissance satellites and, as mentioned earlier, replaced the Vostok design in this role from the late 1970s.

Another version of Soyuz, the "T" model, employed refined electronics, a better propulsion system for maneuvering in space, and more efficient control displays. It was first used operationally in late 1979 when it linked up to the unmanned Salyut 6 space station for final trials prior to manned operation. Earlier, during January 1978, an unmanned tanker-cargo version called Progress was introduced to ferry large quantities of propellant for the Salyut rocket engines and supplies for the cosmonauts on long duration missions. Extended space flight had become a prime feature of Salyut operations late in the 1970s, record-breaking flights extending manned stays to almost six months in duration. The program was also made to embrace the wider political aims of the Soviet Union by allowing volunteers from Soviet "satellite" states and pro-Moscow communist countries to train for flights into space.

Beginning in 1978 the first of these "Intercosmos" flights got under way, eventually carrying representatives of many aligned nations. By 1980 the procession of unmanned Progress and manned Soyuz spacecraft to and from the Salyut stations signalled a major new endeavor to exploit the developing technology of manned space flight. In supporting military operations by providing orbital test-beds for sensors and support equipment, objectives similar to those chosen for the cancelled

Manned Orbiting Laboratory were picked up and exploited by the Soviet Union. The manned space program has had ambiguous responsibilities on both sides of the Iron Curtain but the Soviets are now beginning to advance their capacity to mount large and complex programs with cosmonauts in space.

During the first two decades of space flight, up to the late 1970s, Russian activity with manned operations failed to reach predicted levels. While America accelerated its own manned space effort and rapidly developed a capability to maneuver in orbit, perform space walks, and link up separate spacecraft in space, the Russian cosmonauts were tied to a sequence of missions hampered by limited technology. Early Russian manned flights with Vostok vehicles were little more than passive passenger flights in which the cosmonaut was unable to do very much without commands sent to activate systems from the ground. Even the version of Vostok called Voskhod, used in 1964 and '65 to launch on one flight a three-man crew and on the second a space-walking operation, failed to provide the sophistication imagined from the scale of the operation. The first Soyuz spacecraft crashed to Earth killing its occupant in April 1967, and in 1971 three more cosmonauts died when a valve designed to admit atmospheric air on the way down opened prematurely in space and asphyxiated the crew. After that last disaster the spacecraft was grounded while engineers converted it for two-man operations, allowing both to wear space suits for which there had been no room with a third cosmonaut.

However, the entire thrust of Soviet manned flight languished in the repeated performance of orbital flight for seemingly little gain in capability or research. Not until the Salyut program appeared early in the 1970s did the Russians seem to have a master plan for manned flight. Today, their Salyut operations are a creditable achievement and no doubt reflect a decade of learning new techniques and applications. There is one reason, perhaps, why the manned effort seemed to take longer than expected finally to demonstrate a purpose, although that, too, is open to speculation and debate. Considerable evidence exists that the Russians fully intended to fly cosmonauts around the Moon in the late 1960s before America's Apollo astronauts managed to achieve that goal in December 1968. Recognizing that the engineering techniques to achieve a manned landing were beyond their capabilities, the goal announced by John F. Kennedy in 1961 that America was to place the first astronauts on the lunar surface by the end of that decade doubtless inspired plans in Russia to eclipse the US achievement. Where publicly they denounced the challenge as a worthless product of haste fraught with danger, programs designed to carry a Soyuz-type vehicle around the Moon progressed in actual flights with dummy pilots and animal passengers.

In tests conducted under the Zond program, derivatives of the Soyuz manned spacecraft were actually flown around the Moon and brought back to Earth for recovery in the Indian Ocean. Traditionally, all Soviet manned flights returned their cosmonauts to land, but the type of trajectory necessary when flying to the Moon and back required them to land in the ocean. There was an intention of, eventually, developing the technique of descending over the Soviet Union. The last of those flights came less than six weeks before Apollo 8 lifted away from the Cape Canaveral launch site on December 21, 1968. Its mission, to send the first men out of Earth's gravity field and into orbit around the Moon.

The attempt was an unqualified success and no more was heard of Russia's plans for Moon flight. No more circumlunar Zond missions were flown, and no more research was conducted into very fast re-entry trajectories of the type made necessary when coming back from the Moon. It took a lot of technology to accomplish that feat. Returning from the vicinity of the Moon nearly 400,000 km away, Earth's gravity would speed the vehicle to a record 41,000 km/hr compared with orbital speed of 28,000 km/hr. Temperatures on the outside of the descending capsule would be nearly twice that on a spacecraft returning from orbit and the guidance required safely to thread the trajectory down a narrow funnel through the atmosphere stretched the capability of engineering skill. But the Russians achieved good results with their Zond activity and may well have eclipsed US achievements had anything happened to prevent Borman, Lovell and Anders from flying Apollo 8. Throughout the space era since Sputnik 1, Russia had used the announced goals of America's civilian NASA to upstage the activities likely to gain public acclaim. It had happened with the first multi-man flight. When NASA moved toward first flights with the two-man Gemini spacecraft, Russia's Voskhod 1 beat it into space. When NASA hinted at the possibility of performing a space walk during one of the first Gemini missions, Voskhod 2 was sent into orbit to accomplish this first. That the Voskhod was a stripped-out Vostok, without an emergency ejector seat so that additional couches or the necessary equipment for a space walk could be carried instead, was information which failed to reach the public ear. In fact, only by piecing together various reports from around the world have several specialists been able to prove this. A similar propaganda move was adopted in lieu of a manned Soviet Moon landing. While Zond would capture the glamor of the first circumlunar mission, Russia's propaganda machine similarly prepared equipment to return to Earth with Moon samples before the first Apollo lunar landing.

From the mid-1960s Russia said it had no interest in sending a man to the Moon, thus replacing earlier statements asserting confidence in an imminent Soviet landing. So to endorse the claim that unmanned vehicles could do just as well as men, a Luna series spacecraft was prepared in 1969 for just this purpose. Zond had been eclipsed by an Apollo program spectacular and successful in achieving its goal. But the Russians were determined to get the last available "first" by returning to Earth Moon samples brought back by an unmanned robot. Accordingly, on July 13, 1969, a Soviet rocket of the type used in a different version to place Salyut space stations in orbit, lifted off its launch pad with Luna 15. Three days later, Neil Armstrong, "Buzz" Aldrin and Michael Collins were launched aboard Apollo 11 from the hot shoreline of the Florida spaceport. By this time Luna 15 was nearing the Moon and a day later fired its braking engine to slip into an orbit around the lunar sphere. Four days later, after several maneuvers, it slipped down toward the surface in an attempted soft-landing designed to allow automated instruments to retrieve 1 kg of soil and then lift-off back to Earth. But it never landed, crashing instead at over 450 km/hr. Only hours before, Armstrong and Aldrin had safely touched down. In the light of Apollo's grand achievement, very few even knew about the fate of Luna 15. But it was a bitter blow for Soviet prowess; having stirred up the emotions of their compatriots 12 years earlier with Sputnik 1, they had been beaten to the greatest show of strength yet devised for peaceful means.

For the Russians it was a sad prelude to the arms limitation talks but the hardware had other uses and the following decade was to see an expanding capacity for major Earth-orbit activity. The precise details of the attempted propaganda coup are lost within the secret files of Soviet space engineers, but one reason for the apparent hiatus in solid achievements following early success may well be the effort applied to Moon operations which failed, ironically, to give the Soviets the applause they sought.

Today, the manned space program is dominated by Salyut operations and in effectively re-grouping their technology toward this combined military and scientific research tool the Russians are well ahead of America in exploiting orbital space platforms.

Lieutenant General Thomas P. Stafford, one-time astronaut with NASA and deputy chief for Air Force Research, Development and Acquisition, told a Congressional session in 1978 that Russia "may be developing a manned military space capability about which we know very little. The Soviets understand the force enhancement from space . . . ." Ex-NASA Administrator Robert Frosch, too, is convinced that Russia is deeply involved with manned military space activity and that transfer to a fully operational capability would make people "consider it a serious threat." As we shall see in a later chapter, that capability fits well the broader goals of Soviet policy.

By the end of the 1970s Soviet space technology embraced both manned and unmanned projects enabling the advanced capacity of Soyuz, married to sophisticated surveillance tasks, to give Russian intelligence a spy in space well equipped for growing needs. The Russians were as concerned to keep a photo-file on the Americans as the United States was closely to watchdog impending clandestine activity—for there was no let-up in the latter.

Shortly after the Soviets received a propaganda setback in their Moon plans, Western intelligence obtained information, backed up by reconsat pictures, of a completely new type of bomber using swing-wing technology to achieve a Mach 2 dash capability as well as very low-level subsonic intrusion flights. It was to be called Backfire and it was an acute embarassment to the Soviet delegation at the SALT-1 talks. Deliberate and careful analysis of the Backfire's performance gave intelligence experts the view that here was an aircraft capable of strategic attack on the continental United States, not, as the Soviets said, merely a tactical aircraft designed for European and anti-ship duties. Intensive observation by reconnaissance satellites kept a constant watch on Backfire trials, reporting everything the aircraft was put through in tests prior to operational deployment. If Backfire was deemed a strategic weapon, it would have to be included in the 2,400 strategic delivery systems agreed to in the SALT-1 accord. If not, its operational debut could, like the SS-20 before it, proceed to threaten the European countries outside the SALT boundary. As the 1970s progressed, first President Ford and then his successor Jimmy Carter moved on with discussions for SALT-2. And the Backfire became a thorny issue for both sides. For the Russians had no intention of using it to show strategic intent while the Americans were convinced that, like so many developments in the wake of SALT-1, this, too, would prove an elusive bird of prey.

Careful engineering analysis continued and when SALT-2 was prepared for submission to the US Congress during 1978 it was agreed to exclude the aircraft on the grounds that it was probably similar in role to the F-111 operated as a forward strike and intruder fighter-bomber in NATO countries. That Backfire had the performance to fly a nuclear delivery mission to the United States on a one-way flight seemed not unduly to deter SALT negotiators who agreed, albeit grudgingly, to leave it out of the agreement. But to help ease SALT through a suspicious US Congress, the Russians agreed to remove the air-refuelling probe attached to the nose of production Backfires.

No sooner had the protocol been drawn up than the reconnaissance satellites picked up test flights with a modified Backfire during trials supporting a range enhancement program. And then, while probing the Soviet borders, a Backfire was seen with enlarged intakes and improved engines, first reported by the reconsats. It was a fitting demonstration of the integrated intelligence approach. Information gained first through the spaceborne eyes of Big Bird or the close-look snoopers provides key points to the NATO reconnaissance aircraft dispatched daily to patrol the air border.

Every year, about 300 Soviet aircraft are turned back from attempted intrusion to Britain's air space by Phantoms and Lightnings of the Royal Air Force. Constantly, deeper into European airspace, especially over the Northern Approaches, NATO air forces intercept many more. It was while turning back a Backfire long-range test flight that an aircraft over the Norwegian Sea photographed at close range the new and improved version expected to gain operational status by 1982. At that time, the Backfire will assume strategic importance. More ominous still was the intelligence sent back from a Big Bird which photographed a Backfire from the research base at Ramenskoye performing flight tests with a new cruise missile capable of flying 1,200 km after release.

Cruise missiles are the new development made possible by a unique propulsion system engineered by the Williams Corporation in the USA and fitted to a winged projectile. With guidance logic to allow the missile a circuitous flight path to the target, and a terrain-following capability which keeps it hugging the contours of the ground, it provides a significant advantage over more conventional, and much larger, missiles using rocket propulsion. The cruise missile flies subsonic and can evade defense radars set up to monitor incoming aircraft because of its low flight path. Cruise missiles now being developed in America will carry nuclear warheads ten times the yield of the bomb used on Hiroshima.

Soviet developments in the cruise category imply a major shift away from their total reliance on the strategic missile, and reconnaissance satellites have provided information about a new generation of manned bombers expected to appear in the next few years. In addition to the Backfire B and its new cruise missile, satellites have detected development of a very long-range heavy bomber capable of flying unrefuelled a distance of about 18,000 km with a 20-ton war load. With this aircraft carrying cruise missiles and other stand-off weapons, continental defense would assume radical new proportions.

Existing Soviet bombers, excluding Backfire, are limited in performance and pose little threat at a strategic level. Without the intelligence gathered by the reconsats in this area, SALT-2 criteria would have been judged on existing hardware and stated objectives, which are frequently at variance with the facts. The new delta-wing Model H bomber will supplement the ICBM force in an unprecedented expansion of the Soviet air arm. But debate over the use of the Backfire bomber overshadowed other bones of contention during the SALT-2 negotiations.

For several years, ever since ratification of SALT-1, the Soviets tried discreetly to encrypt telemetry broadcasts from missiles in flight. Telemetry tells all about the performance of a mechanical system either in the event of that system's destruction or during periods when information about its performance must be obtained and cannot be recorded. It is an important part of electronic intelligence and as such emphasizes the importance attached to ferret satellites. Such methods are used to monitor the performance and capability of new Soviet missiles during test.

The Russians never release information to support arms talks and merely agree with intelligence given to the Soviets to show knowledge of their own systems and quantities, etc. An important part of the SALT-1 process was that satellite intelligence, be it photographic or electronic, should be gathered freely without attempted concealment.

But soon after SALT-1 the Soviets began to encrypt certain telemetry transmissions, veiling the nature of the information from US listening posts; two vital installations in Iran being of prime importance in securing data shortly after the missiles ascended from their Tyuratam base. The value of this information can be seen when it is understood that precise details about the performance of the rocket motors, even down to the rate at which propellant is flowing from the tanks to the engines, can be and is obtained through monitoring telemetry channels. Only in this way can Western intelligence sources gather information relevant to arms control agreements. The Soviets would like to deny the West this data gathering capability for the same reason they persistently employ evasive, clandestine and devious tactics to abrogate existing agreements. When the first incidents of encryption were reported, the Russians stopped coding their telemetry. Strong protests through the Standing Consultative Commission, set up to monitor SALT protocol, were effective.

Then, in 1978, the Russians obtained information vital to their next moves. The story begins the preceding summer when the impressionable young son of a Greek immigrant, William P. Kampiles, worked as an operations desk clerk at the CIA headquarters in Virginia. Kampiles joined the CIA during February that year and frequently puzzled fellow workers by his shallow interpretation of truth. He was a strangely dramatic character, seeing in the CIA an opportunity to pull himself from obscurity by seeming to do a vital job. He did not—although Kampiles did have access to secret documents, among them the KH-11 system technical manual. During the summer of that year, Kampiles took Copy 155—some 350 had been printed up for the use of defense agencies and intelligence experts—because, he said, it "appeared to be the most interesting one," and folded the small ring binder into his sports jacket. No one stopped him when he simply walked out and returned to his apartment with the document. Several months later, in October, Kampiles was persuaded to resign on threat of dismissal. He took the document to his mother's apartment (his father had died in 1964) and carefully cut away "secret" notices from the corner of each page to allay suspicion about the book. The following February he took the document on the KH-11 satellite to Athens and, while staying with friends, visited the Russian Embassy. It was around the 23rd of that month that he met with military attaché Major Michael Zavali and offered to sell substantial secrets. Kampiles used a false name to evade blackmail and handed the first few pages of the document to Zavali. The informant was told he would receive no money until the pages had been examined in detail. During the first days in March, Kampiles handed more pages to Zavali who paid him the meager sum of $3,000. Kampiles returned to the United States and began a job with a laboratory in Oak Brook, Illinois. But he could not keep quiet about his adventure and boasted to a girl friend, who just happened to have a friend in the CIA, that he was playing a double game, passing along to the KGB information which he considered of no consequence and which could excite a deal of confusion. Kampiles was mistaken to think his boasts would go unnoticed and, on April 17, 1978, two FBI agents arrested him.

But the damage was already done. The Russians knew at last just what the KH-11 could do and America's most secret satellite was described for them in technical detail, even down to an artist's impression on the second page! They had not known until Kampiles provided the information that the KH-11 had such a remarkable photographic system, neither were they aware of its geographic limitations.

It was the first of two major setbacks for intelligence gathering activity. The second came when agents at the two big listening posts in Iran hurriedly evacuated the site as the Shah fled for his life to the United States. According to former defense intelligence chief Lieutenant General Daniel Graham the stations in Iran were critical "because it represents a tipoff capability to notify other satellites to keep watch or get aircraft out of Alaska to watch the end of the test trajectory." Other listening sites, positioned in Turkey, were unsuited to this ICBM monitoring role because of the mass of the Caucasus Mountains.

There was no alternative but to use U-2 aircraft flying high across the border to gather the intelligence data. But their use was limited, said Lieutenant General Graham, simply because "they can't carry the tons of equipment we had in Iran." Nevertheless, U-2 aircraft were deployed on an interim basis but with new antennae to compensate for the reduced efficiency of the equipment normally carried by this aircraft. It had been planned that U-2 aircraft would operate from Pakistan on flights across Afghanistan and, at other times, along the Turkish border with the Soviet Union, but a decision by President Carter to cut off aid to Pakistan, because the country was trying to acquire a gas centrifuge plant for making nuclear weapons, stalled the effort to maintain a watch on the Tyuratam launch site.

By the spring of 1979, just months after the Shah fled Iran, an interim U-2 based intelligence operation was feverishly trying to patch up the network. In the wake of the KH-11 compromise and depleted capability along the Soviet southwestern border, Russia had already tried to encrypt its missile telemetry once more. While Secretary of State Cyrus Vance was meeting with Soviet Foreign Minister Andrei Gromyko, an encrypted flight test with the massive SS-18 was noted. The Russian position was clear. They would encrypt any telemetry not associated with verifying SALT, and trust America to believe that whatever was in code did not contain information which would change that position.

Throughout 1979 the reconsats worked overtime to plug the intelligence gap. Gradually, relations with Pakistan reached a more conciliatory footing and the Soviets ran into trouble south of their Middle East border. At the same time, it was important for them to secure a more influential control over the people and activity in Afghanistan, about which more later. Attempts to conceal the operating and performance capability of large missiles on test was, however, just one element in a shifting emphasis to shield developments from prying eyes.

Toward the end of the 1970s Western intelligence experts noted increasing use of codes for space activity as well. Hitherto, the Russians had encrypted material from military satellites, like photographic reconnaissance and ferret type vehicles, while leaving uncoded the transmissions from scientific satellites and manned spacecraft. Only the military Salyut stations transmitted coded signals, the others sending information on open channels. But this changed quickly by the end of the decade so the true intent of several programs remained hidden.

Spurred by the loss of US intelligence gathering equipment on their southwestern border and bolstered by possession of detailed information about the KH-11 satellite, Soviet bravado was achieving new heights. In that period, major developments arose with the Russian reconsats. By 1975 they could be separated into three distinct classes. The first category included satellites launched on two-week flights using pulse-duration modulation telemetry broadcasting on 19.994 MHz. The recovery beacon for this type of satellite employed the Morse code "TG" and some would release a sub-satellite into space shortly before coming down. That sub-satellite would continue to operate for a few days before it too returned to Earth.

The second type, being phased out with the adoption of the first and the third categories, lasted about 13 days and similarly returned to Earth. They broadcast on 19.995 or 20.005 MHz a three-letter morse code with a recovery beacon sending the "TK" signal. The third class sends two-tone signals at 19.989 MHz and also lasts 13 days in orbit but an additional subcategory employs a "TL" beacon signal rather than "TF" and releases a sub-satellite at the end of its mission. All three types were based on the Vostok and presented the most effective adaptation of the basic design prior to adopting the Soyuz derivative as a replacement.

Like their American counterparts, Soviet reconsats are frequently launched to spy on events as they happen, whether in support of some new defense activity or a foreign coup. Typical examples reflect the type of attention given to such operations. In October 1967, just days before NASA planned to launch the first manned Apollo spacecraft on an Earth-orbiting shakedown flight, Russia launched Cosmos 246 into a path which would carry it over Cape Canaveral at noon local time. Because the satellite had an extremely low perigee which slowly reduced the orbital period, orbital decay caused the groundtracks to bunch up around the Florida coast. Just 30 minutes after Apollo ascended, Cosmos 246 flew across the Cape area and was returned to Earth a day later, its "TK" recovery beacon being received by amateurs listening in from Stockholm. Cosmos 246 was one of the original type which remained in a fixed path but the use of a maneuvring capability to fix the orbital groundtrack over a specific target can be demonstrated by the flight of two Cosmos reconsats in 1971. It was the time of the Indo-Pakistani conflict toward the end of that year and Soviet intelligence took a close look at the situation with Cosmos 463, launched from Tyuratam on December 6. Inclined 65 degrees to the Equator, the orbit carried Cosmos 463 around the globe in 89.3 minutes. One day after launch, on the 14th revolution, the satellite passed directly over East Pakistan (Bangladesh) and two orbits later the maneuvering engine was fired to lower perigee and reduce the period to 89 minutes. This stopped the daily drift west of the satellite's groundtrack, effectively placing it over this area at the same time each day, timed to coincide with noon when the Sun was high in the sky. For two days the satellite photographed the area taking many more pictures than usual in this period before ground controllers raised the orbit's apogee to resume the westward drift and allow the satellite to be recovered on December 11. One day earlier, however, shortly after

Cosmos 463 "walked" away from East Pakistan, Cosmos 464 was sent up at an inclination of 72.9 degrees. This put the groundtrack on a more north-south orientation since the inclination was closer to the polar axis. With a period of 90.3 minutes, the satellite drifted west at a rate of 5 degrees longitude each day. Shortly after noon on December 13 it passed over East Pakistan and an orbital change was performed three hours later to lower the path, reduce the period, and cut the drift to just 1 degree each day. This effectively synchronized the satellite's path with the target area for a sustained photographic session.

Cosmos 464 was brought back down on December 16. With these two satellites the Russians kept an almost continuous watch on the progress of the war. Two years later, they were to use a similar activity for political ends in a classic example of Soviet lateral-application, where the capabilities of one system are dovetailed with the deficiencies of another to create a workable solution. It was October 1973, and uncompleted hostilities of 1967 provided brittle dialogue between Egypt, Syria and Israel. With the Russian weapons and supplies airlifted into Egypt, President Sadat was planning a military campaign to eject the Israelis from the Sinai once and for all. In a combined attack launched by Egypt and Syria at the same time, Israel would be pressed to defeat and lands acquired in the former conflict regained for good. Or so the theory said. On October 6, during an afternoon which found the Israeli forces unprepared for attack, a massive artillery barrage and intense airborne assault began as Egyptian forces surged across the Suez Canal and quickly destroyed tanks rolling to the defense of the infantry. Within one hour of the attack, a launch vehicle ready on the pad at Plesetsk sent Cosmos 597 into orbit on a photograhic reconnaissance flight. The Russians may well have known the time hostilities were to commence, they certainly knew an assault was in the offing, preferring to maintain passive support by providing intelligence about the war. A reconnaissance satellite was already in orbit when hostilities commenced. Called Cosmos 596, it had been sent up from Plesetsk three days before to take area-survey shots with low resolution cameras. But Cosmos 597 was a close-look vehicle equipped to change its orbit by firing a maneuvering rocket. Two days after the war began, Cosmos 597 was in place over the Middle East, its apogee lowered to cut the orbital period and synchronize it with the Earth below. Being the non-maneuvering type, its predecessor drifted on across the region for recovery on October 9. Cosmos 597 was in a path inclined 65.4 degrees to the Equator, perfectly aligned, as it happened, for the ascending leg to carry the satellite up and across the Suez/Sinai region before sweeping across the Sea of Galilee and over Syria, where mechanized infantry divisions with more than 800 tanks were pressing hard against northern Israeli brigades.

One day after the area-survey satellite (Cosmos 596) dropped back to Earth, Cosmos 598 ascended from Plesetsk to an orbital inclination of 72.9 degrees. Fears that the Syrian forces would be in Israel within two days evaporated when the battle for the Golan Heights slowly went against the attacker. But down on the Syrian front, Sadat's forces were pushing across the Suez Canal with fewer than 100 Israeli tanks to stop the Egyptian armor. Considerable damage had been inflicted on the Israelis by anti-tank missiles procured from the Soviets and this was the more important front. Cosmos 598's more highly inclined path enabled that satellite, just one day after launch, to reach the area and begin extensive photographic activity. One day later its predecessor, Cosmos 597, returned to Earth with packed film cassettes. It was now up to Cosmos 598 to watch the evolving situation in the Sinai where Sadat seemed all set to effect the *coup de grâce*. Undoubtedly the Russians were concerned to monitor the progress of both sides by examining the photographs' real-time, receiving a course image by television at the Yevpatoriya tracking station in the Crimea. Cosmos 598 was just high enough to allow the Soviets a direct surveillance as the satellite scanned the Sinai. It was this satellite which would have provided the images that must have brought consternation to Moscow. For on the 14th, just three days after the satellite arrived over the area, Egyptian armor was all but decimated. In running battles east of Suez, nearly 1,000 Egyptian tanks were in the fray and by the day's end just 20 Israeli tanks had been lost for one quarter of the enemy's total. The following night Major General Ariel Sharon led a force of Israeli paratroopers across the Canal with tanks as a back-up, setting up a bridgehead on the west bank.

Cosmos 598 saw it all and monitored the push before returning to Earth next day, the 16th. A day earlier, only hours before Sharon attacked, Cosmos 599 went up to a 65-degree orbit. It was an area-survey type and not thought to be directly associated with the war. During October 16 the Russians received no pictures—Cosmos 598 had been brought back—but Cosmos 600 was launched that day from the Plesetsk launch site as its replacement. It ran a 72.8-degree path around the Earth and a day later was on station over the battle zone. What it saw was a vindication of Israeli boasts: moving quickly from their newly established position on the west bank of the Canal, the Israelis destroyed large numbers of surface-to-air missiles and other weapon sites. In Cairo, the Soviet military attaché visited Sadat to press upon him the extreme urgency of the situation. Sadat was unconvinced that there was any real danger and only when he saw for himself the satellite pictures revealing the extent of the Israeli incursion did he call at once for full use of the Soviet offer: Russian transport aircraft began lifting arms and personnel to Egypt's aid. But it was a losing game for now the Russians knew the Egyptians stood little chance. They immediately began to press for a ceasefire, gradually swinging round to the US stance. On October 20, Cosmos 602 reached orbit and one day later began to cover the area. Two days after that its predecessor, Cosmos 600, was brought down from orbit. The flight path of Cosmos 602 was adjusted so as to back up the area-survey work still being performed by Cosmos 599. It was a period of intense observation as the situation worsened and Israeli troops moved west toward the Egyptian 3rd Army; the Russians were not risking gaps in coverage.

Astride the Cairo-Suez road now, the 3rd Army's supplies were cut off. Israel had its enemy by the throat. Officially, the cease-fire came into force on the 22nd but sporadic fighting flared to a major confrontation once more as the vanquished 3rd tried to regain glory. Israel pushed hard for Ismailia, placing the 3rd Army in a hopeless position, and Cairo was almost completely cut off from all roads east. On October 27 Cosmos 603 was launched, arriving on station a day later and on the 29th Cosmos 602 was returned to Earth. The former remained in space for 13 days in all, covering the last dying embers of the conflict.

It had been an intense period where Soviet intelligence forced the hand of a reluctant government, already suspicious of Russia's intentions in the area. But it had all been to no avail and when the conflict seemed to go against their protégés, Russia backed away and supported the United Nations' peace-call. The use of reconnaissance satellites to back up foreign policy and to provide a means of convincing national figures of the wisdom in projected coalition was not the sole experience of the 1973 Arab-Israeli war. But this serves as well as any to demonstrate the way satellites can, and do, generate information useful to a foreign power. Without the tangible evidence of the Soviet reconsat pictures, President Sadat would have disbelieved the reports coming from the front. It served the Russians' purpose well to employ this technique for persuasion; they were not to know the Egyptians would turn on their one-time friends in favor of a less demanding West.

During the 1970s, Soviet reconnaissance flights averaged around 30-35 missions each year until the more efficient Soyuz replaced Vostok derivatives. It is difficult to be precise about the exact role performed by all these satellites and some doubtless carry out functions related to electronic intelligence similar to the US ferrets carried piggyback on Big Bird. It is fairly certain, however, that ferrets have been continuously employed by the Soviet Union since about 1967, in which year they put up five Cosmos satellites of this type. One type weighed approximately 400 kg with a length of about 1.8 m and a diameter of 1.2 m, launched by a B-1 rocket into a 71-degree orbit. The B-1 was a developed version of an early ballistic missile, adapted to lift smaller payloads than would normally be economic for the big SS-6 derivative known as the A series launcher, the rocket initially employed to lift Sputnik 1 and of which there were an increasing number of versions.

Later in 1967 a second type of electronic ferret appeared, lifted this time by a C series rocket. About 900 kg in weight, the second type was approximately 2 m long, 1 m in diameter and occupied an elliptical path like its predecessors but inclined 74 degrees. Both were sent up from Plesetsk. The C series launcher was larger and more powerful than the B rocket, respective weights lifted here probably representing their maximum capacities. They were ideally suited to the economic launch of comparatively small satellites.

In recent years, fewer ferrets have been launched, annual total falling from about ten to around six. More frequent, however, are flights of radio store-dump satellites employed by the Soviets to eavesdrop on radio communication for replay over Soviet or Warsaw Pact countries. The Russians face daunting problems in collecting somebody else's communication because of their geographic location. Satellites are ideal for this purpose and annual launch rates average between 20 and 35 flights. This information is used for all manner of covert operations in foreign countries and mirrors the increasing use made of satellites by the CIA in America. The United States monitors foreign communication also, but ground sites and listening posts can more effectively cover wider regions of the globe if only because of the broader distribution of pro-Western states. By the mid-1970s, the Soviets had set up an orbital network of eight continuously operating ferrets in orbit at 45-degree intervals, synchronized across a repeating groundtrack to cover certain areas. With this and other surface-based monitoring facilities the Russians are acquiring an efficient and reliable means of electronically surveying the entire planet.

Some people believe the sophistication of remote sensing has reached the point where telephone conversations can be picked up and recorded aboard satellites developed for this one function. Clearly, there are many opportunities for research into this and other more bizarre forms of spying. With eyes and ears aloft, the passive sensors along orbital space lanes effectively police the world, reporting with clinical precision the smallest object and the most benign events. But there are other, potentially more useful satellites, directly involved with the business of waging a more efficient conflict on Earth.

4. The military mission in space

Ocean surveillance, weather and communications satellites

In debate at the US Congress a few months after the first American satellite went into orbit, Senator John Stennis made a prediction that, in his view: "Space technology will eventually become the dominant factor in determining our national military strength. Whoever controls space controls the world." That was more than 20 years ago. In the period since that day in 1958 when Soviet Russia seemed on the brink of major achievements in space, rapid developments have transformed even the fabric of that prediction. For the stakes are now much higher than those considered by Senator Stennis.

Space has become the crucial theater in which a future global conflict would be decided. Not because the weapons of destruction would be used from space, although that day may well arrive sooner than expected, but because the information and the data necessary to conduct a major war on Earth depend almost entirely now on the satellites orbiting the planet. Above the tenuously thin veil of the planet's atmosphere, silent watch is maintained by reconnaissance satellites and electronic ferrets. But high above these accepted guardians of treaties and agreement, other satellites await the day they will provide expanded vision for large forces on the ground, in the air and at sea.

Reconnaissance has cost the taxpayer little for the value returned. Nevertheless, the development of successive generations of satellites takes a large portion of money the Pentagon spends each year on military space activity. The history of those sums mirrors the changing emphasis on space applications. From the outset, monies given to the civilian space agency (NASA) and the Defense Department space programs have been distinctly separate and quite apart from each other. With the proviso that a limited number of technical developments made possible by the projects controlled at NASA have been of use to the Defense Department, the lines of demarcation are clear, the respec-

105

tive budgets standing to reflect priorities within the national inventory of government-controlled projects. During the Eisenhower era, the first three years after Explorer 1 put America in orbit, funds for respective departments ran approximately the same, although both were increasing. When President Kennedy came to office in early 1961, however, his priorities were different from those of his Republican predecessor. Instead of waiting for a measured Soviet feat, Kennedy decided very early in his term to upstage the Russians with a spectacular demonstration of US technology at its most ambitious. That decision, to send men to the Moon by the end of 1969, prevented the Defense Department receiving the money they wanted for bigger research projects in space, while NASA's annual fund increased from $926 million to a staggering $5,016 million within three years.

Emphasis clearly went on the need to gather adequate intelligence concerning a potential adversary and to that end a capable family of reconsats evolved to the Big Bird, KH-11, close-look and ferret type satellites of today. Throughout the 1960s, the Defense Department consolidated the passive role of support for existing activities it had begun under the improved policies of the Kennedy administration. But still, NASA got the biggest budget, far outstripping the money spent on defense space programs. In fact, by 1965, the latter received less than one quarter of all the money allocated to space that year: $1,574 million of the $6,955 million. NASA received $5,138 million and the balance went to several other government agencies working on information returned by the NASA scientific satellites. This was the peak of spending on Apollo development and NASA's budget declined over the following years. An initial boost given to military projects by the new Kennedy administration, tripling the defense space fund in three years, had not been maintained and by the end of the 1960s the allocation was no more in real terms than it had been at the beginning, despite a sudden influx of money in 1968 and 1969 by the outgoing Johnson administration.

When Lyndon Johnson vacated the White House for Richard Nixon to take over, defense space money took a dramatic tumble. In three years Nixon slashed the annual defense space budget by 30 per cent, more if inflation is considered, and all but crippled new initiatives then being planned by the Air Force. It allowed continued work on the important Big Bird satellites but completely cancelled development of satellites and space vehicles only then coming into operational use. At the end of the 1970s, however, major and alarming new policies implemented by the Soviet Union caused America to find more defense funds. But it went further than that, for what was judged to be a necessary attempt to restore, for all time, the sums essential for matching Soviet initiatives in defense projects began a wave of technology developments which showed how effective a major thrust in defense space planning could be.

At this time, the Russians were openly flaunting before the West a device designed to knock satellites out of operation in the first few hours of a conflict. For the first time, space was becoming a hostile environment rather than the passive haven for observation and coexistence. But more of that later, for the stimulus was seen in major new funding allocations for 1976. Within two years, defense space money had gone up by nearly 38 per cent and in the two years after 1978 it was further increased by an additional 47 per cent. By 1980, the Defense Department was spending about as much as NASA on space projects designed to pull back an increasing lead obtained by the Soviet Union.

In the decade ahead, money applied to military space operations will exceed the annual sums spent on civilian programs. But the picture of a depleted defense budget in the 1960s and early 1970s is not quite the complete story, for NASA was made to spend more than half its money on manned projects for which there was no defense equivalent. If the money used by NASA on the manned projects Mercury, Gemini and Apollo is taken away from the total spent up to 1972, the money allocated to all other civilian projects totals less than that spent by the Defense Department in the same period. In other words, on an equivalent basis, counting only the type of capability acquired by defense space activity, NASA spent less in the same period. For much of the 1970s, NASA was caught up in a funding spiral for the re-usable Shuttle with which it intended to replace all the existing launch vehicles and so the actual sum available for operational satellites was very much less than that available for defense space projects. So where has all the defense space money gone, and what are the major new developments which require such increased sums over the years ahead? To find that out it is first necessary to review the many other satellites which throughout the last ten years have taken an increasing share of the global defense load for both Russian and US forces.

The trends have mirrored changing strategies throughout the globe

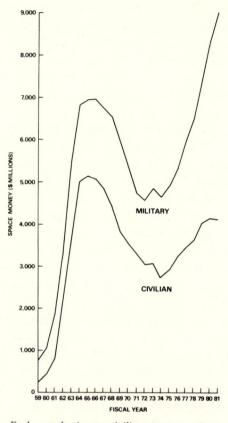

Early emphasis on civilian space projects within the US budget has been dramatically reversed, giving military programs the initiative.

and brought an independence to armed forces in conflicts far from home territory. No better example is available than the Soviet Navy, whose ships and submarines today present a major influence on decisions about foreign initiatives. With four major fleets operating from respective bases at Severomorsk, Baltiysk, Sevastapol and Vladivostok, the Russian surface vessels roam far and wide across international waters. At major yards near Gorkiy, Nikolayev, Komsomolsk and Khabarovsk, ships and submarines roll down slipways in increasing numbers. The Soviet Navy is an instrument of political will for, as Admiral of the Fleet Sergei Gorshkov has said: "The Soviet Navy is a powerful factor in the creation of favorable conditions for the building of Socialism and Communism." Throughout the world, Soviet influence has built up to a global presence and an increasing awareness of the need to keep close to events in the Middle East, from where the West derives almost all its oil supplies, has taken strong naval forces to the Mediterranean and the Indian Ocean. With a large intelligence base at the port of Havana, Cuba, Soviet intelligence ships disguised as trawlers operate up and down the continental United States coast line. Moreover, Soviet reconnaissance aircraft regularly fly into Cuba and use its facilities as a staging post. In the Far East, ports and landing facilities in many locations ensure a continuous presence in that troubled area.

Yet even as the Soviet forces were building up to unprecedented strength around the world, local and regional politics reduced the areas open to United States forces. During the mid-1970s, two major radar stations in Turkey, one at Diyarbakir and the other at Sinop on the Black Sea coast, were closed down. This was the major missile monitoring area for rocket tests in the Soviet Union. At Belbasi a seismic listening station used to monitor Russian nuclear weapons tests ceased to operate and at Malatya a communications station was closed. In the second half of the 1970s, Soviet presence in the Indian Ocean was consolidated. Mooring and logistics facilites were set up at Port Louis, Mauritius, and at Madagascar, with additional sites available on the Chagos Archipelago and the Seychelles. India agreed to support Russia's naval needs at Vizianagaram and Vishakhapatnam along the east coast and tank farms at Chisimaio and Mogadishu in the Somali Republic. But it was in the Middle East itself that the greatest threat was seen.

In addition to a floating dock and refuelling facilites at Aden, missile sites protect a major operational headquarters at Berbera in Somalia where a barrack ship was stationed from 1972 and surface and submarine vessels were dispatched throughout the region. It was the operating center of Soviet activity in the entire Indian Ocean area. But it was at Umm Qasr, at the end of the Persian Gulf, that Iraq provided the foothold where Soviet access would compromise political initiatives toward settling a major crisis which flared in 1980. Russian facilities could accept 6,000-ton ships at Umm Qasr. Only the island of Diego Garcia, 1,800 km south of the tip of India, provided support for US forces which moved in to use British facilities when the host country pulled out and left the entire Indian Ocean available as a Soviet *mare nostrum*.

To counter the expanding threat of Soviet armed forces around the world a reorganization of US defense interests took account of future positions both sides would have in the decades ahead. A shrinking US global presence would come to rely increasingly on remote sensing and long-distance communications and monitoring facilities. There was a need to shift from Earth-based stations and ground facilities to space-borne satellites capable of operating without the risk of losing valuable sites because of revolution or a change of government policy; so many times, facilities had been denied to the US because of sudden political extremism.

With the need constantly to monitor and effectively counter Soviet naval strength throughout the world's oceans, the US Naval Research Laboratory authorized Martin Marietta to build satellites for a unique test, providing the contractor with a valuable facility at the Naval Research Laboratory. The West had, and still has, a commanding lead in anti-submarine warfare but with increasing use of submarines for hunter-killer tasks, threatening the large convoys which would bring US troops and supplies to NATO or Middle East forces, and increasing numbers of SLBM submarines, the Soviet underwater force was of major concern.

The Navy wanted a satellite system capable, like no other system, of monitoring radio communication and radar emissions from underwater submarines and surface ships around the globe. Since Admiral Gorshkov assumed command of the Soviet Navy in 1956 he had effectively built the force to proportions which stimulated early studies of satellite networks for ocean surveillance. Until the 1960s, monitoring roles had been performed by aircraft and other ships, but when "Kresta" Class guided missile cruisers appeared in addition to "Moskva" Class helicopter platforms and the new "Kara" Class cruisers, effectively the most potent ship on Earth, existing methods were no longer plausible.

Under Program 749 the Navy began intensive study of satellite systems proposed by various contractors. At first it seemed possible to integrate surface surveillance with observation of aircraft movements over the same areas; Russian reconnaissance patrols frequently brought Soviet aircraft on probing flights of the US fleet. For some time in the early 1970s, the Navy used photographs returned from Air Force reconsats to monitor Soviet naval deployments, and while the studies for a unique satellite dedicated to ocean surveillance dragged on, the potential threat grew in scale. Finally, when funds began to unlock research projects, the Navy announced it would deploy the White Cloud system and that Martin Marietta would build the satellites. But first, an interim system would be deployed to help stop an expanding gap. There were certainly several possible duties an ocean surveillance satellite could perform. The big nuclear-powered SLBM submarines operated by the Soviet Union in a role equivalent to that of the Polaris- and later Poseidon-equipped boats were virtually undetectable once submerged. And they could easily remain at depth for several months without surfacing, thanks to the nuclear power plant and oxygen production units on board.

However, even nuclear-powered submarines need water taken from the sea to cool their reactors and when this warmer water was put back into the ocean it would quickly rise to the surface. Several commercial satellites developed for locating natural resources used infra-red sensors capable of picking up minute temperature changes. It was no secret that several US Air Force satellites had carried such equipment also. Attached to a naval surveillance network, infra-red scans of the ocean below would conceivably lead to detection of the submerged submarine. Such targets were juicy prizes indeed, for each "Delta II" Class submarine, reportedly the largest boats used for this purpose, had 16 SS-N-8 missiles capable of carrying nuclear charges across a range of more than 7,800 km.

The first steps at proving the feasibility of ocean surveillance were taken in 1971 when, on December 14, a Lockheed Agena ascended on the top of a modified Thor booster with three satellites to eavesdrop on Soviet shipping and direction-find their precise location from space. The aim was to develop an all-weather system capable of mapping the location of every Soviet naval vessel, and if that could be achieved the use of surface-to-surface missiles to knock each ship out in the event of hostilities was a feasible proposition. The tests were sound and the concept proven.

The first pre-operational system got off the ground in April 1976 when three satellites were placed in orbit from the Vandenberg Air Force Base at an inclination of 63.5 degrees. Developed and built by the Naval Research Laboratory they were the first of two clusters scheduled to precede the operational system built by Martin Marietta. When launched, the three 1976 satellites were placed in three separate but parallel orbits displaced in space as well as time. What this meant was that each satellite would be separated from its neighbor so that interferometry techniques could be used to pin-point Soviet surface ships and submarines. The three parallel orbits were all within 46 km of each other and, since they all had the same inclination, the satellites moved around the globe as if in convoy. Interferometry is to radio signals what the telescope is to a source of light. By using several antennae, a small point source of radio emission—in this case a low-energy source from a surface vessel—can be "magnified" for interrogation. The 1976 cluster orbits the Earth about 1,100 km up and at this height the satellites can detect radio signals from surface ships up to 3,200 km away, all three providing good location data in addition to the interferometric capability.

On December 8, 1977, three more Navy satellites reached orbit in a similar spread across three parallel orbit paths, also inclined at 63.5 degrees. The lateral spread in this case was a little less than with the first set but they were deliberately placed in orbit at 113 degrees around the globe, 3,000 km away from their predecessors; while the 1976 trio were monitoring Pacific ships, the new satellites were watching the Atlantic. Thus phased, they established the first pre-operational network, sending their intelligence to the ground at frequencies close to 1,432 MHz on a 1 MHz bandwidth.

The first operational subsets were launched on March 3, 1980, when three Martin Marietta satellites slipped into a 63.5-degree orbit at an altitude very close to the 1976 and 1977 flights. This is but the start of a major effort aimed at plugging intelligence services in to the ocean areas patrolled and used by Soviet naval forces. For their part, the Russians had preceded their naval build-up with surveillance satellites launched under the familiar Cosmos blanket. The first such satellites appeared in 1967 and rapid development led to the operational use of radar units on low orbital trajectories. The use of infra-red or millimeter-length radars can effectively improve the intelligence function by seeking ships and other surface vessels which are electronically quiet. About two such satellites were sent up by the Russians each year, power for the radar being provided by a small nuclear generator on board the satellite. Early tests with Cosmos 198 in 1967, Cosmos 209 in 1968 and Cosmos 367 in 1970 led to operational activities in an expanded role by 1972. The basic operating mode was first to place in orbit a satellite approximately 14 m long and 2.5 m in diameter weighing about 4.5 tons. The launch vehicle employed for this was a specially adapted version of the SS-9 ICBM, precursor to the massive SS-18 introduced as a replacement for strategic defense from the mid-1970s. The SS-9, designated the F series launcher, had been used for other less passive duties as will be seen in a later chapter, but in its ocean surveillance launch role the rocket lifted a combined payload and upper stage to an almost circular path about 270 km high. After carrying out radar scans of the ocean below, and of surface vessels in foreign ports, the radar assembly was separated from the rocket stage so that the latter could fire itself into a much higher orbit approximately 900 km above the Earth. The reason for this was to relieve the rocket stage, and the nuclear power source, of additional weight comprising scanners and instruments used for transmitting the data to Earth, so the stage would have sufficient power to lift itself into a safe path. The use of a nuclear power source required the fissile material to be lifted out of premature decay through the atmosphere where the deadly payload would remain in space for several hundred years, after which time the radioactive source would be harmless.

Initially, in flights from 1967 to 1970, the complete sequence was tested in quick succession. The Russians wanted to be absolutely sure the operation worked well, for it would surely lead to an international incident if the satellite came back down prematurely with its radioactive load. It would, theoretically, have been possible to shield the power source but the extra weight necessary would have been more than the rocket could lift. Beginning in 1971 the Russians flew ocean surveillance missions of this type where increasing gaps were observed between reaching an initial low orbit and final injection of the separated stage into a high orbit. First, Cosmos 402 stayed low for eight days, then Cosmos 469 remained at the lower altitude for ten days. Following this, paired flights each year carried surveillance missions between one and two months in duration, always followed by separation of the stage and its nuclear generator, propelled to high orbit at the end of operations while the instrument package decayed harmlessly back down through the atmosphere.

Until Cosmos 954, launched on September 18, 1977. More than four months later the stage separated from the instrument package and fired its engine as all other ocean surveillance satellites had done before. Only this time it was pointing in the wrong direction and instead of shifting into a higher orbit it slowed the assembly down and the stage fell back into Earth's atmosphere, showering its debris, and fissile material from the nuclear power source, across Canada's North-West Territory. In a combined US-Canadian exercise, scientists and personnel from research laboratories in the two countries scoured the barren countryside for radioactive material, retrieving several kilograms from a wide area. The incident caused an international furor over the use of such materials in surveillance satellites and, in testimony provided to the United Nations, US experts said that not since 1965 had an American military satellite tested any nuclear power source and that none had ever been used on standard operational satellites. The US did admit, however, that an earlier satellite had unexpectedly re-entered the atmosphere during 1962, showering the Pacific with large quantities of radioactive materials.

Sensitive to their exposed operation, the Soviets stopped all further flights with the big surveillance satellites and, in the period of re-design which followed, sent up a pair of interim vehicles in 1979 using ordinary solar cell arrays. Cosmos 1096 launched on April 25, was paired with its predecessor, Cosmos 1094, to perform from an orbital altitude of about 440 km the same type of interferometry function carried out by the US satellites. It was a step back for the Russians, their radar-equipped satellites no longer providing detailed surveillance, but work was well under way to produce a new design equipped this time with very large solar cell panels for the extra electrical energy necessary to run the radar scanners. In April 1980, Cosmos 1176 reached orbit, representing the new generation of Soviet nuclear powered ocean surveillance satellites. It was later boosted safely to high orbit and was followed in March 1981 by Cosmos 1249, which worked alone until joined by solar powered derivatives of the earlier type.

As the new decade of the 1980s began, the US was well into full-scale operations with the White Cloud system while the Russians, initially well ahead in this field with their active radars, were temporarily forced back upon the less accurate system beginning with the paired flights in 1979.

Traditionally, the use of photographs and intelligence gathering activity for information essential to the conduct of a battle relies on fine weather. That prerequisite, present in all reconnaissance missions during World War 2 is no longer quite so important when hour by hour the surface of the Earth is surveyed by satellites in space. Yet careful observation of periodic events or activities, plus the timely watch made of aircraft or ship movements, relies heavily on clear skies through which the oribtal eyes can peer. From the beginning, weather played a fundamental role in just what was available to the intelligence analyst. But more than that, for in the event of hostilities it is important to know the regional weather over bombing targets, or to map the effective cloud system across a battle front. An early attempt at using reconnaissance satellites according to when and where they happened to be over certain areas of the Earth revealed a need for predicted weather patterns. The then existing method employed by the defense establishment, where military stations around the world reported local conditions to a central data facility, were sadly outmoded by the global reconsat. Since most weather is generated and mobilized over large seas and oceans, where few reporting sites or measurement stations exist, the need to sense large areas of land and water remotely assumed paramount importance. Moreover, at a more sinister level, the effectiveness of nuclear weapons depends in large part on the prevailing weather situation and it was deemed wise to maintain a running and up to the minute record of such conditions all over the world. Radiation drift and the colateral effect of comparatively small tactical battlefield nuclear weapons is heavily dependent on these criteria. But the Air Force was slow to adopt weather satellites, relying instead in the first few years on civilian satellites specially developed for this role. The Radio Corporation of America (RCA) maintained an intense research program on weather and its analysis, the company had done considerable work for the armed forces during the 1950s, and when the civilian NASA organization promoted development of the world's first meteorological satellite system called Tiros, RCA got the contract. Launched between 1960 and 1965, the ten Tiros satellites each orbited the Earth in elliptical paths between 680 and 940 km, their orbits inclined variously between 48 and 59 degrees.

For the first few years, the Defense Department used Tiros weather pictures to support their requirements. But the military uses to which Tiros pictures were put soon revealed a specification matched to developments in reconnaissance satellite and battlefield applications. The Defense Department wanted high resolution shots of comparatively small areas so that reconsats could be assigned targets of interest free from atmospheric obscurations; increasing involvement in South-East Asia pressed the urgency of good satellite imagery in that unfamiliar territory.

Under Program 417 the first operational defense weather satellites were designed. Experiments had been going on for some time and the first experimental use of sensors and hardware came in 1962 when a small Scout rocket delivered a 20 kg payload into elliptical orbit. That was followed by several more experimental flights of test sensors and camera systems before the first RCA-built defense metsat lifted off on January 19, 1965, atop a Thor-Altair launch vehicle. Employing the fourth stage of the Scout rocket as an upper stage to a basic Thor, the launch vehicle put its payload in an elliptical orbit 471 km at the perigee and 822 km at the apogee.

Four more were sent up over the following 15 months before the series was replaced by the RCA Block IVA model. There was by now an urgent need for good regional metsat coverage. From the first satellite of this type launched in January 1965, the polar-orbit, Sun-synchronous, path became standard. In Vietnam, American and South Vietnamese forces relied heavily on the daily pictures and soon the Air Force, too, would use views of targets to choose bombing patterns. The Block IVA satellites weighed about 82 kg, were spin-stabilized in orbit—that is, they were made to rotate and maintain their primary axial alignment like a spinning gyroscope—with banks of solar cells covering the outside so that whichever way the satellite was facing, solar energy would be received. In all, four satellites of this type were orbited by Thor Burner II launch vehicles in a 13-month period beginning September 1966. They were replaced by the Block IVB, three of which were launched between May 1966 and July 1969. They differed in that in addition to two vidicon cameras infra-red sensors were also carried, the latter providing information about the changing heat patterns in the atmosphere. That information set up a second dimension for the meteorologists and began a series of improvements which over the next decade would revolutionize the science of weather forecasting.

Next came the Block 5A series, three of which were sent up from Vandenberg on the same type of launcher used for the previous model. But these satellites were attitude-stabilized and controlled by a new digital system. In addition, replacing the earlier vidicon cameras, the Block 5A carried line-scan cameras in the visual and infra-red bands. In late 1971, these were in turn replaced by a 5B/C version, seven going into orbit up to 1976. Because of increasing demand for better and more frequent readouts, the direct transmission system was improved, enabling tactical field units, ships at sea and unit commanders to obtain views they would have been unable to receive a few years previously. More sensors were attached, including an infra-red temperature sounder and an infra-red image channel, with high- and very-high-resolution camera systems.

Beginning in 1976 the Strategic Air Command's 4000th Aerospace Applications Unit began to equip for operations with the greatly expanded capability of a Block 5D series. With specific tasks assigned by the Air Force Weather Service's Global Weather Central, large Univac computers were assigned data processing duties. With available pictures to hand, distribution would go to ground sites in America and abroad, with special readout vans operated by the Army and the Air Force and receivers on board aircraft carriers around the world. In some cases, picture data would travel by satellite to areas remote from land stations. The Block 5D series was an outstanding improvement on earlier classes of military metsat. For the first time it enabled field and unit commanders access to real-time picture readout without waiting for distribution from a central facility. This means, in principle, that remote combat units can call down, from a Block 5D flying overhead, information directly associated with their area and that, even if cut off from all outside contact, they can pursue an independent set of decisions. In the past, pictures were only available from major processing facilities. It is further measure of the changing global strategy where field commanders or local units must be expected to make their own decisions about strategy, even down to a tactical level.

There are two types of Block 5D, the D-1 being replaced by the D-2 in flights commencing 1981, with the second almost identical in design to the first but larger and with greater capacity. Five Block 5D-1 missions were flown between 1976 and 1980. Each satellite comprises three primary elements. At the rear, the main rocket stage responsible for pushing the metsat into orbit forms the structural backbone for attitude control thrusters using hydrazine to maintain a fixed pointing angle when looking down at the Earth. It contains all the control equipment necessary to keep the satellite at the correct position and attitude. Next to it, the equipment support module houses most of the 5D's electronic systems for command and transmission of information from the sensors and for regulating the electrical demands, picture-taking sequences, sensor "on-off" positions, etc. At the front, the precision mounting platform carries the sophisticated sensor packages, each tailored to a specific mission and, as such, completely interchangeable according to needs, with so-called attitude determination sensors for detecting position changes. At the extreme forward end of the satellite, a sun shade is used to prevent backscatter from light which could otherwise degrade performance. At the rear, a single wing of solar cells unfolds in space to present a 9.3 sq m array capable of generating an average 290 Watts of electrical energy; the 5D-2 has 25 per cent more surface area for higher power levels. Because the 5D is built around the solid propellant Burner II second stage, it carries with it into orbit a structural weight not associated with the satellite itself. At launch, on top of the Thor first stage, the combined second stage and satellite weighs a total 2,700 kg (2,900 kg for the 5D-2). After burning away the solid propellant to place itself in orbit, the configuration weighs about 480 kg, although the 5D-2 variant weighs up to 770 kg, of which 180 kg comprises the payload sensors and camera system, up to 270 kg being assigned for the more powerful model. When deployed, the satellite is approximately 3.8 m in length and 2.3 m in diameter. The heart of the system's package is the operational linescan imaging equipment providing pictures in the visible and infra-red areas of the spectrum. The equipment is developed and constructed by Westinghouse Electric Corporation's Defense and Electronic Systems Center and has found application in several other satellite designs operated by and for civilian metsat organizations. It is capable of providing recorded or direct-readout information with a resolution down to 2.7 km, or it can send direct to field commanders, pictures of their local area to a resolution of less than 600 m. Visible images can be obtained with light levels as low as a quarter-Moon while the infra-red scan operates equally well day or night. In itself, the linescanner provides complete and autonomous authority over operations in a remote sector. All that is needed is a comparatively small receiver van with readout facilities. But if the information is sent from a central facility in the United States, global pictures are available for Strategic Air Command bomber crews or personnel on deep intrusion flights of hostile airspace, shaping their flight paths around the meteorological phenomena if required. For ease of navigation duties, the Global Weather Central can convert polar stereographic projection into a Mercator view within 20 seconds by running it through a Univac computer. The display instrument, being a mechanical device, takes fully two minutes to come up with the resulting picture, however! From the Global Weather Central, the most important customer for global data is the Strategic Air Command war room where computers link the facility with the GWC and provide constant projections on a large screen of weather data as sensed and updated. A printer at the command post provides personnel with their own hand copies of the world weather picture on demand.

Orbital geometry for the Block 5D series provides two-satellite operations. One satellite crosses the Equator at a local time of about 6.30 A.M., providing metmaps for early morning combat briefings at air bases in the region and enabling military commanders in the field to plan their daylight strategy according to prevailing conditions. The second satellite has an equatorial crossing time, for that area, at about 12.00 noon, generating information to allow modification of battle strategy to take advantage of the weather conditions, whatever they may be. To accomplish the mission, 5D satellites are placed in Sun-synchronous orbits inclined 98.7 degrees to the Equator, at an almost circular height of 830 km, carrying the satellite once round the Earth in 101 minutes.

In space, operational commands are sent via the satellite's own central computer unit with a capacity to carry 16,000 "words" of information, or 28,000 on the 5D-2. This central processing unit literally takes over at the moment of lift-off and steers the two-stage rocket into orbit. On station, the computer is set to run the meteorological mission by itself if necessary, relying on the ground only for daily updates on its own position as perceived by ground radar installations. But the computer can be re-programmed from the ground, the valuable asset which enabled one satellite to be saved from total failure shortly after launch.

The 5D has no fewer than six communication links with the ground, five sending data from the spacecraft of which three are for transmitting data and two are for engineering telemetry on the status of the satellite; the sixth allows ground controllers to send "uplink" signals to the satellite. Central command and control facilities are based at Offutt Air Force Base, Nebraska, the home of the Global Weather Central. Signals to the satellites are delivered via one of two readout stations: Loring Air Force Base, Maine, and Fairchild Air Force Base, Washington. Data and telemetry can be received and transferred from Kaena Point Air Force Station, Hawaii, while the two readout stations pick up primary data and telemetry for delivery to Offutt by communications satellite.

It is a global network involving ground and space-borne segments with the satellites providing timely coverage of world-wide weather information. The data sent back from Block 5D series satellites is more comprehensive than before, requiring sophisticated instruments covering a broad spectrum of sensors. In addition to the linescan imaging and infra-red equipment, the series carries several alternative instruments. Among these is a scanning infra-red radiometer, capable of telling the ground operator the amount of water vapor in a given vertical column of the atmosphere. It can also judge the amount of ozone present. A passive microwave temperature sounder is also carried, a sensor which measures millimeter wavelength radiation in the atmosphere to set up a temperature profile from the surface to an altitude of 30 km. The limb-scanning atmospheric density sensor is an instrument which looks at the satellite's horizon (or Earth limb) to measure ultraviolet emissions from a band within the atmosphere where large-scale temperature changes occur, providing the user with details of the atmospheric constituents such as nitrogen and oxygen. Another sensor measures the quantity of electrons present on the side facing away from Earth. Yet another device measures electrons and ions on the side facing the planet while an ionospheric sounder determines the effects of ions on radio waves through the atmosphere. Supplied by the Air Force, a seventh detector is designed to pick up gamma radiation of the type produced by nuclear explosions. One satellite in 1979 carried an experimental snow-cloud sensor to see if future instruments could usefully discriminate between the two reflective mediums.

All the time it remains operational in orbit, the satellite maintains a precise attitude-stable orientation, revolving only once on each orbit so that it continually points at the atmosphere directly below. From launch at the Vandenberg complex, a Block 5D satellite passes over the Antarctic and up across the Indian Ocean where it is acquired by a tracking station for telemetry analysis, data sent immediately via a communications satellite to Offutt in the United States. If any unexpected events have occurred, the Indian Ocean station will issue corrective commands, otherwise the satellite continues on its uninterrupted way and within a short time is fully operational.

The Global Weather Central will acquire more sophisticated information during the mid-1980s from a unique Special Sensor Microwave/ Imager (SSM/I), designed and built by Hughes Aircraft Company's

Space & Communications Group. Launched in 1984, a Block 5D-2 satellite will carry the SSM/I into space for tests aimed at qualifying operationally a system built to see through clouds and heavy rain to track weather patterns as they develop. This is more effective than the infrared equipment used hitherto, which can track only the tops of clouds. The new instrument wll map the edges of sea ice, determine the thickness and age of existing ice sheets, measure surface wind speed across open sea, measure the amount of ground moisture in selected areas and report the amount of water held by clouds and the precipitation rate of falling rain.

The US Navy's Fleet Numerical Oceanographic Center, Monterey, California, will join the GWC in using information from the SSM/I. The instrument consists of a parabolic antenna measuring 61 cm by 66 cm and a module carrying electronic components. The satellite will fly in a sun-synchronous orbit over the earth's poles 833 km above the surface. Designed to spin at 31.6 rpm, the SSM/I sensor will operate in four frequency bands and cover a ground swath of 1,400 km. Along with visible and infrared data obtained from other instruments on board, the satellite's SSM/I will transmit information to Air Force and Navy weather stations for rapid processing.

The information now provided by the RCA metsats is more a comprehensive package of environmental reports than the series of weather pictures first used by the armed services 20 years ago. With data from the Block 5D series, the quality of radio transmissions can be predicted, the density of water vapor calculated and the level of chemical contamination obtained. In peace time, the satellites work effectively to provide atmospheric windows for the sensitive scanners of the reconsats, several orbital passages being programmed according to weather patterns. But in time of war, prevailing weather conditions are a vital part of tactical operations.

Upwind of a strong gale, troops could move quite close to a nuclear strike zone without being unduly affected by the radiation, while downwind of the area contamination would extend over greater distance. In this way, environmental access maps can be quickly constructed, showing "red" zones into which troops must be prohibited from moving. Alternatively, it is possible precisely to target nuclear impact zones in such a way that they cause maximum effect on an approaching enemy. But all this applies only to the comparatively small, Hiroshima-size, weapons used for tactical battlefield support.

The larger nuclear charges would create massive fall-out zones. In a period of several days, however, the affected areas here, too, would be effectively mapped out by the metsats. Yet for all that, it is in support of tactical strike roles that the satellites come into their own, providing comprehensive and highly accurate information vital to any airborne operation. Similarly, in a battlefield context, sensors on the metsats would detect and chart out areas where biological weapons were in use, providing information on contaminated areas across wide zones.

Storage capacity aboard the Block 5D is significant. On the basic model tape recorders contain up to 20 minutes of data prior to readout but on the 5D-2 version this capacity is tripled for high resolution data, or extended to 20 hours for low-resolution data. At a tactical level, field commanders can receive real-time pictures covering a swathe 2,963 km wide and more than 7,400 km in length. Long life is a key feature of the 5D, the basic version being designed to operate for 18 months while each 5D-2 will, it is hoped, endure three years of continuous operation. Longevity of operation has been one big drawback with the Soviet military metsats, a type of program run along very different developmental tracks from the US system. Early Tiros semi-operational satellites were supplemented by a series of Nimbus research and development satellites operated concurrently with the Tiros series. The Russians, on the other hand, have preferred to move first through a research phase before designing operational hardware. Consequently, they came to meteorological satellite work comparatively late in the day. Difficult, too, is the prediction as to which satellite carries an essentially military function and which is applicable to civilian needs. It may be that there is an area of activity which can never, in the Soviet system, by separated according to function. The complete integration of both civilian and military responsibilities have apparently generated a family of metsats applicable to both user communities. In this context, it should be said that the United States has maintained an active, and expanding, program of meteorological research embracing operational and research hardware. The latest second generation series of Tiros metsats placed in orbit for purely civilian needs are developed from the Defense Meteorology Satellite Program's Block 5D series, replacing the first generation Tiros series launched between 1960 and 1965, ESSA class satellites operated between 1966 and 1969 and Itos series vehicles placed in orbit between 1970 and 1976. But those are of no consequence here for they form part of the civilian inventory. Suffice it to say that the global weather watch maintained by America's National Oceanic and Atmospheric Administration for civilian users the world over also employs stationary orbit satellites positioned high above the Earth to show top-cover views of the large-scale factors responsible for regional changes; the first was sent up in 1974.

As for the Russian metsats, the first preliminary experiments, using hardware developed for specific instruments lifted into space piggy-back on another satellite, went up on five flights between 1963 and 1965. Between 1966 and 1968 a series of pre-operational satellites was launched into 65-degree or 81-degree orbits prior to an operational commitment with developed hardware. Cosmos 122, witnessed by President de Gaulle, ascended on June 25, 1966, as the first pre-operational prototype. It carried television for cloud pictures and infra-red detectors for day and night scans in three spectral bands. It was placed in a path 600 km above the Earth, comprising a 2-ton structure about 5 m in length and 1.5 m across. The satellite was stabilized about all three axes, unlike earlier US military metsats which were spin-stabilized, and operated only a few months before its successor, Cosmos 144, ascended from the same Tyuratam launch site. But these, it was emphasized by the Soviet Union, were experimental, as were several other similar satellites placed in orbits like their predecessors before the first Meteor-1 operational metsat lifted into space during March 1969, fully 11½ years after Sputnik 1. Weighing almost 2.2 tons, Meteor-1 class satellites have a capacity to scan swathes of the ground 1,000 km wide, with television cameras for global cloud cover pictures, or 2,500 km wide in infra-red. Many supplementary instruments are carried according to the required duties and some satellites of this type can send real-time pictures to simple receivers on the ground. Some instruments are used to measure ice/liquid water balance in clouds while others probe vertical sections of the atmosphere for temperature profiles. Launched first in July 1975, the Meteor-2 version used since then to supplement the simpler model, can carry multi-spectral sounding equipment like Earth-resource satellites now used by the United States for geological studies. In fact, the function of the Meteor satellites is more in line with a broad based scientific study than immediate and timely provision for the armed services. However, perhaps lacking the sophisticated data processing capability of the US military metsats, Meteor vehicles support Soviet military needs too.

The Russians currently employ three ground receiving stations. One is at Novosibirsk and a second at Khabarovsk. Yet, although these stations pick up information direct from the satellites, they are unable to send the data by microwave and must radio the information across to the Soviet Hydrometeorological Service center outside Moscow. The third station, at Obninsk, supplies data direct by microwave, however. The lack of direct data supply from the two remote receiver stations means a long delay between getting the pictures and supplying the information. It is partly for this reason that Meteor-2 series satellites have an expanded capacity for beaming direct to mobile Earth stations the information contained in the recorder system on board the satellite, thus short-circuiting the lengthy ground-transfer process.

There seems to have been some improvement in performance and systems' longevity, for where the Russians launched about six satellites each year up to about 1977, numbers since then have decreased significantly. It is interesting to note that the Russians have so far failed to place global weather satellites in stationary orbit, which, with the enormous land mass under their direct administration, would be of extreme value for mapping large weather systems across central Asia from a satellite positioned over the Indian Ocean (readers will recall that to remain stationary, a satellite 36,000 km above Earth must have its orbit along the plane of the Equator).

The quality of pictures sent down by the Meteors approximates to that of the Block IV satellites, although they obtain wide-angle surveys with a broader format than the US metsats. Like the American satellites, too, Meteor transmits its pictures to ships at sea and small ground receivers world wide. The transfer of meteorological information is one of the more benign data packages transferred across intercontinental distances. Indeed, it could be said that with local picture receivers at hand the loss of communication with a central facility would not seriously handicap field or unit commanders. But information of a more vital kind is used regularly by the military services of East and West and for this a very necessary space application is the communications satellite, suitably screened and hardened against interference.

From the very beginning of space operations, the movement of human communication across international frontiers was an exciting prospect and communications satellites share with weather satellites the distinction of being the most developed application resulting from the space age. Today, in an age of sophisticated high performance weapon systems, communication is a necessary ingredient of military success, be it in the role of deterring aggression or, in the final analysis, as a method of destroying an enemy. The earliest attempt at communication via space involved the inexperienced science of propaganda in its most basic form. In late 1958 the instrumented hull of an Atlas rocket was shot into orbit from where the voice of President Eisenhower boomed a pre-Christmas message, no doubt aimed at those who believed America was in the backwater of technical development. But soon, NASA and the Defense Department were locked in their own, frequently repetitious, research programs to find the best and most applicable means of using space for intercontinental communications.

In 1960, NASA launched a large balloon called Echo and bounced radio signals from it to practice the science of receiving a signal from space, while the Advanced Research Projects Agency, an Army establishment for basic research, lifted Courier 1 into an orbit 1,600 km high. It was apparent that the needs of the two very distinct user communities could not be easily reconciled and while NASA went ahead with projects like Rebound, Relay, Syncom and Telstar, all designed to demonstrate the scientific plausibility of what could become a highly desirable commercial asset, the Defense Department formulated its own programs.

The Advanced Research Projects Agency had set up a communications consultative committee as early as May 1958, just four months after the first US satellite reached orbit, and this led to several different proposals. Culminating in a specification suited to the needs of the Air Force and the Army Signal Corps, three projects were proposed: Steer and Tackle, for basic and advanced polar-orbit duty, respectively, and Decree, a stationary orbit vehicle designed to sit over the Equator and relay communications. They were combined in a venture called Advent just as Project Echo was getting read for launch, combining the research begun under the Courier program with operational needs projected to require a phased program leading to several stationary-orbit satellites. Project Advent lasted barely two years and was replaced by a series of small satellites riding piggy-back in a cluster with several other experimental payloads on primary satellites sent up for other purposes. Combined operating needs were finally honed to a so-called Initial Defense Satellite Communications System (IDSCS) comprising several satellites placed in stationary orbit around the globe.

The experimental piggy-back payloads were, in the meantime, developed by the Lincoln Laboratory and, quite appropriately, called Lincoln Experimental Satellites, or LES.

There are several different orbital options available for communications use. Very low orbits at comparatively high inclinations would provide very limited use, but high orbits would ensure increased time above the user's radio horizon. Ideally, stationary orbit was the best possible place since satellites in this type of path would remain permanently fixed with respect to facilities on the ground. This was the type of orbit, and the very application, proposed by Arthur C. Clarke at the end of World War 2. On the other hand, because the satellite is so far from the surface of the Earth, very sensitive receivers are necessary to pick up the signal. Satellites are unable to generate the large power outputs of a ground transmitter so signals picked up and amplified before re-transmission back to another site on the ground will be weak by comparison with conventional transmissions. It is possible to use a point in space merely for bouncing signals from one location to another, but that has little application where the signal is likely to travel in an artificially hostile environment calling for resistance to deliberate jamming. In any event, the received signal strength would be considerably weaker than by the direct radiation method.

So, for the first pre-operational defense communications satellite system, the Air Force equipped small 45 kg satellites with transponders receiving signals from the ground at 8 GHz and re-transmitted at 7.2 GHz. Each IDSCS satellite was a symmetrical polyhedron shape with 24 sides covered by solar cells, 81 cm high and 91 cm in diameter. Launched by a Titan 3C-Transtage rocket capable of lifting 1.6 tons to stationary orbit, the plan envisaged a total 26 IDSCS satellites in an equatorial path just below stationary altitude. From a height of about 34,000 km they would continuously lose out to the spinning Earth below, an observer on the ground seeing them move from one horizon to the other in a period of about 4½ days. The powerful launch vehicle used for this program was to carry seven or eight satellites at one time in a dispenser attached to the front of the Transtage, the last stage, employed to circularize the path of the complete assembly.

The first cluster of seven ascended on June 16, 1966, but a second attempt two months later failed when the Titan rocket blew up. Eight more were, however, sent up in January 1967, and three more joined the group in July before the last eight ascended in June 1968. With this flight all 26 satellites were in space, separated from each other by on average nearly 14 degrees of longitude, slowly rotating around the spinning Earth. During this period, additional research satellites under the LES category continued to develop new communications technologies applicable to the second phase which, re-named the Defense Satellite Communication System, would use true stationary orbit positions and much larger satellites.

The initial set of 26 IDSCS satellites were all built by Ford Aerospace with a design life of 18 months. The communications capacity of the IDSCS set was strictly limited, only one circularly polarized torroidal antenna being carried by each satellite. The Phase 2 satellites of the DSCS network were to carry the load for at least a decade, beginning late 1971, and represent the strategic communications system for worldwide teletypewriter, data and voice contact with Army, Navy, Air Force and Marine units.

Controlled and operated by the Defense Communications Agency, DSCS-2 satellites were built by TRW at their Redondo Beach plant to exacting specifications. Six satellites were ordered at first, each to a common specification built around the stipulated need for two steerable narrow-beam dish antennae and two wide-beam horn antennae, one for receiving and the other for transmitting. The dish antennae were to concentrate their respective beams on comparatively small regions of the Earth, making possible the use of small ground stations or mobile receivers. The horns would serve to provide broad and uniform coverage to the side of the Earth visible to the specific satellite. Each narrow-beam antenna would illuminate an area of the surface 1,600 km in diameter.

Communications equipment and the antennae were placed on a platform separate from the main body of the cylindrical satellite which was made to spin and so stabilize its position, or attitude, in orbit. The de-spun section allowed the fixed antennae to point Earthward with a high degree of accuracy, while the cylindrical body would generate electrical energy from the solar cell panels wrapped around the exterior. Eight separate solar arrays were designed to generate more than 500 Watts but continued use over several years would gradually degrade the efficiency of respective cells so that at the end of its planned five-year life, generated electrical power would average only 390 Watts, more than enough, however, to provide for the 245 Watts necessary to power the satellite's systems.

Because the DSCS-2 satellites were to be placed 36,000 km above the Earth at an orbital inclination of 3 degrees to the Equator, they were not strictly positioned in a stationary path but would weave a figure-of-eight up and down the equatorial latitude, moving 3 degrees north and 3 degrees south as the Earth spun on its axis. The narrow-beam antennae incorporated a nodding mechanism designed to compensate for this movement and keep each beam locked on to its respective co-ordinate.

Compared to the IDSCS satellites, each Phase 2 vehicle was large and heavy. With a height in orbit of nearly 4 m and a diameter of nearly 3 m, each DSCS-2 weighed 570 kg. Special coded signals were to be transmitted so that Earth stations could lock on to the satellite. Ground stations would transmit at 7.2 GHz to 7.4 GHz for the wide-beam or 7.5 GHz to 7.7 GHz for the narrow-beam antenna and the satellite would transmit that signal to a second ground station, perhaps across the other side of the Pacific, at 7.9 GHz to 8.1 GHz for wide-beam or 8.1 GHz to 8.4 GHz for narrow-beam.

Ground terminals compatible with this system were provided for fixed locations with 18.3 m diameter antennae down to highly mobile terminals with a 1.8 m dish, the type fitted to a ship. From the outset, DSCS-2 was intended to carry strategic and tactical communication between fixed and mobile stations supporting defense needs around the world, in greater volume and with more services than had been possible hitherto, certainly under the quasi-experimental interim system and its 26 little satellites.

Because fewer DSCS-2 satellites would be involved with carrying the global military traffic, each carried a small propulsion system designed to move it from one stationary position to another. Should one satellite fail, say an Indian Ocean carrier, one from the Atlantic region could be "walked" around the planet by taking it temporarily out of its synchronous path until it reached the correct longitude, at which point it would be repositioned as a stationary satellite for sustained communication.

In this way, too, true global facilities were to be available for the first time, the beams fixed to common ground sites so that a signal from one side of the Earth could be sent to the other by hopping from station to satellite and on through the system until the message reached its destination.

DSCS operations were to be controlled via the Air Force Satellite Control Facility, a unit of the Air Force Systems Command headquartered at Sunyvale Air Force Station, California. Around the world, stations at New Hampshire, California, and on Hawaii, Guam, Greenland, and Diego Garcia in the Indian Ocean would track, communicate, command, and process orbital data to and from the DSCS network. Each of the two 1.1 m diameter dish antennae would be steered on instructions from one or another of these stations.

The Air Force had mixed fortunes in beginning deployment of the global net. The first two satellites were successfully launched by a single Titan 3C on November 2, 1971, and the second pair reached orbit as planned following launch on December 13, 1973, but the third pair failed to reach orbit because of a failure in the Titan guidance system shortly after ascending from Cape Canaveral on May 20, 1975. By this time, TRW was working on a second batch of six satellites and the first two from this set were fired from the pad on May 12, 1977. Two more were launched on March 25, 1978, but the launch vehicle's second stage failed and they too were lost. A successful dual launch in December of the same year completed the production batch with the initial model.

In 1977, the Defense Department authorized fabrication of four more DSCS-2 series satellites, bringing the total production to 16, and TRW incorporated modifications into this batch further to increase the effective radiated power. The first pair from the third, modified, set ascended in Nobember 1979, to supplement the existing satellites, not all of which were still working at this time. The Defense Communication Agency's plan envisaged four operational DSCS satellites in space, with one each over the Atlantic and Indian Oceans and two stationed to cover east and west regions of the Pacific, plus two orbital spares ready to "walk" to any assigned longitude and take up duty.

The lack of adequate coverage, theoretically not achieved even with the November 1979 launch because one spare was inoperable and others had reached the end of their useful lives, necessitated the Defense Department assigning roles anticipated for DSCS to other satellites of the NATO series, discussed later in this chapter. Delayed initially by low funds from the Pentagon, the DSCS Phase 2 program limped along from one technical or production problem to the next, falling far short of objectives laid down originally.

The "domino" effect of several unpredictable troubles pushed the Phase 2 program on into preparations for Phase 3, a distinctly separate generation of communications satellites designed to replace the

DSCS-2 series from the late 1970s. Trouble there too, and severe funding cutbacks, delayed the program to a first flight attempt in 1981 and deferred production beyond two test vehicles designed to a "fly before buy" concept. Only after proving themselves in orbit would the Pentagon decide one way or the other on production models urgently needed by the Defense Communication Agency.

Unlike Phase 1 and 2 satellites, which were spin-stabilized at 150 rpm and 60 rpm respectively, Phase 3 satellites are attitude stabilized, completing, like the Block 5D weather satellites, a transition to a more satisfactory form of stabilization. They are manufactured by General Electric, who gained valuable experience in attitude stable platforms by building the Nimbus weather research satellites and the Landsat Earth resources spacecraft, and received the contract to build DSCS-3. Each satellite comprises a box-like structure 1.9 m by 2.8 m by 1.9 m tall, supporting two extended solar panels folded against the main structure for launch. When deployed, the DSCS-3 spans 11.6 m and weighs 885 kg at launch; after orbital insertion and the consumption of expendables, the satellite weighs about 748 kg, approximately 220 kg more than the DSCS-2 it replaces. Because of three-axis attitude stabilization, the DSCS-3 can remain pointed at the Sun continuously and, since channel capacity is proportional to the electrical power available, the large solar array surface finds useful application for the more than 1,100 Watts generated in flight.

In fact, DSCS-3 carries six channels, two more than the DSCS-2. Moreover, performance is improved by system reliability, each satellite being designed for a life of ten years, twice that of its predecessor. Two multiple-beam, electronically maneuverable, transmitting beams will together carry 19 elements, effectively working as a 19-beam transmitter; the single receive antenna carries a 61-element capacity, or 61-beam capability, with both phase and amplitude control for compatible Earth terminals which can also be directed at enemy jammers. The satellites also carry a 91 cm dish antenna for transmitting a more powerful signal at small mobile terminals. Extra support in the system is provided by two transmit and two receive horn antennae for Earth illumination. Frequency switching facilities include the ability to receive signals at UHF (ultra-high frequencies) for re-broadcast at the same frequency, or reception at SHF (super-high frequency) for re-transmission at UHF. Four primary travelling-wave-tube amplifiers generating 10 watts and two more generating 40 watts provide a maximum total radiated power of 120 watts, three times that of the DSCS-2 series.

Complete switching capability enables any number of combination of TWTs or antennae to be interlinked between receive and transmit functions. For instance, a signal picked up via the 61-beam receive antenna can be sent to the 40 watt TWT for transmission over one of the two 19-beam capability antennae or the gimballed parabolic dish or both. Receive and transmit frequencies are the same as those applicable to DSCS-2 with an additional telemetry tracking and command capacity on SHF.

In the two years by which the program was delayed beyond the anticipated first launch date of 1979, minor re-designs and other delays provided time for significant modifications to protect the satellites from jamming and strong electromagnetic pulses aimed in time of hostility with the purpose of disabling the communications or electrical equipment. This "hardening" is made all the more necessary by developments within Soviet defense science which threaten to knock out satellites performing critical functions. In time of war the Russians are expected quickly to attempt the destruction of communications and reconnaissance functions which, among others, are now increasingly dependent upon oribital operations. DSCS-3 program schedules were significantly modified when the Defense Department decided to build only two prototypes before committing to a production decision. Now, the first DSCS-3 is expected to lift off a Canaveral launch pad packaged with the third modified DSCS-2, both lofted simultaneously by a Titan 3C. The launch vehicle will have an improved third stage to allow it to carry the added weight of the DSCS-3. The second package comprising the second prototype DSCS-3 and the fourth and last modified DSCS-2, is expected to fly in 1982, about one full year after the first. The launch vehicle for this second mission will be a new derivative of the Titan rocket, a version called the 34D especially developed as a stand-by in case of trouble with early flights of the NASA Shuttle, built to replace all current expendable launchers.

However, the Defense Communications Agency wants additional Phase 2 satellites built while the Pentagon studies the two Phase 3 models for, in the period immediately following 1983, the communications traffic will threaten to outpace available hardware. If extra

DSCS-2 satellites are ordered, they will be sent up on an early Shuttle flight but the Defense Department is concerned not to spend money on a satellite it already sees as an outdated design.

Defense Satellite Communication System hardware supports the strategic, national defense, and global communications network for the US armed services, preserving the infrastructure of the National Command Authority, the big voice of global war. The rather special needs of the US Navy are a little different and call for a unique satellite communications capability epitomized in the Fltsatcom design, a name derived from the function: fleet satellite communications, pronounced "fleetsatcom."

Early recognition of the expanding role of naval commitment in a world increasingly populated by Soviet warships stimulated the basic satellite specification in the late 1960s and following further analysis and successful lobbying at the Pentagon, the Navy was allowed to commission TRW to build the Fltsatcom system in 1972. At that time the satellites were to be available for launch by 1975 and to form a network of five vehicles in orbit.

When delays hit this program too, the launch date slipped and the Navy was forced into the self-descriptive Gapfiller program, leasing capacity aboard a civilian maritime satellite network called Marisat; the Defense Department has been forced to lease capacity on several commercial satellites, paying market prices for channel capacity it has been unable to provide for its own needs, further reflection of the appalling funding schedule generated by diffident White House administrations in the past.

Fltsatcom is designed to provide a UHF and SHF global communications network supporting high priority requirements of the US Navy and Air Force, the latter through Afsatcom, although this does not call for special satellites but places transponders on several other satellites, Fltsatcom included. The Naval Electronics Systems Command has overall management of the program and NASA launches each satellite atop an Atlas-Centaur launch vehicle from the Cape Canaveral launch complex. The basic idea behind the network is to position at least three satellites at all times in strategic locations around the world at stationary orbit altitude for fixed communications between ships, aircraft and the National Command Authority. Each satellite comprises a six-sided structure supporting the payload module, or communications equipment, and an apogee kick motor. This, also known as the AKM, is designed to provide the final shove necessary to circularize the satellite's orbit nearly 36,000 km above Earth. The Transtage third stage to the Titan 3C launcher has the capacity to circularize the path of a satellite without additional hardware being necessary but the Atlas-Centaur can only inject the satellites to a path in which the stationary orbit altitude is the high point of an ellipse.

When the satellite coasts to apogee an extra thrust is needed to bring perigee (the low point) to the same height so that the orbit is circularized. At launch, with the solid propellant apogee kick motor installed, the Fltsatcom satellite weighs about 1,860 kg but after burning the propellant necessary to circularize the orbit, the satellite weighs only 840 kg.

At the opposite end, the satellite supports a stainless steel mesh parabolic antenna folded for launch but deployed in space by 12 ribs to a maximum diameter of 4.9 m. The helical UHF receive antenna is deployed through release of spring-loaded hinges positioned to one side of the parabolic dish. Two large solar array paddles are also folded around the spaceframe for launch, deployed in orbit to generate an average 1,260 Watts from 2,940 separate solar cells feeding the primary electrical distribution system or three batteries for storage.

With a design life of five years, each Fltsatcom satellite is three-axis stabilized by hydrazine jets which also provide the energy to "walk" it from one stationary orbit location to another. Normal operations would keep the satellite stationed within 1 degree longitude through commands generated at the Air Force Satellite Control Facility. Each satellite provides 23 communication channels in the UHF and SHF bands, with ten channels used by the Navy and others leased to the Air Force as part of the Afsatcom system to maintain contact between nuclear strike forces. A single channel is reserved for the National Command Authority, through which word would be given for nuclear strikes.

The first Fltsatcom was successfully launched in February 1978, followed by second, third and fourth in May 1979, January 1980 and October 1980 respectively. A fifth satellite was launched in August 1981, but a violent jolt during ascent partially damaged it. Fleet deployment of Fltsatcom broadcast receivers is now complete, with more than 300 ships and 150 submarines and shipboard terminals now operated through both the Defense Department's Fltsatcom and the Marisat systems, the latter on lease.

Owned and operated by a consortium of US communications enterprises, the Marisat Corporation purchased three satellites from Hughes, each to provide three channels for US Government use and two for ship-to-shore communication with the merchant fleet. All three Marisat satellites were sent up in 1976 and are to be replaced by a new European system in the early 1980s. But DSCS and Fltsatcom represented only the US-based leg of a communications triad involving Britain and NATO.

Developed by the UK Ministry of Defence and the Ministry of Technology, Skynet emerged in 1969 as a military communications program designed to link Britain's home and overseas forces at sea and on land. As early as 1966 the British Government entered into an agreement with the United States about the procurement of a stationary orbit system from Ford Aerospace, the transaction carried out by the US Air Force on behalf of Britain. Operating at frequencies between 7 GHz and 8 GHz, Skynet 1 was delivered to orbit in November 1969, and served over the Indian Ocean to link stations in the Middle and Far East.

Skynet 2, sent up nine months later, was stranded in an elliptical path when its apogee kick motor failed to fire. This was the second of a pair built to provide UK military satellite communication needs for up to five years but loss of the second satellite compromised plans for a replacement pair in 1973. Instead, the program was reorientated and not before November 1974 did Skynet 2B get off the launch pad and into stationary orbit; the first attempt ten months earlier failed when the US launch vehicle put the satellite on the wrong path, stranding Skynet 2A.

Skynet 2B is now stationed over the Seychelles for communication between a wide range of facilities from the mid-Atlantic to Australia. Communications take place on two channels, one at 20 MHz and one at 2 MHz with a separate beacon signal used for tracking the satellite. Another element of the West's communication systems involves the use of NATO satellites paid for through the usual channels of combined North Atlantic Treaty Organization funding. Development grew from UK research work at the then Ministry of Aviation's Signal Research and Development Establishment, Christchurch, Kent. From this emerged the Skynet program and, in turn, NATO countries were encouraged to support the idea of a satellite system binding together the separate North American and European countries. Understanding was reached in Bonn during 1967 after preliminary meetings with representatives from the seven countries involved: Belgium Canada, Federal Republic of Germany, Italy, the Netherlands, the UK, and the USA. It was agreed that the satellites would be built by the United States because at that time there was little experience elsewhere with hardware of this type. Test instruments were launched on two Lincoln Experimental Satellite flights in 1967 and 1968; Ford Aerospace received the contract to build and test the NATO satellite. Designed to link the capital cities of NATO countries, NATO-1 was launched in March, 1970 on a Thor-Delta rocket from Cape Canaveral. It was stationed over the eastern Atlantic from where it was initially controlled by the US Air Force.

NATO-2 was sent up in February 1971, and the two were used together, one for testing new ground stations, the other for operational communications primarily through NATO headquarters in Brussels. The second satellite was employed to cover NATO facilities from the United States to Turkey and both served to carry traffic until the second program phase began in April 1976, when the first of three NATO-3 satellites lifted off the launch pad on top of a Delta rocket. It was considerably larger than the two earlier satellites, weighing 705 kg at launch and 385 kg on station above the Atlantic, about three times that of its predecessors. Spin-stabilized at 90 rpm, NATO-3 carried a three-horn antenna on a de-spun section and two transponders operating in the 7 GHz to 8 GHz region. Power was provided by solar cells generating 425 Watts and the satellite in total measured 3 m tall with a diameter of 2.2 m. NATO-3B was launched in January 1977 and was followed by the third and last in this series, NATO-3C, in November 1978. By arrangement with the United States, the US gained exclusive use of NATO-3B from 1977, allowing reciprocal use by the NATO countries of equivalent channel capacity on a DSCS-2 satellite over the Atlantic. NATO-3C was considered a spare.

Because all DSCS series, Skynet and NATO series satellites operate from stationary orbit high above the Equator, polar regions of the globe are not well covered and the paucity of ground stations across high latitudes in the northern hemisphere brought urgent need for a special satellite to cover the strategic needs of the US bomber force. Accordingly, in March 1975, the first Satellite Data System (SDS) satellite was placed in a special orbit to cater to Afsatcom requirements. All Strategic Air Command aircraft and missile launch control centers were tied to satellite terminals for speedy communication in the severest environment.

Because of the need to cover flight paths across polar regions, the SDS-1 operated from an elliptical path between 295 km and 39,337 km in an orbit inclined 64 degrees to the Equator. In the event of a major war, redundant communications could be the deciding factor in just how soon and effective the retaliatory strike could be and the ability for individual aircraft to maintain constant communication, if necessary, with the National Command Authority ensures the continued survival of the strike force, be it ICBM Minuteman or Titan or the SAC B-52 fleet.

The problem of communication via stationary orbit satellites for communites and forces beyond 70 degrees N latitude highlights the difficulty for Soviet communicators. The system selected by Russia is based on an elliptical 12-hour orbit inclined 63 degrees or 74 degrees to the Equator. The disadvantage of non-stationary orbits, calling for active tracking facilities to keep pace with the satellite as it travels from one horizon to the other, is largely avoided because the Soviet satellites are positioned at sufficient height usefully to reduce the transit time, providing about eight hours of continuous tracking before the satellite disappears.

Tests began in 1964 with hardware designed to prove the feasibility of satellite communications. Three years later the operational Molniya system emerged as the first of a series placed in highly elliptical paths, about 500 km above Earth at perigee and 39,000 km high at apogee, with an inclination of 65 degrees.

Because Russia had the use of very large rockets early in its space program, Molniya satellites took advantage of combinations utilizing the basic Sapwood ICBM with additional upper stages. Accordingly, engineers designed Molniya to a weight of more than 1½ tons, far exceeding the capacity of US systems at that time. Molniya is a complex shape employing deployable solar cells on six main panels designed to provide 500-700 watts of electrical power. Because the satellites were large, a major problem afflicting US systems was avoided from the outset—high radiated power levels providing strong signals to more conventional receivers.

The elliptical path selected for Molniya allows the apogee to be placed over northern latitudes, so increasing the time the satellite remains within view of a ground station. This allows the eight hours' visibility for each pass, quoted earlier. The original Molniya network provided a system of satellites with orbital planes spaced 120 degrees apart, then a system of 90-degree spacing was introduced further to improve coverage. Twelve satellites were a part of this system until 1976 when a 45-degree spacing was set up. Three types of Molniya were involved in this constellation.

Molniya 1 was the pioneer for the complete operation and was used primarily for military communications. Molniya 2 was first launched in November 1971, representing a more powerful design with 50 per cent more electrical power. Molniya 2 did not replace Molniya 1 but was used to supplement the earlier system. At first, Molniya 1 satellites were flown in groups of three, hence the 120-degree spacing, but when the 90-degree spacing was adopted, with four groups of three, the triplet cluster was populated by a single representative of Molniya types 1, 2 and 3.

The latter emerged in November 1974 with provision for color television relay and higher communications frequencies. From this it has become clear that Molniya 1 represented the military leg of the system, with other class 2 and 3 satellites supporting domestic civilian needs.

The Russians had not attempted to use the stationary orbit slot during the first 16 years of space activity but their first application of this fixed position came with the successful flight of Cosmos 637 in March 1974. Dubbed Molniya 1-S, it was positioned to cover Eurasia, Africa and Australia, serving as a prototype for the Statsionar series then being planned. Stationary orbit satellites followed projected development plans leading toward a commercially competitive system to counter an international telecommunications consortium set up by more than 100 countries in the free world. As such they do not represent a part of the military network, although here, too, the precedent set by weather satellites prevails and it is difficult to discriminate between civil and military equipment. In 1978 the Moniya 2 series was phased out but military communications continued to be carried by the class 1 satellites. A major development effort is now under way to launch a series of four Gals stationary orbit satellites for relaying global communications to Soviet armed forces. Two will be stationed over the Indian Ocean at 45 degrees and 85 degrees east, with one each over the Atlantic and the Pacific. They will serve a similar role to the DSCS-2 series launched by the United States.

In addition, three domestic commercial programs called Ekran, Raduga and Gorizont are given high priority by the Soviets while the Louch system designed to take custom from US networks in securing foreign participation continues the attempt to erode Western programs.

Communications are a vital part of maintaining peace, one Molniya network carries the US-Soviet "hot line" between Washington and Moscow, but it is increasingly exploited for political gain as more and more traffic moves via space. The most sobering realization is that 80 per cent of all military communication in the West now goes by satellite. If the network was to fail it would be almost impossible to conduct a measured response to aggression. In the past 15 years, the Russians have been working deliberately to effect such a breakdown.

5. Sentinels and killersats

Early warning and anti-satellite vehicles

On August 21, 1966, at 5.30 P.M. Greenwich Mean Time, Moscow Radio broadcast the following sentiment: "It is quite clear that these mad plans and insane aims of the nuclear maniacs with regard to space and the celestial bodies must alarm world opinion. All of mankind is interested in barring the road toward transforming space into an arena of military rivalries. The USSR, which was the first to open the way into space, has always been careful to conduct research and the conquest of space for peaceful purposes, for the good of mankind."

Exactly 27 days later the Soviet Union became the first nation to place in orbit a shell representing the nuclear warhead of a ballistic missile. It would have contravened an agreement between the super-powers not to orbit "weapons of mass destruction" had the shell been a real warhead and remained in orbit for a full revolution of the Earth. Instead, it was brought back to a target in the USSR within that first orbit by firing a braking rocket to slow it down and so allow gravity to pull it back through the atmosphere. It was a classic example of the best form of defense: attack. For in wild accusations aimed at the "nuclear maniacs" the Russians were previewing their own tests with what is known as the Fractional Orbit Bombardment System, FOBS for short. The idea of orbiting nuclear bombs hanging above the heads of an enemy population excited fiction writers and extremist military planners in the early days of the space program. But no one seriously considered putting a nuclear bomb into orbit simply because it would be less responsive to an urgent call for action. In the lowest path possible, just grazing the atmosphere, an object takes almost 1½ hours to circle the Earth. Moreover, with the Earth spinning on its axis once every 24 hours, during long periods each day the orbiting bomber would be inaccessible. Paradoxically, it would take such a weapon longer to get down on to the target from even the most favorable position in orbit than it would take an ICBM, launched from a silo, to reach its target 10,000 km away. Nevertheless, there was great concern at the United Nations that new developments would make orbital weapons a practical reality and, in October 1963, the General Assembly called upon all nations to "refrain from placing in orbit around the Earth any objects carrying nuclear weapons or any other weapons of mass destruction."

Only a few months before, Deputy Secretary of Defense Roswell L. Gilpatric said that the United States had "no program to place any weapons of mass destruction into orbit . . . The United States believes that it is highly desirable for its own security and for the security of the world that the arms race should not be extended into outer space, and we are seeking in every feasible way to achieve that purpose. Today there is no doubt that either the United States or the Soviet Union could place thermonuclear weapons in orbit, but such action is just not a rational military strategy for either side for the foreseeable future."

Within four years the Russians were actively testing an orbital bombardment system, not one based on the old concept of a constellation of nuclear weapons orbiting the Earth, but rather a system designed to sneak in the back door of Western defense systems, unannounced and without detection. The radar defense networks of the United States and NATO were designed from the beginning to counter a threat from the East. Any world globe will reveal that the shortest distance between Russia and America is the so-called "great circle" route over the polar regions. This is the logical route along which the several thousand ICBMs would travel going in opposite directions.

Accordingly, in the early 1960s, North American Air Defense Command (NORAD) was set up to watch for incoming warheads and provide the by now famous "four-minute warning." Watching through huge radar eyes beamed from antennae at Fylingdales Moor (England), Thule (Greenland), and Clear (Alaska), the Ballistic Missile Early Warning System (BMEWS) stood guard on the gateway to Europe and the United States. But only from one direction, the favored route over the northern approaches.

Cemented within US nuclear strategy was the dogma that because all-out conflict was unthinkable, defense was the surest safeguard since it implied a capability to respond before the means to retaliate had been destroyed. Awareness of this, it was said, would deter the potential agressor since he would bring upon his own head a reign of unimaginable terror. The only problem with that was when the Russians openly said they were not at all horror-struck by the prospect of a nuclear war and that if nuclear weapons were the logical choice for a given tactical or strategic need then they would perhaps be a strategic necessity, and so matured the selection of the FOBS concept tested from 1966.

Because the Russians were prepared to strike first without warning it made good sense to eliminate the means of detection, not by destroying all the defense radars (for that would have eliminated the disguise), but rather by coming in from the south where nobody expected to detect an ICBM assault and where there were no radars watching space. Because the trajectory of a strategic ballistic missile quickly reaches a height within range of defense radars, early warning becomes possible; anything coming up over the horizon will be picked up by these powerful beams. As an example, taking the case of a US Minuteman missile launched from its silo, the rocket will reach a height of about 840 km traversing a distance of 3,300 km, or an altitude of more than 2,200 km for a more normal range distance of 14,000 km. Coasting far out into space before completing the curving trajectory back down into the atmosphere, slightly uprange of the designated target, warheads would be easily detected with sufficient reserve time to authorize a reciprocal attack. However, by boosting the warhead to orbit speed it need not expose itself by flying a high, arching, trajectory and, so long as the warhead was de-orbited uprange of the target, the system need fly no higher than the equivalent of a near-Earth orbit.

The Russians conceived the idea that they could sneak in undetected by launching their missiles into orbit, travelling south-east across the Indian Ocean. Getting into orbit before reaching the Antarctic region, the warhead would coast on round the planet in an inclined path which would carry it up the South Pacific and over the southern United States. This type of "depressed trajectory" appealed to the Russians and early in the 1960s they began a major propaganda campaign to sow seeds of discontent in the West about proposed defense systems in the United States.

Using the familiar Soviet ploy of lambasting the political opponent for ills perpetrated by the home side, verbiage and hostility directed toward "nuclear maniacs" reached outrageous proportions. In the 1965 May Day parade through Red Square, the Soviet commentator provided an intriguing preview of Soviet plans:

"Three-stage intercontinental missiles are passing by. Their design is improved. They are very reliable in use. Their servicing is fully automatic. The parade of awesome battle might is being crowned by the gigantic orbital missiles . . . For these missiles there is no limit to range. The main property of missiles of this class is their ability to hit enemy objectives literally from any direction, which makes them virtually invulnerable to anti-missile defense means."

The Russians were still 18 months away from the first tests of this system and the rocket which stimulated the Soviet announcer was, in fact, never developed for operational use. Called the SS-10 Scrag, it was replaced in the FOBS tests by the SS-9. Before the end of the year, the Russians announced test activity with "space vehicle landing systems" where rocket stages would fall into the designated Pacific danger zone. From later events it would appear that this was an SS-9 flight leading up to FOBS activity the following year. However, whatever it was it did not complete one full revolution of the Earth and so require the Soviets publicly to announce the flight.

The following May Day parade still had the Scrag trundling through Red Square but this time the commentator made only passing mention of its capability. Throughout the remainder of that year the Russians developed elements of an orbiting weapon system about which very little has emerged through intelligence reports or surveillance. In fact the Russians were so sensitive about their activity they broke traditional agreements formally to acknowledge hardware placed in orbit and sent up two payloads without announcing the events. One was on September 17, 1966, the second on November 2. This placed the United States in a compromising position. The normal publication of orbital elements of satellites launched from anywhere on Earth was a visible, highly exposed, way of showing the public that US space activity was completely open and did not contain hidden projects of the type the Russians accused the West of possessing; it also showed the Russians that defense radars were capable of acquiring and logging every object sent up from the ground wherever that launch site might be. If the US published reports which deliberately ignored the Soviet violations by leaving out the two launches, scientists and astronomers would observe the debris of spent rocket stages and payload in space and the US would be accused of compliance. The United States first published situation reports without listing the secret flights and then retrospectively applied numbers out of sequence to the normal chronological order. Three years later the Russians launched another mission with almost identical characteristics, only this time they simply announced it as Cosmos 316. From this clandestine activity, and through the tests associated with flights U.1 and U.2 in 1966, the Russians evolved the FOBS system which got its first full workout in January 1967. Nobody was sure just what the Russians were up to when the SS-9 ascended with its undeclared payload. Launched from Tyuratam, the rocket flew across Siberia, from north-west to south-east across the Pacific, up over South America, the Atlantic, Africa, the Mediterranean and back on to Soviet territory. The basic carrier rocket was in an orbit inclined 50 degrees to the Equator with a perigee of 144 km and an apogee of 210 km.

Before completing one full revolution, the payload section, simulating a nuclear warhead, was brought back down to a target in Russia, leaving the terminal stage of the carrier rocket to continue orbiting the Earth. Some of these fragments passed over the United States on successive revolutions as the Earth rotated beneath the fixed orbital plane. Four months later, a second flight was made, this time with an apogee as low as 177 km, followed by another seven over a four month period. Considerable speculation surrounded the flights and not until the Secretary of Defense publicly declared them to be FOBS flights, carefully pointing out that they did not contravene any agreement on the use of space for military tests, were they officially counted as the first test of an orbital space weapon.

In the next four years, six additional FOBS tests were carried out, the last flying just nine months before the SALT-1 treaty was signed by the Soviet Union and the United States. There was nothing in the agreement about this kind of activity, indeed the Russians had even outlawed discussion of multiple warheads like MRV or MIRV, but the fact that no more tests were conducted was interpreted by some as perhaps a show of intent, a conciliatory gesture on the part of the Soviet Union; in the light of subsequent weapons expansion this may be considered a premature conclusion! Undoubtedly the peak of FOBS activity came within the first ten months of 1967 and by 1971 research was at an end. There is no indication that the Russians ever intended to deploy the FOBS concept operationally, indeed it reduced the efficiency of the rocket itself.

A standard SS-9 could send a 25 MT warhead across intercontinental distances using conventional ballistic trajectories carrying it high above the Earth; with the depressed trajectory technique the SS-9's throw-weight was cut by 30 per cent, reducing the potential explosive yield of the warhead to 10 MT. While the Soviets may not have found any strategic purpose for the bigger head, the increased throw-weight allowed the rocket to carry more heads of a smaller yield.

So, having experimented with at least the precursor to the much discussed "orbital bomb" the Russians found, as had previous theorists, that the concept had little benefit to offer. Especially since the main advantage was made redundant by the use of stationary orbit satellites for early warning duties. Where once the Ballistic Missile Early Warning System fed NORAD the information on missiles ascending over the horizon, satellites now looked directly down upon the planet, never blinking for an instant in their vigilant watch for signs of a mass attack. For here was one area where space techniques had virtually replaced a complete segment of the defense net.

Through the evolution of reconnaissance, weather, electronic ferret and communication satellites, defense had taken on a radical new meaning for space industries capable of supplementing or improving the state of the art. Communication satellites came close to providing a completely new capability, where truly global voice, teletypewriter and telex facilities were available to unit commanders around the world. But early warning satellites achieved a complete transformation which few believed was possible just 20 years ago, stimulating a science which would almost exclusively depend upon the orbital eyes.

In the event of nuclear attack the ground radars would not for long maintain their vigil on the horizon and it would be up to the early warning satellites in space to keep up the constant flow of reports about what was being launched from where and to which targets the warheads were moving. WS-117L, already seen to have been responsible for starting reconsats on the road to a viable observation system, embraced the Midas early warning objective when Lockheed got the contract in October 1956 to build the Agena rocket stage as a main "bus" for several different roles.

Discoverer paved the way for Samos, the Space and Missile Observation System, and provided research platforms leading to the Midas (Missile Defense Alarm System) series which were to have pioneered the application. Midas requirements stemmed from the need to get the big bombers airborne as quickly as possible in the event of a major attack from Soviet Russia or Communist China and for that reason the few minutes remaining between detection through the BMEWS radars and arrival of the first ICBM warheads was considered too close for comfort.

At this time, in the late 1950s, the arrival of the big ICBM was still a few years off; only test shots with Atlas had been carried out to prove the feasibility of the concept, while several hundred intercontinental bombers were already waiting to deliver the strategic punch. The days of quick reaction times where more than 1,000 land-based missiles waited in underground silos were nearly a decade away. Because of this, and the significant time it would take to get the heavy bombers airborne, development of a satellite early-warning system to extend the available reaction time was considered a priority.

The basic idea which evolved as America was getting ready to launch its first satellite, and being surprised by the ascent of Sputnik 1, adopted a simple principle. By placing infra-red detectors aboard a satellite, hot rocket exhausts from missiles fired at the United States could be detected and tracked as they ascended. But it was not so simple in practice. Built for Midas by International Telephone and Telegraph, the infra-red sensors required complex equipment to ensure a stable temperature on board the satellite, for without this the system would be inoperable. That called for considerable engineering to pack the system into the Agena-based housing and weight soon grew beyond the specified limits.

Lifted on the first leg of its journey by an Atlas booster, the Agena A stage would propel itself and payload into orbit 3,600 km above the Earth. At this height, the maximum for this launcher with a 2-ton payload, the satellite would slowly move from one horizon to the other at which point another satellite of the same type would be spaced so as to come up over the first horizon and replace it. And so it would go on, a string of up to 15 Midas satellites continually covering the Earth from polar orbits watching for signs below of unfriendly missiles being fired.

Initial tests with the satellites, the sensors and the ground systems were to be conducted with hardware in almost equatorial orbits, only the operational vehicles being placed to fly across both poles. The initial test launch got off the pad on February 26, 1960, but the Agena blew itself up and not until the second attempt did the Air Force get to run the system through its paces. Midas 2 performed well, for a day, and then trouble with the transmitter put it out of action. It was the beginning of a spate of disappointments, for at this time the Discoverer research and development program exposed basic flaws with early Agena models which effectively grounded further flights until the problems were sorted out.

Not for almost a year did another Midas shot get under way but when it did, in July 1961, the satellite's performance gave only cautious optimism about the viability of the entire concept. Midas 4, three months later, had limited success with picking out the launch of an early Titan rocket but this was under ideal conditions where the test was set up for known events. Over unfamiliar territory and assigned to watch for unknown activity, Midas results gave no cause for elation. For several months, scientists and engineers performed tests and carried out research to see if the system could be improved and somehow made to overcome a basic flaw: its inability successfully to discriminate between hot rocket exhausts and sunlight glinting off the cloud tops.

It was at this time that the defense programs begun under WS-117L were veiled by a security screen mimicked by the Soviets with their Cosmos designations. Flights after this were not named, nor was the purpose of the attempt disclosed. But much of the research into early-warning technology which went on during the 12 months beginning late 1961 sought solutions to the sensor problem. In a complementary program using U-2 aircraft to test various sensors, the Air Force made little headway. And it was a bad time for getting money to spend on exotic defense systems, for the original estimates about Soviet strategic capacity were already being replaced with more realistic figures derived from reconsat photographs which showed the invalidity of claims about a "missile gap" supposedly threatening the United States.

Early-warning research was put under a development effort catalogued as Program 461. Pessimism prevailed. In 1962 John H. Rubel, the Assistant Secretary of Defense, outlined the "greatest technical difficulties and disappointments" concerning the early warning plans. A year later, Dr. Harold Brown, Director of Defense Research and Engineering, testified before a Congressional committee that up to half the money already spent on Midas was a total waste.

Also in 1963, author Vernon Van Dyke, while writing a summary of US space plans to date, asserted a common belief of the day that: "Even if such an early warning system were developed, it is doubtful how much operational significance it might have." Moreover, he went on, "it would take a very rare and extreme circumstance to justify the United States in launching a retaliatory strike with nuclear missiles simply on the basis of warning signals from a Midas satellite; the system could scarcely be absolutely reliable."

Nevertheless, theory predicted the feasibility of eradicating the several problems related to the infra-red sensors and a major development effort went over into the mid-1960s. The last two successful Midas-type launches came in May and July 1963, and President Johnson supported a continued effort to find a viable system when he assumed office at the White House toward the end of that year. Using Agena D stages, two interim flights were conducted three years later utilizing orbits very similar to those employed for the Midas concept. This resulted from the development of what was by then considered a working design under the code of Program 266.

Re-designated Program 949 at the end of 1966, it led to TRW getting the prime contract for development and fabrication of the precursor test satellites designed to fly the sensors and scanners intended for a stationary orbit successor situated over the Equator. The interim program got under way in August 1966 and included, over the next four years, a total of six experimental payloads, some launched on Atlas-Agena D rockets and others adopting the rocket scheduled to carry the fully operational version, a Titan 3C which had the capacity to lift 1½ tons to stationary orbit.

Under Program 647, the Air Force put together the instruments and the equipment to be used for the definitive role, so long in reaching the assured level of perfection necessary to fund the project. Phase 1 would lift three separate satellites into stationary orbit to cover possible launches from Russia and China and from underwater submarines; Phase 2 would include additional refinements if and when Phase 1 proved itself in operation. A single Phase 1 satellite would be built for ground tests and qualification.

Before looking further at the 647-series satellites, which still today provide the backbone of missile early-warning, it would be useful to consider a category of military satellite incorporated into the Phase 1 hardware. They are the family of nuclear detection satellites built to monitor weapons test agreements. Although basic research had been conducted by the Army and the Air Force since late 1959, it was not until the end of 1961 that TRW received a contract for Vela satellites from the Defense Department. In August 1963, the United States, Russia and the United Kingdom signed a Partial Test Ban Treaty and just two months after that the first pair of Velas were launched from Cape Canaveral.

They were lifted into space aboard an Atlas-Agena D, each satellite weighing just 135 kg, to work from opposite sides of the Earth between 100,000 km and 115,000 km above the surface. In this type of orbit, the highest used for defense purposes, each satellite would fail to keep pace with the spinning Earth and seem to an observer on the ground to move in the opposite direction, although this would be an illusion created by the planet rotating faster than the satellite's orbital speed.

Each Vela satellite of this initial series comprised a 26-sided structure, 24 sides populated with solar cells for electrical power. Two nickel-cadmium batteries were built in for power during eclipses and for maintaining a constant voltage to the detectors. With a command capability by which instructions sent from the ground could be stored on board, Vela satellites carried very sensitive detectors looking for X-rays, gamma rays and neutrons created by nuclear explosions. In less than one year after launch, the performance of the first pair had exceeded the best achieved by any other satellite project, inspiring a reduction from a planned five dual flights to just three launches with the initial model.

Major General Ben I. Funk, head of the Air Force's space effort, said that "performance of this caliber, coupled with a scientific and technical readiness to proceed to the next phase of the program, promises to reduce the system development time cycle and—to reduce the system development time cycle and—consequently—to save substantial money." It was put to good use, for while it was not necessary quickly to launch the other two pairs, TRW was commissioned to move on with the second generation Velas lifted by the more powerful Titan 3C. These would incorporate additional command and control capability, carry better and more sensitive detectors, and ensure even longer lifetime before replacement.

The second and third pair of first-generation Velas were launched in July 1964, and July 1965, respectively. Originally designed to work for six months, they were already showing a capacity for almost a decade of continued service. Outstanding performance for the day and, at the time, a very real boost to confidence in the ability of engineers to build lasting capabilities in spaceborne equipment. In fact, success brought its own reward in the form of accelerated plans for the second generation model, a need acquiring new roles in the form of proliferation sensors to watch a world fast witnessing the spread of nuclear weapons.

In April 1967, almost two years after the launch of the final first-generation Velas, a Titan 3C successfully sent up the first two improved satellites. Growth in the first model carried the weight from an initial 135 kg per satellite to approximately 151 kg; the second set of six weighed between 230 kg and 350 kg each. They were a little different in design, with a three-axis stabilization and control system and a spin rate of about 1 rpm.

Each satellite carried the usual complement of X-ray, gamma ray and neutron detectors, plus optical and electromagnetic pulse sensors, background radiation counters (to measure the radiation field), and an improved logic circuitry better to discriminate between natural events and man-made bursts of radiation. Like the first six, the second generation Velas performed exceptionally well and were followed by second and third pairs in May 1969, and April 1970. It was at that point the development of nuclear detection sensors merged with the Program 647 early-warning satellites, for with the introduction of Phase 1 stationary orbit vehicles the duties of the Vela hardware were taken over. Officially at least, for such was the outstanding performance of the Velas that in 1979 they detected in the South Atlantic what was considered by many intelligence experts to be the detonation of a comparatively small nuclear device on test by the South African Government; second generation Velas were built to last 18 months!

But it was under the guise of the Defense Support Program that dogged determination to expose a viable early-warning system provided Program 647 with the appropriate hardware. The first TRW satellite was launched on November 6, 1970, but a launch vehicle failure prevented it reaching the intended orbit, providing the Air Force limited opportunity to test the sensors and system operation; TRW was requested to bring the single test satellite to flight standard just in case it was needed. As it turned out the others performed well following ascents in May 1971, and March 1972, and the spare was never used.

In 1972 the Aerospace Defense Command took over full operational control of the two 647 satellites from their stationary orbit positions: one over the Indian Ocean to watch for Soviet or Chinese missile attack, the other over Panama to detect SLBMs launched from Russian submarines which, because of the lower range capability, had to move close to the US mainland to reach useful targets. It had taken a long time to develop, but at last the Air Force could provide early-warning top-cover for the BMEWS radars positioned to look for missiles coming over the northern horizon; jettisoned too, was any implicit advantage in the Soviet FOBS, or depressed trajectory, delivery system.

With satellites on high to look for missile ignition, a pre-emptive first strike would never get below a 30-minute warning to the West. Or would it? Just how good was the infra-red eye at discriminating between a massive oil fire and a missile ascending in flight? That issue was put to the test in late 1975, but first what of the satellites? Each series 647 satellite consists of a 3 m cylinder, 2.7 m in diameter, supporting a large Schmidt telescope equipped with a two-dimensional array of lead sulphide detectors to focus the energy emitted by a ballistic missile in flight. The total vehicle is 4.3 m tall, weighs about 1,000 kg, and carries four paddle-type solar cell arrays in addition to similar cells wrapped around the cylindrical exterior. A Schmidt telescope, named after the Estonian instrument-maker who perfected the system 50 years ago, is designed to eliminate spherical aberration which normally occurs where comparatively large areas are to be surveyed.

Where a conventional telescope is limited in practice to a field of view only arc minutes across, the Schmidt is good for fields 10-20 degrees across. This capability is perfect for the early-warning system through which the array of 2,000 infra-red sensor cells observe the Earth's surface. Approximately 3.6 m in length and with an aperture of 91 cm, the Schmidt telescope is offset from the central axis of the satellite by 7.5 degrees. Because the satellite is designed to spin at 5-7 rpm, the telescope sweeps a conical scan in looking at the planet below. Each infra-red cell looks across an area only 3 km wide.

To keep the satellite aligned properly, two star sensors shrouded from stray light are fixed at right-angles to orientate the attitude control system. The infra-red array observes events around the 2.7 micron region on the electromagnetic spectrum with nuclear radiation detectors attached to two of the four paddle-type solar cell arrays. Additional Earth-pointing radiation detectors supplement the space-view from the paddle-mounted sensors and provide a Vela-type watch for nuclear tests.

A true measure of the early-warning system is the time it takes to respond to a suspected attack, or to discriminate between some entirely natural event, a missile launch, and intentional blinding. On October 18, 1975, and again on November 17 and 18, US satellites detected energy levels up to 1,000 times as great as that typically emitted by an ICBM launch. The first, October, event, was the most important for it was sensed by one of the interim early-warning satellites developed under the Program 949 code and launched in September 1970. The energy level was of such intensity that it immediately led to suspicion that the Soviets were intentionally blinding the infra-red sensors. Considerable speculation surrounded the events and the Russians would merely affirm their original explanation, that an enormous oil leak created a fire plume which was seen by the early-warning satellite. Yet, coupled with other intelligence information about Soviet tests with chemical lasers using hydrogen-fluoride, the reports seemed to indicate excessive testing prior to development of an operational laser weapon for knocking out defense satellites.

The Indian Ocean early-warning satellite was not permanently blinded by the energy but the fact that on at least one occasion the "beam" was observed to last four hours incited grave concern that, under a veil of this intensity, the Russians could quite successfully mount a massive attack on the West. Nobody satisfactorily determined the exact cause of the detected emissions, the Russians simply refused to hear alternatives to their stated explanation, but the event was a somber object lesson about the reliability of such valued satellites.

In achieving great success with eliminating the probability of a pre-emptive strike, the early-warning satellites which sealed the fate of FOBS heightened awareness of the fat targets sitting in space ready for attack. However, in the absence of an alternative, plans for a Phase 2 series materialized in June 1973, when an improved 647-type satellite was launched to stationary orbit by Titan 3C. Others followed in the years ahead while engineers worked out the details of a much improved sensor designed to track a missile for more than the first few minutes of flight. For this was the one big drawback with the 647 satellites.

By looking for infra-red emissions the missile could be tracked in powered flight. But when its engines were switched off for the long coast across the top of the atmosphere, the satellite was unable to observe subtle changes in the trajectory which could be made by blipping another small propulsion unit. Thus, predictions on the missile's aim point could go disastrously awry by the time it dropped its charge. This so-called mid-course guidance tracking would be a vital ingredient of the next generation early-warning satellite, but more on that later. For their part, the Russians seem to have spent little effort on early-warning space technology. Information on more than 3,000 Soviet missile and space rocket launches has been gathered by the series 647 satellites employed by the United States in the past decade and there is no reason to assume the Russians would have willingly denied themselves a similar capability.

But, as related earlier, the use of stationary orbit by Soviet satellite planners has been retarded by the limited advantages for that country in adopting an equatorially-centered position above the Earth. It is highly probable that satellites developed under the Molniya communications, or Elektron scientific, designations carry sensors which provide some form of early-warning. The Soviet Union genuinely suspects the West of aggressive intentions and is likely to regard an orbital tripwire as necessary and timely warning of a pre-emptive strike by the United States or NATO. Such a view is made easier for the Soviets to accept when several times in the past few years military leaders in the West have openly professed a desire to hit first before the Russian armory acquires many more tools for its dubious trade.

Doubtless too, Cosmos launches veil the flight of early-warning sensors on modified Sapwood rockets launched from Plesetsk, although there are only seven suspicious candidates between the first in 1967 and 1975. In October 1975, Cosmos 775 was placed in stationary orbit over the Atlantic where it could watch for SLBM attacks emerging from the deep. This is the first known example of a stationary orbit slot used by the Russians for an early-warning satellite, but the function it performs could not readily be provided by the more usual elliptical orbit types under the Cosmos designation, two or three of which are launched on average each year.

The Russians are as aware as their Western counterparts that timely recognition of an impending attack does not rest alone on the unpredictable game of estimating through reconnaissance photographs the intentions of an enemy purposely aiming to evade detection. In the final analysis, a massive first strike attack, still the best option for winning a global war, rests on the ability of the early-warning sensors to provide information in time to hit back. But whereas the FOBS system took a back-door route to evasion, the elimination of sensors and "national technical means" of intelligence gathering can, at a stroke, so confuse the enemy that he may be unsure of the level of hostility aimed at him and unwilling to risk an all-out exchange in those vital minutes before an armada of nuclear charges fall to their respective targets.

For, having waited for a command decision, or authority from above, field commanders may be quickly denied the use of weapons designed to deal an unacceptable blow in return. The majority of strategic ballistic missiles are aimed at the silos of the supposed enemy and would fall to Earth on the concrete doors which protect the underground force. It is because a war could inflict major damage on an enemy within a few hours of attack that the opportunity to knock out the eyes and ears which warn of such a strike has been too tempting to avoid.

As we have seen, space has been used for at least a decade effectively to provide the cutting edge necessary to win any major war. Reconnaissance satellites provide global intelligence for deploying forces at a tactical and strategic level, and give timely notice of the enemy's dispositions. They show how the fleets are deployed, the moves they make to seal access routes, and they sniff out the communications which carry the enemy battle orders. Weather satellites provide the important details of the environment in which the host and enemy forces confront each other, and about the climate in zones to which forces must be quickly deployed. They tell the strategic command what subtle weapons are being employed by recording the use of chemical dispersants and they map out the moving zones of dangerous radiation.

Then there are the communication satellites which carry eight-tenths of all military voice and teletypewriter transmission in the West and an uncertain percentage of Soviet command instructions. Without the stationery orbit relay platforms, war would quickly decay into an uncertain and spontaneous anarchy where control or direction was totally abandoned for "last-ditch" techniques. This could have the most devastating and profound effects upon the terminal stages, where field and unit commanders, aircraft pilots, submarine captains, and marine forces assume maximum effort to destroy what they perceive to be the enemy. It is precisely this level of anarchic war which it may be in the interest of an enemy to incite.

Having set in motion the familiar boxed-crossfire techniques employed throughout every major conflict this century, good surveillance and communication via satellites could allow an enemy very effectively to set up an element of induced fratricide, where tactical nuclear weapons are turned unwittingly upon the home forces. In a classic situation where rapid movement of Warsaw Pact armor penetrates the NATO central front, absence of adequate intelligence could lead to boxed killing zones where NATO weapons are turned upon West European forces. This assumes that Russian-backed Warsaw Pact armies have the full advantage of surveillance and communication via satellite while NATO has no such system and can, therefore, be denied the means to survive militarily.

Of course these projected scenarios are at best mere examples for a more complex, interlocking, series of eventualities which would inevitably form the nucleus of global conflict. But the lessons are there in almost every campaign and military operation since World War 2. Too much dependence on irreplaceable technology brings an inevitable lack of redundancy, and nowhere is that dictum seen to better effect than in the myriad defense functions now exclusively conducted via a space-borne system.

The Russians were quick to recognize the need to eliminate orbital support equipment and from the outset kept alive the options for war in space. Not by physically transporting into orbit the combatants into whose unhappy hands World War 3 would be delivered, but rather by retaining or being denied the irreplaceable dependence upon the space systems essential to war on Earth. So far, all the systems described here with the exception of FOBS have been passive in concept and principle, effectively exploiting physical laws to aid military needs. Not one is exclusively used for waging war, yet neither is any specific category immune to the consequence of being denied to its owner in time of conflict. Consequently, the prospect of destroying the satellites of a potential enemy may provide a pivot around which the entire fortune of war could turn to face a new direction.

When serious consideration was first given to sending satellites into space the inevitable value such a capability would have for the nation clever enough to perform such a feat inspired thoughts of anti-satellite weapons. Yet even a cursory glance at the problems involved gave grave cause for concern and while politicians and soldiers confidently predicted a new arms race in space, technical studies were consistently unable to show just how an anti-satellite weapon could work. Yet for all the many problems lurking on the horizon, there was an intense will to possess such a weapon.

General Curtiss LeMay, when Chief of Staff of the Air Force, asserted that the United States "will need in being forces that can control each stratum of aerospace." The Office of the Secretary of the Air Force issued a statement in 1961 to the effect that "military supremacy in space is as essential to our security as military supremacy at altitudes near Earth," and just one year later General Thomas S. Power, Commander of the Strategic Air Corps, asserted his belief that: "Absolute superiority in space is essential to the future welfare and security of the Free World . . . and we must achieve a strategic space capability of our own . . . ."

One of the earliest practical attempts at developing an anti-satellite capability evolved under Program 706, also known as Project SAINT (Satellite Inspector Technique). This included theoretical study of the ability of ground controllers to launch and guide an interceptor toward its target, a function considered every bit as important as the actual destruction of a satellite. The role of inspection provided serious study of rendezvous and docking, an unknown art on which the Air Force encouraged analysis during the early 1960s.

Program 706 began in 1960 and was to have led an Agena B rocket stage to rendezvous with a target in space two years later but the effort was cancelled. As the civilian space agency, NASA, was to find out, the technique of rendezvous was no mean feat, but with a well thought out test vehicle in the form of the Gemini manned spacecraft, astronauts repeatedly proved the ability of one vehicle to find and link up with a second.

It was all very different to simply pointing the nose and firing in the direction of the target. In the bizzare world of orbital mechanics a satellite climbing to match lanes with a second satellite will actually drift further away if the thrusters are fired *toward* the target; paradoxically, only by firing a braking maneuver will the satellite drift up to rendezvous. All this had to be learned and practised through several complex rendezvous missions with Gemini spacecraft and the Air Force played a prominent role in developing the mathematical models for achieving this difficult feat. One of the most important exponents of the developing art of orbital rendezvous, Edwin "Buzz" Aldrin, accompanied Neil Armstrong on the first lunar landing in 1969.

But while the Air Force ran into problems with Program 706, and seemingly left NASA to sort out the techniques for rendezvous, an alternative method of reaching a satellite in space—the concept of the direct ascent—evolved through several different projects. These were the only two modes by which an interceptor could reach an orbital vehicle and the precise targeting from ground level of a specially designed rocket seemed the least complex; rendezvous over several orbits was a complicated business and required several hours between launch and arrival.

Under the guise of Program 437, the Air Force developed a system using a Thor rocket to intercept a satellite in comparatively low orbit. In 1963 the operation was tried out when a Thor ascended from a launch pad on Johnston Island in the Pacific closely to approach a US booster already in orbit. It came within the range necessary to destroy the target and could have done so had it carried a warhead. Considerable interest surrounded this demonstration and both Presidents Kennedy and Johnson referred to the concept that year and the next.

In a definitive system developed under Program 922 the Vought Corporation built four rockets designed to detonate a warhead close by the target satellite, thus disabling it. Two were launched but neither performed well because of technical difficulties. By this time funds for military space programs reached a low level and in the interest of keeping alive imperative developments elsewhere, the direct-ascent killersat work was temporarily shelved. Later in the decade, the US Army conducted studies employing Nike Zeus and Nike-X anti-ballistic missiles. These rockets evolved from a requirement to seek defense against incoming warheads and date from a requirement set down as early as 1956 to deter the missiles believed to be rolling from Soviet production lines.

Designed by Bell Telephone Laboratories, Nike Zeus was an improved version of the Nike Hercules anti-aircraft missile and worked in cooperation with radars built to acquire incoming warheads at a range of 2,400 km. Local radar units would then discriminate between real charges and decoys so that Nike Zeus missiles could be fired from underground silos to destroy the warheads at a range of up to 400 km. It was a perfect system for killersat work in that the rapidly accelerating missile could reach heights populated by reconnaissance and weather satellites, knocking out the orbital vehicle rather than a ballistic warhead; the target was different but the principle was very similar.

Between 1964 and 1968 Program 505 provided a semi-operational capability with Zeus hardware but the phenomenal cost of both the anti-satellite and anti-ballistic missile equipment brought both to extinction. Before the end of the 1960s the anti-satellite role was abandoned and within the next six or seven years the missile defense work was also shelved. A major reason for disinterest in a fully operational anti-satellite system was that the total reliance on space-borne equipment now experienced by all defense agencies had not properly matured by the time Nike Zeus was cancelled. It was simply too costly a project to pursue for so little tactical or strategic gain. That position is reversed now that satellites form the life-blood of military strength and the United States is fast catching up with Soviet developments which were sustained throughout the period of killersat decline in the West.

Russia's interest in acquiring a killersat doubtless stems from its own increasing dependence on spacecraft and satellites to maintain contact with and control forces remote from the Soviet command centers. Until now, the Soviet Navy has been the prime exponent of this ambassadorial function but events have taken the Red Army deep into Afghanistan and there are increasing numbers of troops on loan to several Third World states with a need to communicate over great distances. So far, Russia is alone in having demonstrated repeatedly to those appropriately concerned that it has the ability to intercept and destroy orbiting satellites up to 1,000 km above Earth. In repeated tests, flaunting before the West a capacity so far unique, Russia has ignored political gestures made both formally through embassies and informally through the back door of foreign diplomacy. The Soviet Union, in showing a readiness to turn near-Earth space into a lethal medium for hot-war conflict, has invited the full weight of US technology in a desperate race for supremacy in the killersat league. Ironically just when the United States gave up all plans for deploying a satellite interceptor/destructor the Soviets formally began a series of flight trials which has gone on continuously since that time.

Where the US Air Force and the Army preferred the cheaper and less sophisticated technique of direct-ascent for a killersat vehicle, the Russians developed a true satellite interceptor placed first in orbit before maneuvering in for the *coup de grâce*. The Soviet killersat program can be seen in retrospect to have divided itself into three trajectory profiles across three distinctly different test patterns. The first tests were run between 1967 and 1970, the second between 1971 and 1972 and the third between 1975 and 1978; a fourth series is probably now just getting under way with more ominous overtones than the threat presented by the first three test series. By comparison, it should be noted that the FOBS tests were carried out between 1966 and 1971; that point is of interest because the prime launcher for the killersat tests used the same basic SS-9 Scarp rocket originally developed as an ICBM and used for all Fractional Orbit Bombardment flights. As a satellite launcher it was known as the F class space booster, the derivative F-1-r employing a retro-package for FOBS and the F-1-m variant utilizing a maneuvering stage for killersat missions.

The first F-1-m flight came on October 27, 1967, under the disguise of the Cosmos 185 designation. That vehicle went into a 546 x 370 km orbit inclined 64 degrees to the Equator; all killersat trajectories used orbital planes close to this inclination. A short time later the payload section was maneuvered up into a higher, 888 x 522 km, path and the mission seemingly ended there. Later analysis would reveal it to be a test precursor for the actual killersat flights.

Six months later, Cosmos 217 was put into a 262 x 144 km orbit before the Russians announced it had been moved to a higher path 520 x 396 km about the Earth. However, Western trackers, both amateur and professional, could find no trace of anything in that higher orbit, only debris remaining at the original altitude. Again, nothing dramatic emerged from the flight.

Six months after, in October 1968, Cosmos 248 shot into a 551 x 490 km orbit similar to that claimed for its predecessor. One day later Cosmos 249 was put into a 254 x 136 km path before separating from the final main rocket stage and maneuvering itself to a highly elliptical path 2,177 km at apogee and 514 km at perigee, the latter very close to the average altitude of the Cosmos 248 launched the day before. So effective and accurate was the flight path of Cosmos 249 that less than four hours after reaching orbit it had performed a close fly-by of Cosmos 248, overshot the target and been purposely detonated to destruction on command from the ground.

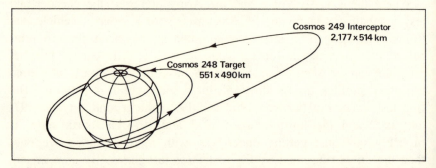

In the first successful demonstration of a Soviet killersat system, Cosmos 249 intercepted its target, Cosmos 248, from above.

The Cosmos 248 target remained intact, but clearly Cosmos 249 had been the first interceptor/destroyer, demonstrating an interceptor capability on the scheduled fly-by and a destruction facility by blowing up. The fact that it did not destroy the target but was itself only destroyed when a safe distance away suggested a plan to use the target on another interception. At first, observers believed the missions to have failed while performing some incomplete activity, but when a similar mission profile was flown with Cosmos 252 making a high speed flypast of the same target, Cosmos 248, before itself blowing up, the intention was clear.

Only the previous year the Russians had experimented with rendezvous and docking between the two Soyuz vehicles then being introduced as the Soviet manned spacecraft designed to carry men around the Moon (see Chapter Four) and to Salyut space stations. The same basic principles of orbital law were being applied to rendezvous between non-cooperative satellites: one the hunted, one the hunter.

Shortly after killersat tests began, but just a month prior to the first successful interception by Cosmos 249, an East German newspaper commented that it would not be too difficult to destroy unfriendly satellites "with the help of weapons systems which, for example, the Soviet Army has at its disposal."

Just one year after the Cosmos 249 mission, Radio Moscow launched a blistering attack on the United States which was "dragging its NATO pact allies into its strategy of total espionage and is successfully ferreting considerable funds out of them to cover the cost of espionage centers," by developing the NATO communications satellites, a move which would incite "armed forces of the Warsaw Pact member countries . . . to undertake reliable measures to protect themselves from the aggressive activities . . .": clearly a reference to killersats with a capacity for destroying the NATO communication hardware in stationary orbit. But that optimism was ill-founded in reality, for the killersat missions were flown on interceptions in low orbit while NATO satellites were stationed more than 35,000 km above the Equator.

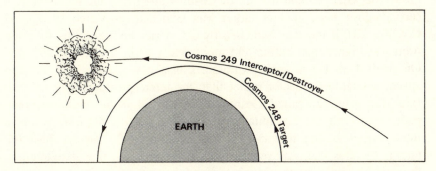

Descending from a higher path, Cosmos 249 passes its target and explodes, demonstrating a destructive potential but preserving Cosmos 248 for another interception test by Cosmos 252.

Following the successful interception of Cosmos 248 by Cosmos 252 in November 1968, Soviet killersat tests were quiet for almost two years, a period broken only by the apparent failure of a target vehicle launched in August 1969. But in October 1970 the last round of the initial test pattern got under way with the launch of Cosmos 373 to an elliptical orbit of 1,102 x 510 km. Shortly thereafter the path was made nearly circular at 553 x 490 km and three days after reaching orbit its interceptor, Cosmos 374, shot up from the Tyuratam launch pad. From an initial orbit of 1,053 x 530 km it rose to a 2,153 x 536 km path where, like its successful predecessors two years earlier, the perigee point hovered around the average altitude of the target. Again, a fast fly-by was performed and the interceptor blown up.

Seven days later Cosmos 373 was the target for a second rapid fly-by and interceptor explosion when Cosmos 375 flew a similar profile to its immediate predecessor. And that was the end of the first set of tests where on two separate occasions a single target had been the objective for two high-speed interceptions several days apart.

A new format emerged in 1971 when, on February 9, a target was sent to a 619 x 574 km orbit on top of a C series launcher. This type of booster evolved as a two-stage space rocket from the single stage SS-5 Skean, an intermediate range ballistic missile much smaller than the F-1-m hitherto employed for target launches. Moreover, Cosmos 394 was sent up from Plesetsk. Sixteen days later an F-1-m lifted into orbit with an interceptor/destroyer satellite as payload. Designated Cosmos 397 it began life in a comparatively low orbit but soon moved up to a 2,317 x 593 km ellipse from where it performed the normal fly-by and detonation, blowing itself into a myriad fragments. But then the format changed and instead of Cosmos 394 being the recipient of a second close pass, another target was launched on March 19. Called Cosmos 400, it too was launched by a C series booster. This time the orbit was higher than before and more nearly a circle, 1,016 x 995 km. On April 4 an F-1-m from Tyuratam sent a new class of vehicle into space, a satellite inspector rather than the interceptor/destroyer used so far. That satellite, called Cosmos 404, moved from an intermediate path to an orbit not dissimilar to the target: 1,009 x 811 km. Whereas interceptions before had caused the satellite to fly rapidly past the target, Cosmos 404 was so nearly in the same path that it loitered in the target's vicinity, the relative speed between the two being quite low. After some time the inspector satellite, Cosmos 404, was moved to a very different path (799 x 169 km) and a further maneuver was made to bring it down through the atmosphere, the first "chase" vehicle in the killersat tests to be delivered back to the planet. It plunged into a particularly deep part of the ocean from where it could not be recovered.

There were now two distinctly separate roles played by the F-1-m launched killersats: a fast, high-explosive carrier and a slower inspection vehicle. On November 29, 1971, another variation emerged when a C series launcher from Plesetsk put Cosmos 459 into an orbital path less than 250 km up; this was considerably lower than any previous target. It was part of another high-speed interception and Cosmos 462 launched four days later moved into a highly elliptical path with the low point, or perigee, of the orbit down around the average height of the target.

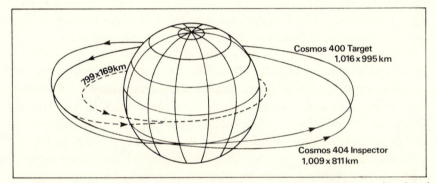

In a similar path to that of its target, Cosmos 404 dropped down to a lower orbit (dotted line) and then was returned through the atmosphere in tests of an inspection concept.

Less than a year later the last of the second set of tests saw Cosmos 521 go into an elliptical path similar to those flown by Cosmos targets 373 and 400. Only this time no interceptor or inspector launch followed and it was impossible to determine if the flight was a success. Nearly three years were to elapse before the third set of tests began in a flurry of Cosmos flights designed to explore yet another flight profile, a period during which the first SALT agreement was being ratified. .

If the dubious Cosmos 521 mission is left out, for it is just possible that the flight was nothing to do with killersat tests, the gap from December 1971 to July 1975 represents considerable development time in which new operating procedures were worked up and the associated hardware prepared. But intelligence experts watching with interest the onset of a new set of tests were mindful of the suspected blinding by laser of sensors in October 1975, carried aboard an early-warning satellite in stationary orbit. Was it all part of a major research and development effort to test under operational conditions equipment designed to knock out defense satellites? It began to look convincing when three different modes of killersat attack were tested in one ten-month period beginning February 1976. The opening shot in the third series of tests had put a single target into orbit during July the previous year but no other launch was associated with this flight, seemingly a repeat of the last in the second set of tests flown in September 1972. That was followed in February 1976 by the flight of Cosmos 803 into a 620 x 550 km orbit and four days later by an inspector satellite dubbed Cosmos 804. After moving away it was casually returned through the atmosphere but a second satellite, Cosmos 814, more than two months later performed a rapid fly-by and re-entry within the first orbit. This was quite a new technique and seemed part of a more broadly based capacity to knock out satellites without warning. Because NORAD maintains a constant vigil on all satellites placed in orbit, and because it tracks carefully every object circling the Earth, analysis of a killersat's flight path would allow defense analysts quickly to compute the course and predict the target satellite. But the first-orbit rendezvous technique would allow insufficient time accurately to determine the killersat's course, thus giving the Soviets the advantage of surprise; most Soviet military doctrine supports the element of pre-emptive attack or surprise assault.

Three months after the first-orbit fly-by, Cosmos 839 was put up as a target for Cosmos 843 launched 12 days later; it failed to repeat its predeccessor's success. And then, in December 1976, Cosmos 886 flew rapidly past Cosmos 880 and blew itself up at a safe distance, repeating the more conventional killersat operation. In the ten months concluded by that dual flight, the Russians demonstrated a slow inspection mission, a rapid fly-by on the first orbit, and an interceptor/destroyer capability.

There was yet another mode due for test, one in which the so-called "pop-up" technique was explored. It began with the launch of Cosmos 909 in May 1977, to a highly inclined orbit of 2,102 x 996 km, very much higher than earlier targets. Four days later the chase vehicle, Cosmos 910, arrived in a comparatively low orbit, 506 km high at apogee, with the intent that it should put itself into an elliptical path for a quick fly-by of the target high above. It failed to perform this function and returned to Earth in one revolution. Following almost a month of modifications and data analysis from this failed test, very similar to the failure of Cosmos 839/843, Soviet engineers prepared another chase vehicle designated Cosmos 918 when it ascended in June 1977. This time the system worked and the interceptor moved first to a 197 x 124 km path before suddenly popping up to the much greater height at which the target resided. The orbit was so elliptical that the interceptor fell back down through the atmosphere during that same orbit without exploding.

More conventional killersat trajectories exploited from the beginning of such tests had the interceptor climb high over the target for a high-speed dash from above; the new technique put the interceptor initially far below the target so that in the ensuring engine burn it would climb fast to reach the higher satellite. Operationally it was a more flexible mode of operation, for the altitude to which the interceptor could be moved depended only on the energy available in the killersat's booster engine. Almost all defense satellites were now within striking distance of the Soviet killersat and the new hunter-killer variant was a flexible system capable of threatening the electronic eyes and ears of military personnel.

That the Russians did not have it all their own way, and that Cosmos 839 had been the target for the first, failed, pop-up technique, is endorsed by careful analysis of tracking data. Whereas the more conventional targets in comparatively low orbits weighed about 900 kg, the higher targets used for hunter-killer tests weighed between 400 kg and 500 kg; Cosmos 839 weighed 400 kg. Interceptors consistently weighed about 2 tons.

Before the end of the year a second hunter-killer class test began with the October launch of target Cosmos 959 into an intermediate orbit of 834 x 144 km and was followed by the interceptor, Cosmos 961, to a lower, 309 x 291 km, path. Within one orbit the chase vehicle burned its propulsion system and moved quickly to fly rapidly past the target before plunging back down to Earth. Newspapers in Japan were full of flying saucer reports as the fragmented debris from the interceptor, which broke up when it passed through the atmosphere, showered the Pacific Ocean.

It was clearly a low-orbit demonstration test of the high-orbit pop-up

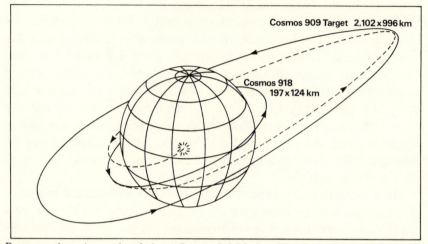

Demonstrating a 'pop-up' technique, Cosmos 918 lifted itself to the higher path of Cosmos 909 and within one revolution fell back down through the atmosphere (dotted line).

technique. Another test in December 1977, probably of an inspector mission involving slow fly-by, failed before the final mission in the third killersat test series got off the ground in May 1978, using the same target for a new interceptor which this time successfully closed to within 1 km of Cosmos 967 before moving away and re-entering over the Pacific.

The intense activity beginning in February 1976 deeply concerned US defense officials who successfully convinced President Carter of the urgent need to look again at parallel killersat technology before the West was held to ransom. In preliminary discussions with Russia, the United States openly stated its belief that the Soviets had developed an operational capability which was considered "somewhat troublesome." When approached on the issue of killersat limitation talks, the Soviets responded favorably and a first meeting was arranged between Paul Warnke, director of the US Arms Control and Disarmament Agency, and Russia's representative, Oleg Khlestov. They began discussions on June 8, 1978, in Helsinki, for sessions considered a preliminary statement of respective viewpoints. But more detailed debate was made difficult by the Soviets' insistence that the US Space Shuttle be considered a potential killersat too! The Shuttle, built as a re-usable launch vehicle, could, they said, be used to carry big anti-satellite weapons into orbit and the Russians refused to dismantle their own killersat hardware unless the United States agreed to include this winged transporter in future discussions. The proposal was absurd but it was a useful ploy to inhibit talks. By the end of 1978 the Russians were well aware of a new drive in the United States to develop quickly the technology which had been kept on the shelf for more than a decade. There was a lot of catching up to be done and Carter decided to negotiate from strength while developing the capability to deploy a US killersat system should limitation talks break down. But whereas to the Western view, negotiation from a position of equivalence is a sound basis for reciprocal withdrawal, the Russian view runs contrary to this and demands negotiation from a position of Soviet supremacy. Soured by the sudden upsurge of research on a US system, talks became more difficult to arrange. It had suited the Soviet purpose temporarily to halt killersat tests when the delicate SALT-2 negotiations were being finalized. But when, in the wake of flagrant Russian aggression in the Middle East, the United States Government decided temporarily to cancel plans to have the treaty ratified in Congress, Soviet leaders gave the go-ahead to a new series of tests.

On April 3, 1980, Cosmos 1171 put a target into space and 15 days later an interceptor sped away from the Tyuratam launch pad. Cosmos 1174 failed in its attempted fly-by when it came no closer than 8 km, outside the range at which shrapnel from an explosion would disable the target. Having successfully shown intent to pursue the pop-up technique, however, it moved away and was intentionally detonated two days later.

By this time all hope of getting killersat limitation talks together again had evaporated under one international crisis after another. Reluctant to continue not only killersat talks but a complete range of negotiations involving the United States and NATO, Soviet Russia invited the reciprocation which President Carter authorized in full. The resumption of Soviet killersat tests in April 1980 was the stimulus necessary to tip the balance in favor of a major US commitment to an inventory of anti-satellite weapons.

It was certainly bad timing on Russia's part, for two months after the Cosmos 1171/1174 mission major decisions were due about the US program. The White House considered it an answer in full to their demand in late 1978 for a complete halt to Russian tests before formal negotiations could begin. A massive effort to exploit new technology for war in space was now inevitable and one by one the supporters of detente slipped away from the White House.

In April 1980, Secretary of State Cyrus Vance resigned over the new

new "hawkish" policies of the Carter administration, opening the President to greater influence from his hard line security adviser, Zbigniew Brzesinski. It had taken the Pentagon several years to convince the US political camp of Russia's determined bid for global superiority. But the writing was now clearly on the wall, in Afghanistan, in the Indian Ocean, in blatant violation of SALT agreements, and in flagrant disregard for all attempts to keep space a peaceful preserve for science and application.

In late 1980, Americans elected a new President and firmly rejected the naive policies of the Carter camp. In came Ronald Reagan with firm deliberation and an unexpectedly large following. His policies were unambiguous and a clear indication to the Soviets that much had to change before another US administration would offer concessions unilaterally. For their part, the Russians responded with a new wave of killersat tests, beginning January 21, 1981, with the launch of target vehicle Cosmos 1241 into an elliptical, 1,009 × 973 km, path. On February 2, the interceptor was launched, under the guise of Cosmos 1243, to a path of 1,013 × 294 km, flying within 8 km of the target two revolutions later before returning through the atmosphere less than twelve hours after lift-off. It was a variation of the pop-up technique, one in which the interceptor was sent on an inspection misson before first occupying a low altitude orbit.

Cosmos 1241 was also the target for Cosmos 1258, sent up on March 14, 1981. Using a radar seeker, the interceptor was successful in demonstrating full operational capability for the Soviet killersats. But the ground-launched concept, utilizing targets and interceptors sent up on converted SS-5 and SS-9 missiles, were not the only vehicles being developed for anti-satellite operations. At the conclusion, in early 1981, of manned operations with the highly successful Salyut 6 space station, military activities increased to effectively develop a precursor manned satellite hunter directly applicable to a new generation of advanced killersats.

Salyut 6 had been launched in September 1977, and, by late May 1981, five long duration occupations of the station had accumulated 670 days of operational space flight. Ten teams of cosmonauts had been sent to visit the long duration crews and 12 unmanned Progress tanker supply ships had been launched in support of the program. When the last crew returned on May 26, 1981, the second-generation killersat was already in space, waiting to dock with Salyut 6. Weighing nearly 15 tons, Cosmos 1267 had been launched on April 25, 1981, and on June 19 it linked up with the space station. Several times a maneuvering unit on Cosmos 1267 was used to shunt the docked assembly into different orbital paths, as complex engineering tests got under way. But the real purpose of Cosmos 1267 emerged over the following months when operational evaluation began of a hitherto unsuspected role. Cosmos 1267 carried ejection ports for small infrared homing torpedoes capable of destroying military satellites on impact. With the enormous maneuvering capability of Cosmos 1267, even stationary orbit satellites would come within range of the high-powered interceptor.

Free now to express his full opinion about the Soviet threat, Major General George J. Keegan, Jr, Chief of Air Force Intelligence until his retirement in 1977, catalogues primary zones of concern thus: "Antisatellite weapons to deny our use of space for warning and command; pioneering research in directed energy weapons to kill our retaliatory missiles; an omnipotence on land; an ability to deny our use of the seas and a continuing projection of power into the Third World representing the greatest imperialism in history. Deny the reality if you will. I cannot."

For 20 years, military space missions hinged on the availability of Titan derivatives, typified here by the first Titan 3C in 1965.

Massive solid rocket boosters attached to the Titan 3A converted it into a heavy launcher capable of lifting more than 13 tons into space versus 1½ tons.

The basic core of
the Titan 3C and
3D models was the
3A, a two-stage
launcher without
supplementary
boost.

Titan 3C military launcher.

U. S. AIR FORCE
TAN III COMPLEX

Above *Titan 3C has been the largest military launcher since the first flight in 1965, employed for a variety of Air Force payloads. It is marginally less powerful than the Soviet Salyut launcher.*

Above right *The first military weather pictures were taken by civilian Tiros satellites, the views finding wide application with both user groups.*

Right *Under the Defense Meteorological Satellite Program, RCA built the Block IV military weather satellites, first used in 1965.*

Above left *First launched in 1971, the Block 5B/C military weather satellite carried improved direct transmission capability with temperature sounders and high resolution camera systems.*
Above right *The Block 5A weather satellites carried line-scan cameras and produced views in visible and infra-red portions of the spectrum.*

Below left *The RCA Block 5D-2 represents the most sophisticated military weather satellite built to date, with broader and more substantial coverage than any earlier model.*
Below right *The Block 5D-2 carries a bank of solar cells deployed in orbit and has considerably enhanced qualities over its immediate predecessor, the 5D-1.*

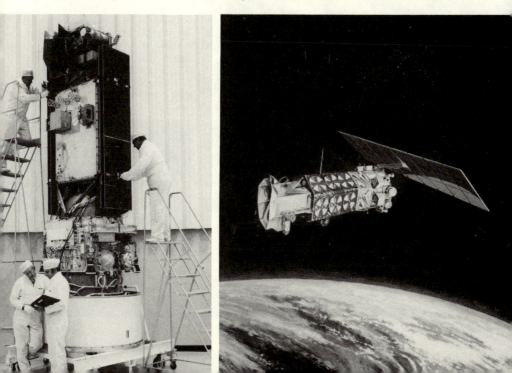

Above *Launched by Titan 3C, this Transtage upper stage carries IDSCS satellites into orbit.*
Above left *Technicians put finishing touches to an engineering model of the military IDSCS communication satellite.*

Below left *This artist's illustration shows how a single Titan 3C launched eight satellites on a single flight, dispensing each to a specific location.*
Below *This drawing shows IDSCS satellites girdling the globe as part of the initial US military communication satellite system.*

Fltsatcom was built by TRW to link elements of the National Command Authority with ships and aircraft around the world. It employs a large mesh antenna reflector seen here during test.

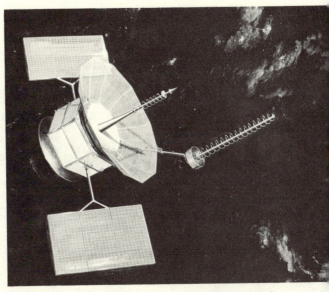

Fltsatcom's antenna is 4.9 m across when fully deployed in space and the satellite carries a helical receive antenna to one side, power provided by two large solar panels.

Fltsatcom communications satellite.

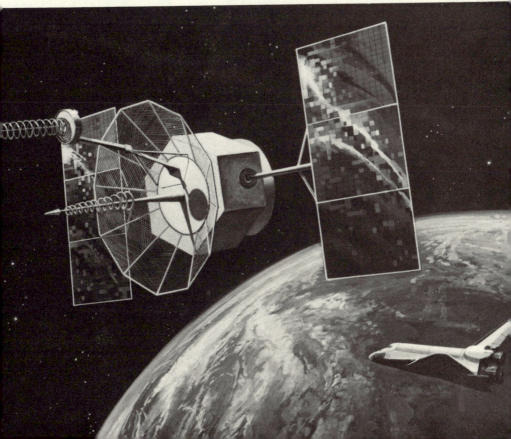

The current NATO-3 satellites were built by Ford Aerospace and launched from Cape Canaveral.

NATO satellites are currently launched by Delta rockets purchased from the civilian space agency. In this way, when the Shuttle takes over launch duties from all expendable rockets, military users will pay for the availability of that winged transporter.

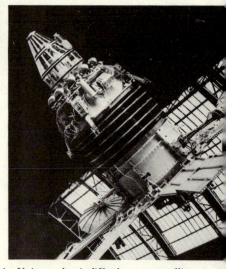

Right *Because the geographical location of the Soviet Union makes it difficult to use satellites in stationary orbit, Molniya communication satellites are placed in elliptical, inclined, paths crossing Russia.*

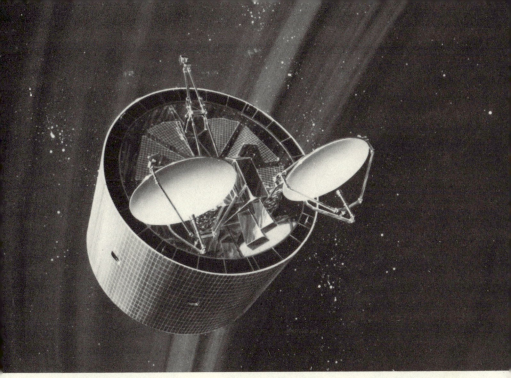

Above *TRW built the DSCS-2 series military communication satellites. A great improvement on the IDSCS series, each spin-stabilized DSCS-2 received its power from solar cells around the exterior.*
Below left *Although experimental in concept, the Hughes Tacsat satellite was launched in 1969 to demonstrate the use of a stationary orbit satellite for tactical communications between mobile field units.*
Below right *The NATO satellites are used to relay communication between units in the United States and Europe and for strategic and tactical communications with ships at sea.*

Above *Deep inside the Cheyenne Mountain complex, North American Air Defense (NORAD) personnel watch every satellite and space vehicle, hoping not to see in the constellation of objects ascending from the horizon Soviet ballistic missiles on their way to US targets.* **Below** *SS-9 Scarp rockets were used for Fractional Orbit Bombardment tests between 1967 and 1971, but the concept was not adopted operationally.*

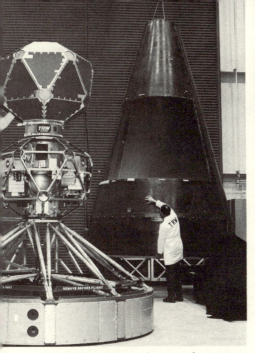

Designed to detect nuclear tests from space, Vela satellites have policed the globe since 1963. Here two satellites are seen in the configuration they would assume for launch.

Vela nuclear detection satellites have been launched by Atlas-Agena and Titan 3C rockets, the latter representing a more powerful satellite design. One is shown here before fitting inside the launcher's shroud.

The idea of combining early-warning, nuclear detection, reconnaissance and weather observation in one manned space facility did not stop at the aborted Manned Orbital Laboratory project, as evidenced here by this Lockheed proposal for a massive orbital complex.

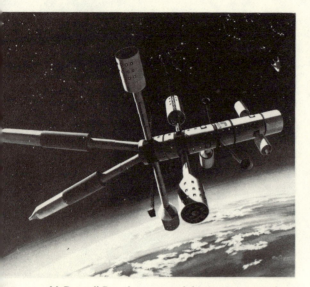

Rockwell International's space station proposal carried large solar cell arrays but, like McDonnell Douglas designs, would have had several ports at which unique sensor modules could be docked.

McDonnell Douglas proposed this massive space base for about 100 people in 1969, with many capabilities appropriate to the military mission in space.

The preferred Rockwell space station proposal would have been a multideck structure capable of accepting separate modules.

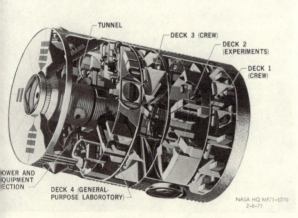

TUNNEL

DECK 3 (CREW)

DECK 2 (EXPERIMENTS)

DECK 1 (CREW)

OWER AND QUIPMENT ECTION

DECK 4 (GENERAL-PURPOSE LABOROTORY)

NASA HQ MF71-5270
2-8-71

When serious design studies evolved on large space stations, the facility was seen to benefit from a basic core module structure to which could be attached separate sensor modules as necessary.

Modular elements docked together for habitation would provide a military presence in space deemed necessary for many unique operations impossible with unmanned systems.

As studies progressed through 1971 on the type of orbital facility to use with the Shuttle, engineers proposed the use of this reusable transporter for carrying into space the several separate elements needed to assemble the facility in orbit.

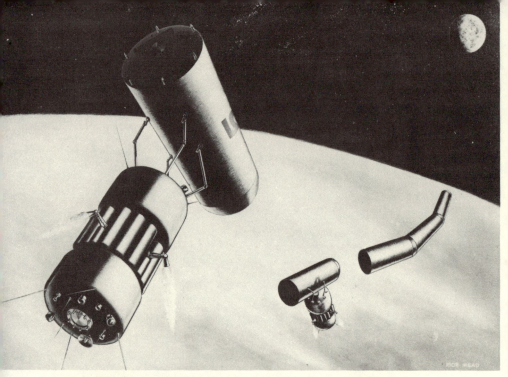

Orbital space tugs have long been recognized as essential to the construction in orbit of large structures designed to provide a manned platform. This early Lockheed drawing typifies the kind of operation such tugs would perform.

Manned space tugs would use manipulator arms to accomplish construction tasks in orbit.

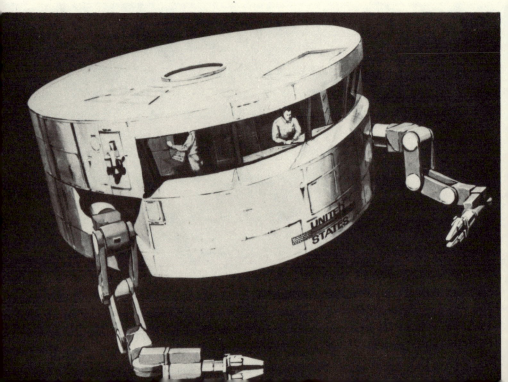

Rockwell International's Navstar global positioning system satellite.

Increased operations with an integrated manned and unmanned military space program require the Soviets to control more hardware at any single time than their US counterparts. Control facilities like that shown here are used to monitor Soyuz/Salyut operations.

Opposite page *A key element in the success of the Shuttle is the high performance rocket engines, three of which are carried at the rear of the orbiter.*

Above *Designed and built by Vought to a specification from the US Air Force, this anti-satellite device would be used to destroy Soviet hardware in space by firing solid rocket projectiles around the exterior to propel it on a collision course with the satellite.*

Below *Civilian projects designed to improve technical services on Earth would be especially vulnerable in time of open war; and increasing dependence on space systems means that, should these facilities be denied, the ability to control civil order would rapidly evaporate.*

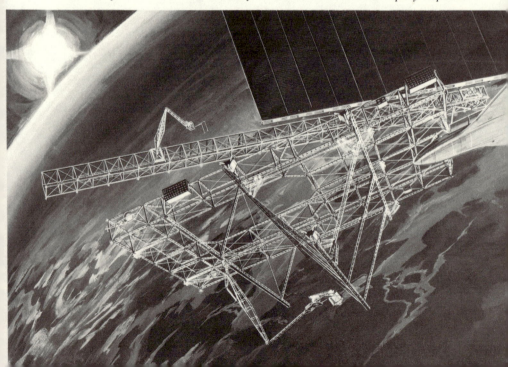

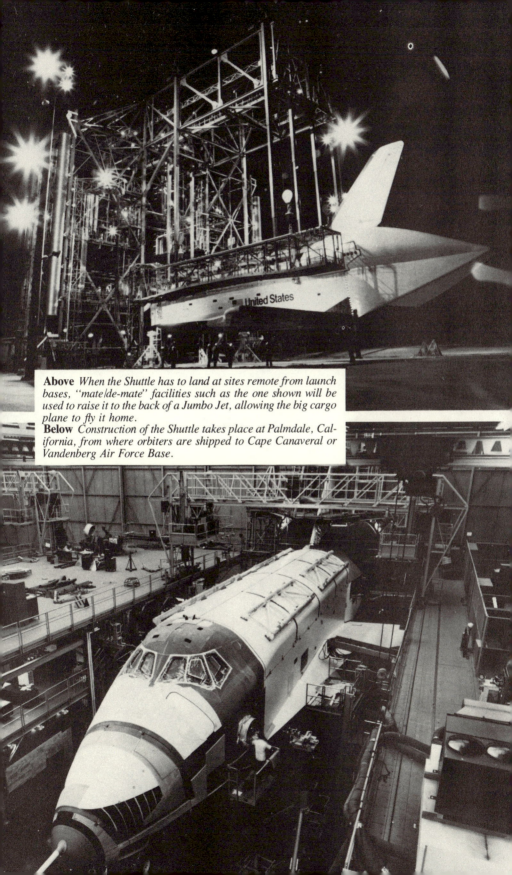

Above *When the Shuttle has to land at sites remote from launch bases, "mate/de-mate" facilities such as the one shown will be used to raise it to the back of a Jumbo Jet, allowing the big cargo plane to fly it home.*
Below *Construction of the Shuttle takes place at Palmdale, California, from where orbiters are shipped to Cape Canaveral or Vandenberg Air Force Base.*

Preparing the Shuttle for launch.

As depicted in this cutaway illustration, the Shuttle not only provides a reusable launch system but also a capacity for carrying several people into space. In this view, four crew members are seen working on the flight deck. Note the forward facing seats used by the two pilots during launch and re-entry.

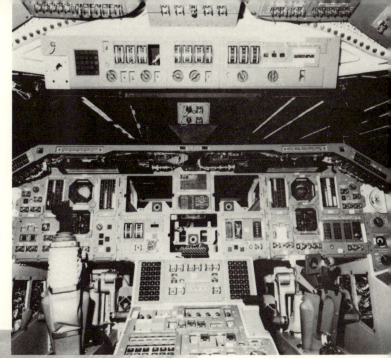

The Shuttle's flight deck is greatly simplified by the use of cathode ray tubes which can present many different displays upon command, deleting a need for several hundred different instruments and dials which would otherwise have to be incorporated, as they were for Apollo spacecraft.

The prime function of the Shuttle orbiter is to carry into orbit the satellites which to date have been launched by expendable rockets.

At the end of a mission the Shuttle returns to land like a conventional aircraft, gliding in without power, and carrying cargo returned from space.

The Shuttle is launched on its historic mission. The successful conclusion of this venture put America back on a path toward military equality with the USSR, as well as providing a vital tool for the peaceful use of space.

Critical to the Shuttle's safe return through the atmosphere are the individual thermal protection tiles seen here applied to the exterior of Columbia. More than 30,000 such tiles are carried by each vehicle.

Solid propellant rocket units like this IUS are designed to lift satellites to higher orbits than can be reached by the Shuttle alone.

At the launch site, Shuttle systems are checked by automated ground equipment. The large square structure at left is designed to pivot round, enclosing the orbiter cargo bay to allow satellites to be moved across and installed for launch.

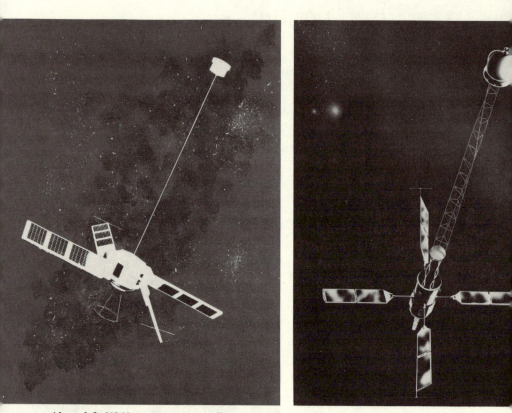

Above left *US Navy navigation satellites are used to provide precise, all-weather information, a constellation of five transmitting signals to computers via Earth tracking stations.*
Above right *This advanced US Navy Nova navigation satellite is designed to provide significantly improved services and has been developed for the Navy Strategic Systems Project Office.*

Navsat integration and assembly, like most satellite jobs, calls for extreme cleanliness and great care with checkout equipment, as evidenced by this view of RCA technicians.

Above left *Rockwell International's Navstar global positioning system satellite is the most accurate, and potentially most useful, navigation satellite built to date. It will form the base upon which new and important weapon system guidance packages will be operated.*

Above right *High reliability is a key feature of the Navstar program since several satellites will be required to operate simultaneously from orbit, and exhaustive tests are a prerequisite for this assurance.*

Below *Testing a Navstar global positioning system satellite.*

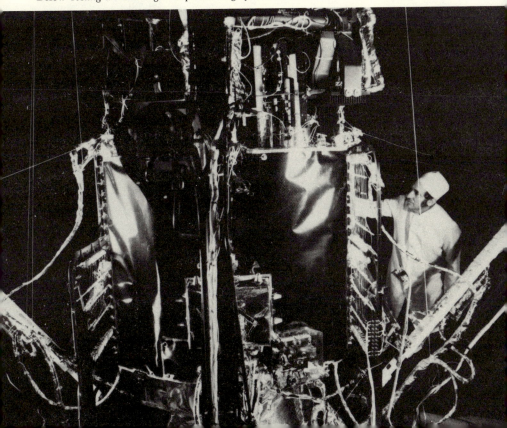

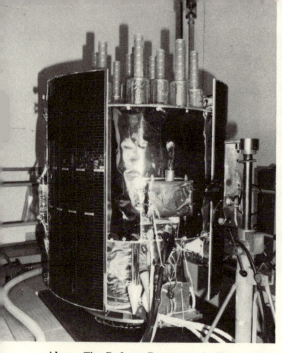

Above *The Defense Department's Navstar program calls for a comparatively large production run since 18 satellites must be fully operational at any one time and the global positioning system must serve user needs throughout the coming decade.*

Above right *Topped by a shaped-beam helix antenna array, Navstar satellites will provide guidance information accurate to within a few meters.*

Right *Navy Tomahawk cruise missiles will use Navstar to integrate a precisely routed course to the target.*

Below *An air-launched cruise missile drops from the bomb bay of a modified B-52. By 1989, the US Air Force will have 3,400 rounds.*

Above *In 1979 the Soviet military reconnaissance program adopted production modules from the manned Soyuz spacecraft to carry cameras and sensors for Earth observation.*

Above right *The orbital module, carried on the front of the manned Soyuz crew module, has been adapted for a variety of unmanned roles including reconnaissance duty.*

Right *Military spacecraft are vulnerable to impact because of appendages which, once destroyed, completely invalidate the function of the satellite, as seen here with these two satellite booms.*

Below *Although shown here releasing an AIM-7 Sparrow air-to-air missile, the F-15 will carry the anti-satellite weapon in a similar under-fuselage location for release at extreme altitude.*

Above *Large solar power satellites, if built in space, could be directly threatened by hostile weapon systems.*
Below *Satellites like particle-beam and laser gunships would need large electrical systems and could derive power from panels deployed in orbit.*

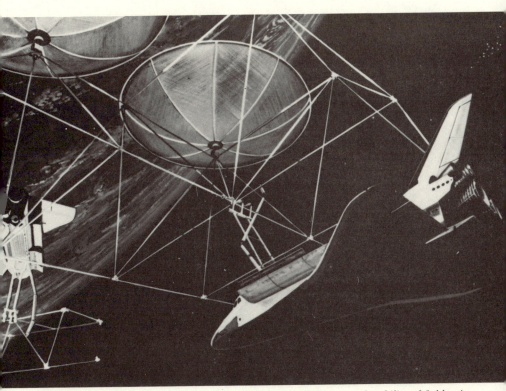

Above *Large antenna forms like these would dramatically improve the ability of field unit commanders to maintain channels of communication.*
Below *The Inertial Upper Stage is capable of propelling more than 2 tons from an initial low Earth orbit attained by the Shuttle to an altitude of more than 30,000 km.*

SS-10 Scrag missiles trundle past the Kremlin in this 1968 Red Square Parade in Moscow, rockets identified with the Soviet orbital bomb tests.

Antenna platforms built in orbit could greatly expand the communications net available to tactical military forces on Earth.

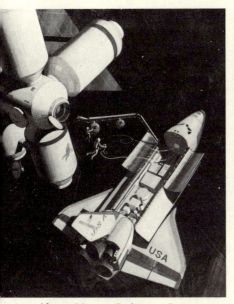

Above *Many Defense Department tasks now conceived for the 1990s will require the use of a permanently manned orbital facility, like the Soviets achieve in part already with their Salyut station. Here, a supply Shuttle brings equipment to the orbiting astronauts.*

Above right *To effectively move one satellite, or space structure, from orbit to orbit a mini-tug will be developed and carried in the Shuttle. In this way, satellites can be retrieved for return to Earth and repair or refurbishment.*

Middle right
Star Raker, the logical development of the Shuttle, will have a highly developed defense capability. This will be one of the most impressive weapons of the future.

Right *The last major rocket to be developed for space transportation is the Titan 34D, which will be designed to back up the Shuttle in case of failure with the reusable launcher.*

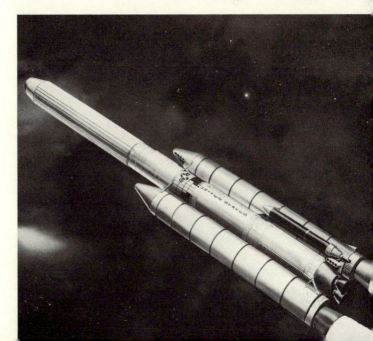

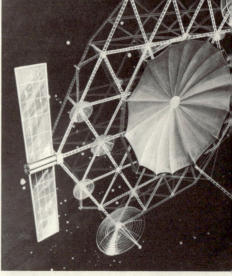

Above *Adaptations of existing Shuttle hardware are seen here lifting a heavy payload into space, albeit with an unmanned configuration. Note the modified liquid boosters replacing the solids now used with Shuttle.*
Below *Massive space freighters like this design from Boeing probably would be launched from a dry-dock facility.*

Above top *Massive orbiting space structures like this stationary orbit platform will require the use of larger delivery capacities than the standard Shuttle can achieve, thereby promoting the development of new launchers.*
Above middle *The single most important element in the emerging space program of the 1980s will be the ability of human beings to participate in almost all space operations, rather than flying along on a few selected trips as they have in the past.*

6. The big lift

Lazer weapons and the reusable Shuttle

A decade ago most scientists considered the possibility of a space-borne laser weapon with the same credulity as that afforded the Buck Rogers ray gun. In the last ten years, however, major strides have been made which promise to ensure the use of a particularly efficient laser for the fully operational killersats now planned by the United States and the Soviet Union. The need for weapons to disable satellites has never been clearer. As early as mid-1976, US Navy Secretary J. William Middendorf testified to the American Security Council that: "There's no question the Soviets have developed satellites that give them real-time, mid-course guidance for their incoming missiles," and that in the event of hostilities, "we've got to work like mad to get them down real fast."

The ability to "get them down real fast" has only since the mid-1970s been sought with sufficient determination and resolve to produce an operational killersat. For when the Russians repeatedly tested several different methods for disabling defense satellites in a burst of shrapnel from a detonated interceptor, the United States vacillated while politicians, convinced of the sound reasoning behind detente, talked and signed agreements. Only in the second half of the last decade has it become apparent that Russia has applied more military uses to space than has the United States in the same period.

In any future conflict involving direct confrontation between the super-powers, satellites will be used to provide highly accurate information by which tactical and ballistic missiles are delivered to within a few meters of their designated targets. Not through passive, informative, data streams to operators, but on direct links with the missile in flight, elim-inating the human element once the commitment has been given. In this way, satellite systems of the future will command increasing importance for the conduct of war on Earth, and it is for this reason that both America

169

and Russia seek a means of eliminating each others' spaceborne capability. There are several ways this can be achieved, in two operating mediums: ground-based systems designed to destroy the satellite itself, or spaceborne interceptors working from an orbit around the Earth. The former, for reasons discussed later, are limited to hot-kill mechanisms or enhanced radiation-type weapons fired into space by missiles; a variation on this theme is the air-launched anti-satellite weapon carried to extreme altitude by a high performance jet. Hot-kill mechanisms are the type used by Russia in its extensive killersat tests incorporating an explosive device discharging a burst of shrapnel. It is necessary for detonation to take place quite close to the target, thus demanding accurate and reliable guidance.

Perhaps more forgiving in guidance needs are the enhanced radiation weapons, one example being the neutron bomb where a fission charge creates a fusion reaction—in effect, using an atom bomb to trigger a hydrogen bomb. With an unusually low fission yield, the device produces more deadly neutrons than the conventional nuclear bomb and has enhanced range. Trading blast for radiation, a weapon of this type could be used to destroy the electronics or delicate sensors employed by military satellites. Space-borne interceptors can use both hot-kill and enhanced radiation weapons too; but they can also employ lasers, thereby eliminating the need to get within close range of the target.

The initial series of US anti-satellite tests described in the previous chapter were limited to the ground-launched, direct-ascent, hot-kill type. J. William Middendorf's statement that the Russians have tested satellite-based missile guidance systems was not primarily responsible for re-energizing US interest in anti-satellite weapons, but it certainly contributed to a growing unease about Soviet endeavors. The argument that a defense system is necessary in an age of force equivalence not only because it has some strategic advantage but also because the potential enemy has it, carried the day for killersat protagonists. In fact it is a weapon which only deters if the opposing forces also have a killersat capability, for then the system's activation would merely establish a status quo through reciprocal destruction of the enemy's satellites.

Early in 1975 the Air Force set up contractor teams to study in a four-year period various technologies for disabling satellites in space, effectively starting again on the road which earlier terminated with the Nike Zeus and Nike X concepts. Rockwell International proposed a large metallic net deployed from an interceptor to snag a hostile satellite and disable its functions. By August 1975, however, the hot-kill impact interceptors looked the most promising and General Dynamics competed with LTV Aerospace on a 12-month examination of alternative designs using this ground-launched technique.

As work progressed the political climate for decision ran counter to expedient anti-satellite development; Jimmy Carter formally became President in January 1977, and his dove-like policies were considered by the Pentagon a restraining influence on operational deployment. Carter was adamant that he should personally review all pending military developments, especially in arms and weapons procurement, and showed a preference for limiting new and agressive systems which might, he thought, be construed by the Soviets as a hostile move. Over the next few years that mood changed dramatically and by the end of the decade the President had formally approved major increases in defense expenditure including anti-satellite weapons. But back in 1977 the Pentagon waited its appropriate moment, the National Security Council had already given tacit approval but the final stamp awaited a Presidential review. The Air Force had already conducted feasibility studies and the aerospace contractors proved the concept was possible as an effective anti-satellite weapon.

The preferred concept embodied a ground-launched device using rocket propulsion for a direct-ascent through the atmosphere, into space and up to the target, at which point it would drive a non-nuclear warhead directly into the satellite and put it out of action. Terminal guidance could be either an infra-red seeker or some form of active homing radar, designed of course to work with a non-co-operative target.

By autumn 1977, President Carter gave approval for a research and development effort to prepare the hardware for operational deployment should anti-satellite limitation talks break down. The Air Force got its program and moved to find appropriate contractors to build a test system involving the homing head and the boost unit as one integral package and a set of targets on which to test the interceptor. During the first few months of 1978, the President became totally convinced of the need for a US anti-satellite system and while the Defense Department briefed him on the escalating Soviet killersat trials, State Department officials studied the repercussions on SALT-2.

The first Strategic Arms Limitation Talks agreement had been signed in May 1972, and the second set of talks were held back by differences of interpretation about the Backfire bomber and deployment of a mobile ballistic missile force called MX, proposed as a counter to increasing numbers of Soviet ICBMs and multiple warhead combinations. For once, Russia's insistence that specific agreements and treaties should be concerned solely with the stated issues worked to the benefit of the West; killersat developments by either side were of little interest to SALT negotiators and the Russians were not tempted to embrace them in the strategic arms talks, there being a separate set of discussions planned for killersats.

During 1978 the Pentagon set up computer models for war-game scenarios to show the President just how anti-satellite warfare would fit in with established US and NATO strategy and how the Soviet Union would probably turn their killersats on Chinese spacecraft operating as veiled back-ups to US satellites. One line of interpretation stressed the application of Soviet killersats to China's expanding space program, seeking to show how Russia would gain more by eliminating that country's spaceborne surveillance.

It was becoming a complex problem where the Soviet Union might have to fight separate forces from opposing sides. With this detailed evaluation of how future global conflict may emerge, final plans developed for an interim anti-satellite weapon. The transformation imminent as Air Force officials put together the basis of an anti-satellite system is reflected in a clinical but historic statement incorporated among National Security Council conclusions on future war scenarios:

"The US space defense program will include an integrated attack warning, notification, verification and contingency reaction capability which can effectively detect and react to threats to US space systems."

The "reaction capability" emerged in the form of the direct-ascent, hot-kill interceptor which, by this time, the Air Force had decided to build around an active radar seeker to guide the warhead to its target. There was no compromise; the Defense Department was committed to building a system specifically designed to counter threats in space. It was a significant step, for once deployed the near-Earth space lanes would never again be a solely peaceful preserve.

By January 1978 the US Air Force Flight Test Center at Edwards Air Force Base, California, had put together the nucleus of a test program in response to Pentagon directives. Now the Vought Corporation had been brought in to adapt an anti-ballistic missile device developed by that company during the early 1970s but which had never been pursued. The basic design included a cluster of solid propellant rockets grouped around a small package of sensors which were to steer the complete assembly toward the target and then fire again to ram the metal object fully home. It called for considerably better guidance and tracking than anything achieved with the Soviet killersat for those only had to get within 1 km of the target for a theoretically successful kill from the detonated warhead.

The Vought weapon could be launched by a Minuteman 3 ICBM housed in a hardened underground silo, or it could be fired from an aircraft in flight at high altitude. Careful study of competing modes favored the air-launched concept and plans were made for a McDonnell Douglas F-15 Eagle to carry the weapon on test. It was in preference for the highly mobile deployment capability afforded by the Eagle that Air Force officials chose that concept over the fixed-base method; in the first wave of a major strike, anti-satellite weapons could be knocked out in their silos. For more practical reasons too, it was cheaper and easier to hang the weapon on an airborne platform than adapt a complex ICBM system.

The Vought device was to be propelled to its target by two solid propellant rockets adapted from other programs in a package 5.4 m long, 51 cm in diameter and weighing about 1,200 kg. The first stage would be a modified Thiokol motor from the Boeing short-range-attack-missile, or SRAM, while the second would be essentially the same Altair 3 motor used as the fourth stage of the Scout launcher. SRAM was an Air Force stand-off missile carried by B-52 and FB-111 bombers, generating thrust equal to half that of the wartime V-2 missile. The Scout launcher was capable of lifting 180 kg payloads into orbit, a small rocket but one used by NASA and the Air Force at the bottom end of the booster league.

In 1979 the Air Force selected the Avco Corporation to design and fabricate ten anti-satellite targets which the Vought interceptors would destroy in simulation of a hostile attack upon Soviet satellites. Scout rockets would be used to put the warheads in orbit and the F-15 would carry the rocket-boosted projectile on the first leg of its flight. In a similar flight profile to that adopted for the earlier anti-ballistic missile device, the solid propellant motors would ignite upon release from the F-15, carrying the Vought warhead on and up to its target. Guidance information prior to release from the F-15 would be provided by a head-up display in the cockpit and at an appropriate point a simple pull-up maneuver would present the booster/warhead package in a vertical mode which, when released by the pilot, would simplify the missile's own guidance requirements. Steered to the general vicinity of the target satellite by computed commands, the Vought warhead would incorporate its own computer for terminal homing on instructions from the active radar. Close in, the cluster of solid rocket motors, each no bigger than a bullet, would be fired together, effectively killing the target on impact. The twin-solid rocket motor boosted Vought head is cylindrical in shape, 30.5 cm long and 33 cm in diameter.

Phase 1 of the anti-satellite program ended in June 1980, with completion of the design details and preliminary hardware development; Phase 2 is scheduled to end in 1985 by which time the entire system will have been tested using live Vought warheads to kill Avco targets. The Russians have never destroyed one of their own satellites in space, probably because of their preference for a second use of the same target, but also because the target possibility carries complicated equipment for monitoring performance and test results.

Total funding of anti-satellite work increased dramatically at the end of the decade, going from $2.6 million in all previous years up to the end of 1977 to $9.8 million in 1978 and $14.5 million in 1979. In January 1981, Vought received a formal contract to build and test the anti-satellite device for $268 million. But the F-15 launched system was just the start of a major program aimed at boosting satellite warfare. The interim design could only seek out comparatively low targets and was specifically aimed at Soviet ocean surveillance satellites no more than 1,000 km high. Russian satellites used in war to target naval vessels on US objectives would be a priority for the Vought kill system but, like Soviet killersats, the high-altitude strategic targets covering global communications and early-warning functions would be left untouched.

There are growing signs that Russia is in hot pursuit of a stationary orbit killer system whereby sensitive and complex satellites nearly 36,000 km above Earth would be eliminated in the opening phase of a nuclear exchange. And if the stationary orbit satellites are threatened, every other defense function performed via space would be in similar peril. Accordingly, the United States is pressing ahead with a follow-up system which could be used both to replace the interim design and provide reciprocal stationary orbit kill capability. But this will not emerge before the second half of the decade because it relies on wholly new technology involving advanced concepts in physics. For this is where the laser comes in as the logical choice for a roving battlesat patrolling the orbital space lanes, liberally equipped for observing, computing, checking and responding to an implied threat from any spacefaring nation.

In August 1962, Air Force General Bernard A. Schriever said that the laser "may prove to be even more important to the world than the development of the ballistic missile, the discovery of the transistor, or the reality of Telstar." If present trends are continued to their logical, technical, conclusion, that predicition will almost certainly come about within the next ten years, for against all scientific opinion of recent history, research laboratories, military test facilities, and defense establishments across the United States are unanimous in their belief that laser weapons are here to stay.

The prime value in developing at great expense just one more way to destroy a complex piece of engineering lies in the ability of a laser selectively to pluck out targets distributed across a wide area and at varying distances. Moreover, the vacuum of space is an almost perfect medium in which to operate a laser.

For more than 20 years, Soviet scientists have concentrated enormous resources on the development of high-energy physics, nuclear physics and laser technology. Consistently, the Russian scientific presence at international conferences embracing this type of work impresses Western observers with its advanced capability; several times the Russian scientists have shown themselves to be involved with concepts alien to their contemporaries in other countries. It is partly because of this, and partly because defense intelligence agencies continue to receive details of highly advanced Soviet research at several discrete facilities, that the Defense Department is alert to any weapons development US laboratories come up with.

Intelligence estimates from the Pentagon put Russia's expenditure on lasers at a total $6,000 million, research which is producing suspicion about development of several different weapons applications. These include ballistic missile defense, satellite sensor blinding, cruise missile defense and anti-satellite operations. In the latter category, defense experts are concerned that Russia will soon have a stationary orbit killer without the need to fire an interceptor 36,000 km from Earth, a feat demanding uncommonly accurate guidance requirements for any hot-kill system demonstrated to date. In a single step, Russia would have the ability to destroy at will the more important defense satellites operated by the United States and NATO.

However, lasers are powerful devices calling for large amounts of electrical energy and cumbersome equipment difficult to minaturize. Yet progress here has already reduced the size of such designs to allow them to be installed in large aircraft. Within the next few years scientists hope to have lasers applicable to the anti-satellite role packaged in a container not much bigger than existing rocket payloads.

Lasers, defined by the concept of Light Amplification by the Stimulated Emission of Radiation, fall into several different categories. But all operate on the same basic principle calling for light to be made directional and coherent. Ordinary light, from a bulb say, is a jumbled mixture of photons released from some material in what is called spontaneous emission. It is incoherent, it canot be modulated like radio waves and it is a very inefficient use of the potential energy involved. If the incoherent spontaneous emission is made to pass through several different filters, each of which removes some part of the spectrum—white light contains all the available colors—a series of monochromatic waves would be left. If those few waves were presented to a pinhole in some material, most would be blocked off and the few which passed through would be more or less in step, providing coherent light. Although very different in function, the principle is identical in concept. By producing coherent, phased, wave forms the light can be focused to phenomenally small points. In this way, the total energy present is packed into a thin beam and so the energy per unit area increases dramatically. Ordinary light is the product of *spontaneous* emission of atoms but the laser light is much more powerful, even if not focused in a narrow beam, because it is the product of *stimulated* emission. Atoms of certain materials are made to take up the correct amount of energy, store it and then expend it at the appropriate time. Albert Einstein published a paper in 1916 to show that controlled emission of light energy could be obtained from an atom at the correct condition. Not for more than half a century did anyone take this up seriously, until in 1951 Charles H. Townes, a faculty member of Columbia University, concluded—whilst seated on a park bench—that whereas all normal molecules of a material are in low-energy states he could rearrange them to provide an abnormal quantity of high-energy molecules. By exciting them with microwaves he was able to produce the first maser (Microwave Amplification by

Stimulated Emission of Radiation) in 1954. Two years earlier, two Russian scientists prepared a paper with the same independently derived conclusions. All three, Townes, Basov and Prokhorov, were awarded the 1964 Nobel Prize in Physics. Before the end of the decade, work at Bell Telephone Laboratories provided the working principles of an optical maser. T.H. Maiman, then with the Hughes Aircraft Company, successfully demonstrated this device in 1960 and the laser was born. The active substance used at the time was a single crystal of ruby, an aluminum oxide where a small quantity of aluminum atoms are replaced with chromium atoms. In principle the device worked by presenting a ruby rod to a spiral flash lamp so the ruby atoms were raised to an excited state. When an excited atom emits a photon, or small particle of light, parallel to the axis of the crystal it stimulates another in its path, and another, and so on until they are reflected back and forth between the ends of the crystal rod. When the amplification is great enough it flashes through a partially reflecting mirror at one end, generating a narrow beam of coherent light—a laser. After emitting photons, each excited atom returns to its initial state.

There are several types of laser, all potentially applicable to anti-satellite operations. The first to be successfully developed was the solid-state laser and this type can produce a very intense beam of energy as pulsed light, ruby or garnet being possible for excitation. A second type incorporates a semiconductor material producing laser light in infra-red bands of the spectrum. The third type is the gas laser where high voltage currents are passed across a column of gas contained within a tube. These produce enormous quantities of power as a continuous beam rather than the pulsating energy of the solid-state type. Continuous beams are not, however, as high in output as pulsed lasers.

A derivative of the gas laser has the greatest promise of all for military applications. As early as 1971, Soviet scientist Nicholas Basov presented a paper at an international conference in which he claimed to have used xenon in an early form of what is now called the excimer laser. The word is coined from the dimer, or compound which will only exist when one or both of its constituent elements are in an excited state. Thus, an excited dimer, or excimer laser, gives up its energy as laser light and then returns to its former low-energy state where it can no longer bind with its partner. The apparent success in developing a demonstration excimer inspired scientists the world over to study the Basov technique. One year later the Russian scientist withdrew his claim, evidence, some said, that the Soviet research base was well advanced and very firmly under the control of political authority. Nevertheless, the enormous amounts of energy possible with this type of device pressed home the value to military applications and the Defense Advanced Research Projects Agency concentrated on developing this technique. The high-energy light is in the ultraviolet portion of the spectrum and provides a pulsed beam excited by electrons aimed at the gas.

One major drawback at present is the extremely short duration of the pulse and while intense research continues, military technologists are concerned more to develop the deuterium fluoride laser emitting a continuous wave beam at 3.8 microns in infra-red. By 1977, hydrogen fluoride lasers emitting at 2.7 microns had demonstrated their worth for spaceborne applications and in the following years scientists concentrated on reducing the size of the equipment package. The two very separate categories—excimer lasers at 0.5 micron; hydrogen fluoride laser at 2.7 microns—represent different applications.

In space, where there is no atmosphere to attenuate the beam or distort the emission, the hydrogen fluoride laser wins out and the continuous wave form propagates energy to the target at a constant rate. Air is particularly unkind to lasers and can cause the beam to spread out due to turbulence or because the beam itself heats the atmosphere and "bends" it out of focus. As much as 85 per cent of the emitted energy can be lost in this way. Consequently, high-energy pulsed beams are better for use on Earth because they send a single bullet of light which does not allow enough time for the atmospheric tunnel through which the beam is transmitted to heat up and distort the photons coming behind.

As an example, less than half the energy received at the end of a 3 km hydrogen fluoride beam transmitted in a quiet and clear atmosphere gets through in a turbulent, hazy atmosphere. Energy loss is appreciable with this type of device and this is where the pulsed excimer comes into its own. Such a design would be appropriate to the defense of prime targets on land or to the defense of large ships at sea.

Ruth M. Davis, the Defense Department's deputy under-secretary for research and development, is keen to promote the concept for use against fast intruder aircraft from remotely controlled turrets designed to lock on and kill the target. A beam control system built in 1978 by Hughes showed how feasible this was and the Air Force have already converted a redundant Boeing KC-135 tanker aircraft to carry a laser built by United Technologies Corporation. By carrying the device up through the denser layers of Earth's atmosphere the equipment can be made to perform better than at the surface because of the more rarefied air.

Tests like this have convinced defense scientists of the feasibility of placing laser guns high up mountain slopes and on military installations. The advantages are theoretically enormous for not only will the laser kill its target at any line-of-sight range, it can do so at the speed of light because light itself is the death ray. As one example, an aircraft travelling at twice the speed of sound 25 km away from a laser would move less than 6 cm in the time it would take the beam to leave the gun and reach the target. There would be no need for track compensation or trajectory computation. Theoretically at least.

To see just how valid this is, and to refute once and for all the few pessimistic scientists still unconvinced of the laser's value as a weapon, the Defense Department set up an impressive test at San Juan Capistrano in California. Situated at the TRW Systems laboratory, a 3.8 micron deuterium fluoride laser with a beam strength of several hundred kilowatts, was given the task of gunning down in flight a supersonic anti-tank missile only 1.2 m in length during a series of tests carried out in 1978. Coupled to the Hughes pointing/tracking system developed in response to Defense Department contracts, the system stopped the missile precisely as planned and in a stunning series of examples which followed, proved a 100 per cent success rate at killing the target. But while the Air Force was primarily interested in developing the laser for use as an air-borne defense weapon carried to protect large jumbo-jet size cruise missile carriers, Pentagon studies continued for space applications. It was comparatively easy to use extant technology, plus available hardware, to develop a low-altitude anti-satellite weapon. That has already been done with the Vought device launched from an F-15 Eagle. But knocking out of action satellites 36,000 km above Earth calls for a very different assemblage of equipment. Here, the laser would be most effective because it could be carried into a residential orbit far below the stationary orbit path but in the same plane so that hostile satellites would be knocked out of action before they could inflict damage on US defense satellites. In this way, the laser-equipped battlesat would not only destroy the enemy's valuable sensors, but Soviet killersat's too. Discriminating between passive enemy defense satellites and potentially hostile killer-sats would require precise tracking from the ground, or satellites in low orbit, to see the exact pattern of orbital changes. For instance, a satellite ostensibly launched to fill a stationary orbit slot for some monitoring function would have a different trajectory to that of a killersat maneuvering to get within range of a US defense satellite also at stationary orbit altitude. By accurately tracking the ascending vehi-cle, defense radars could theoretically pick out potential adversaries and, if the satellite was deemed to be an offensive device, call up the battlesats in lower orbit which would disable the suspected vehicle by hitting it with a laser burst. The entire system would need a very sensitive surveillance technique, however, because it would call for precision and assurance of identification; the consequences of knocking out an unmanned satellite which was later found to be quite passive in design would not have the internationally disastrous repercussions of a similar incident on Earth, however.

The surveillance system chosen by the Defense Department involves three separate programs: satellites in low orbit constantly tracking every object at or near stationary altitude; active radar surveillance from ground sites; ground-based electro-optical deep space surveillance (GEODSS). The Air Force is now busy developing the deep space surveillance satellites which will be sent up in the second half of this decade, each requiring complex and weighty radar equipment for tracking cooperative and non-cooperative satellites. By the time the system goes operational, certainly this decade, Soviet and perhaps Chinese satellites may well be transparent to radar detection while others could lurk close by sensitive sensor packages in case they were knocked out by killersats and had to be replaced. For that reason the ground based radar is considered a back-up to the spaceborne segment. Surplus to their original purpose, Advanced Research Projects Agency tracking and instrumentation antennae are being upgraded for this purpose and in some cases air-lifted to different sites. One will remain on station at Kwajalein Island in the Pacific, another will be operated from Guam and a third previously based in Thailand is being placed at a secret location.

The optical tracking program represents the third leg of the support base for better identification of roaming killersats sneaking up on stationary orbit satellites. Begun more than a decade ago, GEODSS is designed to replace four existing sites in California, New Zealand, South Korea and Italy. All are equipped with Baker-Nunn telescope systems with film cameras for showing unidentified satellites among a host of stars or other space objects. Developed nearly 30 years ago, the existing equipment requires 1½ hours operation successfully to plot a new object and can observe only one satellite every six minutes; the delay arises from the need to process the film and scan it with a microscope.

Contracted to TRW Incorporated, GEODSS employs five sites, each equipped with two 101.6 cm telescopes possessing a focal length of 2.18 m and a 2.1 degree field of view. These will be used to search for distant, faint, objects moving slowly in high orbits. The specification calls for identification of the shape and size of an object as small as a soccer ball, 36,000 km from Earth. A single 38.1 cm diameter auxiliary telescope, with a 76.2 cm focal length and a 6-degree field of view, will be used to search for lower objects moving fast across the sky.

The five new sites have been chosen both to provide global sky coverage and to obtain the best possible viewing conditions, compromise being necessary where requirements conflict. Beginning in early 1982, the Air Force activated GEODSS sites in New Mexico, South Korea, Hawaii and one site each at an east Atlantic and Middle East location. The five sites are each manned by 35 civilian personnel and five or six Air Force officers. The new optical system will detect satellites within a few seconds and track one every two minutes, while radiometers on each large telescope will tell operators whether the object is debris, a spinning satellite, a stabilized satellite, a rocket stage, or a killersat.

By 1985 the Air Force will be ready to move into the second phase of its anti-satellite operation, replacing the existing Vought impact device with a ground-based laser system capable of knocking out satellites in comparatively low orbit. The stationary orbit satellites will be covered initially, in that second phase, by a very high altitude hot-kill impact device developed from the Vought system and using that same basic principle. Because of the much greater distance involved, however, the impact head would be launched by a silo-installed missile like the Minuteman ICBM or the Trident C4 SLBM at present going into service as a Poseidon replacement for nuclear powered submarines.

The space-based laser battlesats are now in the development stage and while the stationary orbit hot-kill mechanism is operational, orbital tests will be carried out with the battlesat. The precise type of laser has yet to be selected but will conceivably be the deuterium-fluoride device propagating a continous wave of energy. When proven, the space-based battlesat will open a completely new spectrum of opportunities by releasing the ground-based segment to look after comparatively low orbit satellites.

There may always be a place for the air-launched, hot-kill device, however, since only a few modified aircraft would be necessary to cover wide areas. The flexibility of having a piloted aircraft fly to a discrete release point would place added pressure upon the enemy, calling for several interception penetrations of hostile airspace to knock it out because the anti-satellite aircraft need never leave its base country.

Already, early-warning satellites of the Program 647 type placed in stationary orbit to look for signs of a pre-emptive strike, have been equipped with impact sensors to tell operators if they are being hit by shrapnel from a Soviet killersat. No Russian vehicle of this type has operated remotely near stationary orbit but the Air Force is convinced the Soviets are on the verge of deploying a stationary orbit killer. One suspicion relates future stationary orbit killersat development to dramatic improvements in masking the electronic presence of a satellite in space and if the Russians ever show they have perfected the technique of launching a hidden satellite veiled from radar detection it would force US reciprocation. Already, aircraft can be made virtually transparent to hostile radars and if a similar capability were applied to space vehicles, invisible sniper-sats could be sent into space riding piggy-back on bona-fide flights. But the prospect of this happening in the next decade is remote at best and for the present attention focuses on the ability to knock out defense satellites put up by the Soviet Union or killersats in hot pursuit of US targets.

The invigorating addition of important roles and functions presaged by the advent of killersats, antisatellite hot-kill warheads, battlesats and laser gunships, together with a major new advance on all fronts of the military space satellite scene, has brought an urgent need for the Air Force to reorganize its command structure. As noted at the close of Chapter One, the Air Force's Ballistic Missile Division was given responsibility for the military US role in space, an organization formed in July 1957, from the Western Development Division of the Air Research and Development Command set up three years earlier.

In 1961 the Ballistic Missile Division was functionally divided into the Ballistic Systems Division, looking after rocket technology and missile equipment, and the Space Systems Division, responsible for orbital operations and the development of spaceborne sensors. Six years after that, in 1967, the two were merged to become the Space And Missile Systems Organization (SAMSO). For 12 years, SAMSO epitomized the Western military presence in space and from its head-quarters in El Segundo, California, set up the research programs which led to the revolutionary new developments now under way. For much of that time the organization monitored ICBM research rather than production, for the big missile programs were only a shadow of the former days when Titan and Minuteman rolled from contractor factories to underground silos. By the end of the 1970s it was time again to separate the two functions; a major new missile development program was gaining momentum to augment and partially replace Minuteman with the mobile MX system, and the sudden upsurge in new military space hardware called for unique facilities and management structures. In October 1979, SAMSO was deactivated and its responsibilities divided between the Ballistic Missile Office at San Bernardino, California, and the Space Division at Los Angeles. It was also time to improve the control aspect; with significant new missions to perform, the Air Force had need of an integrated command network.

Close by the space defense operations center deep in the Cheyenne Mountains, Colorado, an existing facility called Peterson Air Force Base was chosen for construction of the North American Air Defense Command's Consolidation Space Operations Center (CSOC, pro-nounced see-sok). Operational by 1985, CSOC will employ about 1,800 personnel of which the majority will be contractor employees monitoring specific space-borne systems. It is the first uniquely mili-tary space command post set up in the United States. It is also the site from where Air Force astronauts will coordinate their mission roles with manned flight in space.

Denied the right of human access to the space environment they have defended for two decades, the United States Air Force is now heavily involved with final plans for the Space Shuttle. Designed to replace all existing expendable, launchers like Delta, Atlas-Centaur and Titan derivatives, which for a quarter of a century have been the only means of delivering military or civilian satellites to orbit, the Shuttle is considerably more than just an economical means of gaining regular access to space. For with it comes the capacity to expand, in a

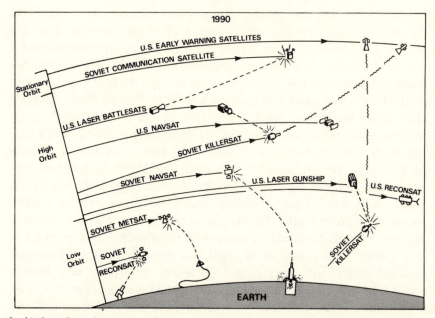

In this hypothetical scenario, offensive space systems possible by 1990 are shown in simulated combat. In low orbit, a Soviet reconsat is destroyed by a ground-based laser while a metsat is knocked out of action by an air launched anti-satellite weapon. In high orbit, a Soviet navsat is knocked out by a silo-launched anti-satellite missile while a US laser gunship, acting on information from an early warning satellite in stationary orbit, destroys a Soviet killersat ascending toward a US reconsat, which proceeds on its way. Elsewhere, a Soviet killersat in high orbit, on course for a US navsat, is itself knocked out by a laser battlesat while another battlesat zaps a Soviet communication satellite in high orbit. In this illustration, US early warning satellites provide top-cover eyes to watch for pop-up killersats.

manner impossible hitherto, everything which is done in space and to introduce within the very near future an exploitation likely to change the very nature of war for all time.

But although that revolution is a phased transformation extending over at least two decades, the first steps have been taken already. The Shuttle emerged in the late 1960s when the men who put the civilian NASA program on the road to the Moon sought ways to capitalize on the rich investment made over the preceding decade in complex and demanding space systems, launchers and hardware. Instead of looking around for some completely different role in space, why not use the basic Moon project Apollo hardware to develop a major Earth-orbiting space station starting with a project like Skylab, they said?

Skylab was an outgrowth of Apollo in that it used redundant rocket stages and spacecraft and kept momentum going while Congress debated. As it turned out, Skylab was all that NASA got; Congress was disenchanted with being tied to expensive technology programs for years on end and had only just been asked to consider a major undertaking which would give America a supersonic airliner. It turned out that this too received a rebuff when costs escalated and gloomy predictions about growth rates jettisoned optimism in favor of a mood of entrenchment. But all the while, NASA kept up its appeal for money to develop the space station which would, said NASA management, need a winged space transporter for flying back and forth with cargo, supplies and personnel to man the orbital facility. Soon after the first Moon landing was over in mid-1969, and deeply involved with funded contractor studies to test the feasibility of a space station and a transportation system, NASA was informed by the Nixon administration that it would have to moderate its plans for the future. Realizing that it would be left without a manned space program after a decade of developing experience in astronaut operations. NASA looked for other uses to which the transporter could be put.

It looked as though there would be no money to build both station and transporter so the space agency opted for a phased development plan where it would design and build the transporter and then ask Congress for money to build the big space station. By late 1971 NASA was ready with its design plan and went to the White House for permission to proceed; the administration's Office of Management and Budget, the White House purse-carrier, had blocked NASA at every turn, fearing another Apollo-type commitment which would tie up large amounts of government money.

President Nixon was joined at his San Clemente retreat by NASA Administrator James C. Fletcher who received the formal go-ahead during the morning of January 5, 1972. The new transporter would be called Space Shuttle and within ten years or so would replace the complete inventory of existing rocket launchers. Instead of merely feeding the big station, which NASA failed to secure, the Shuttle would be used to launch every satellite and space probe sent up from the surface of the Earth.

During the preceding two years, NASA had carried its ideas to the Air Force, seeking support for what it saw as the only hope of staying in manned flight operations. What the Air Force saw was the instrument it had campaigned for long to obtain, and been denied through cancellation first of Dyna-Soar and then the Manned Orbiting Laboratory. At several meetings, Air Force and NASA personnel worked out a specification which could serve the needs of both user communities, settling on a lifting capacity at least 29.5 tons to low Earth orbit with a cross-range capability of about 2,700 km.

Cross-range was the distance the Shuttle would have to fly to compensate at the end of one full orbit for the movement of the Earth on its axis: in a 90-minute period the plant would spin east by approximately 2,700 km and the Air Force had a mission which would call for the Shuttle to land back at the launch site after one orbit. Because of this requirement, the design evolved with a double-delta wing supporting a cargo bay 18.3 m long and 4.6 m in diameter. The delta wing was necessary to allow the Shuttle to fly left or right of its ground track by the specified 2,700 km.

Following a competition, Rockwell International won the design and development contract in July 1972 and rolled the first Shuttle out of the factory doors in September 1976. That vehicle, called Enterprise, was used for air-lifted drop tests from the top of a Boeing 747, simulating the speed and descent profile when a later Shuttle returned from space.

This was one revolutionary aspect about the entire program, for where launch vehicle stages were normally thrown away at the end of the boost phase, and manned space vehicles were previously designed to fly only once back through the atmosphere, each Shuttle would be used for at least 100 missions and provide a thermal protection which could safely return the vehicle to a conventional landing. Moreover, the three main rocket engines at the rear would be reusable and throttleable so that the overall acceleration could be kept low, thus permitting ordinary personnel to fly into space.

Protection from the heat of re-entry would be provided by more than 30,000 separate "tiles" bonded to the exterior. Designed on the heat-sink principle, unlike earlier heat shields which burned away during descent, the system would remain intact for most of the Shuttle's life.

By 1979 the first flight-rated Shuttle, called Columbia, had been delivered to the Kennedy Space Center ready for tests that began with the first flight on April 12, 1981—exactly twenty years after Yuri Gagarin became the first man to orbit the earth. During the mission, a few thermal insulation tiles at the rear of the Shuttle were observed, in TV pictures from space, to have come off during the high stresses experienced during launch. To check on the status of tiles underneath the winged vehicle vital to Columbia's safe return, a KH-11 reconsat was maneuvered sufficiently close to get a look at the vehicle and confirm that all silica tiles were intact and where they should be.

The Shuttle came home to a triumphant welcome two days after launch and was back in space on November 12, 1981, the first manned spacecraft to return to orbit. Third and fourth test flights were planned for 1982 before fully operational missions could begin. Because the Shuttle is essentially a NASA project, and because there are strict lines of demarcation which prevent the civilian agency from pursuing, or significantly contributing toward, military space activity organized by the Air Force, a code of operation was set up to prevent objections from Congress or foreign governments.

Most Shuttle flights will originate from the Kennedy Space Center in Florida, using launch pads and assembly buildings set up for the Apollo Moon project, but beginning in 1986 flights will also take place from Vandenberg Air Force Base in California. The reason for the two launch sites mirrors existing rules which prevent space rockets flying over populated land. Sited, as it is, south of the eastern seaboard, the Florida base cannot accommodate launches at an orbital inclination greater than 57 degrees. Flights to polar or Sun-synchronous orbit must begin by flying south over the Pacific from California. The phased introduction of the two sites is brought about by the need fully to qualify the Shuttle under conditions of reduced stress before committing it to the higher velocity demands of the polar inclinations.

A second Shuttle (Challenger) was delivered to the Kennedy Space Center in 1982, and was to be followed by a third (Discovery) in 1983 and a fourth (Atlantis) in 1985. The third and fourth Shuttles could have a better payload capacity than the first two by incorporating additional boost motors under the main propellant tank to which the winged vehicle is attached. Baselined to a 29.5 ton lifting capacity, the augmented Shuttles could carry more than 32 tons to a due east orbit from Cape Canaveral's Kennedy Space Center, or place more than 20 tons in a polar orbit from Vandenberg. But NASA is also looking at the possibility of raising performance by increasing the thrust of the main engines and considerably reducing the weight of existing elements, thereby allowing the Shuttle to lift more cargo. Most flights will carry civilian payloads but defense missions will account for about one quarter of the total traffic model and on those flights only Air Force personnel will preside over satellites and space vehicles placed in the cargo bay. There will be no payload mixing, only dedicated missions for either NASA or Air Force use. Military missions will be paid for by the Air Force and controlled from the CSOC in Colorado, with facilities for preserving the security blanket now placed on most military space operations.

NASA estimates both users will fly a total of more than 400 Shuttle missions up to 1993, an average of one every week from 1988. About one quarter of all flights will take place from Vandenberg but these are not solely military missions for NASA, too, has several scientific and applications flights which it intends to fly to polar orbit from this site. Ordinarily, two Shuttle vehicles will operate from each launch facility, although there will be times when three are at Cape Canaveral; on average only one flight a month will leave Vandenberg from 1988.

Because the Shuttle is built to place very heavy payloads in low Earth orbit, it is effectively limited to an operational altitude of about 1,000 km, but this with a minimum payload in the cargo bay; with the maximum design load, Shuttles will not get above 400 km. This is acceptable for the basic mission. It is not good enough for medium-orbit altitudes or for stationary orbit 36,000 km above the Equator. To accommodate the increasing number of satellites designed to sit high above the planet, the Air Force has developed a supplementary solid propellant booster called the Inertial Upper Stage, or IUS. This has the ability to sit inside the Shuttle's cargo bay with the satellite or space vehicle on front. The IUS takes up less than one half the available space in the bay, allowing plenty of room for a large payload. In orbit, when the cargo doors open, the IUS and its attendant satellite are removed by an extendible manipulator arm fitted as a standard accessory to the door hinge line. Thus deposited, weightless, in space, the IUS and satellite are left alone while the Shuttle moves some distance away. Commanded to fire by instructions from the Shuttle, the IUS ignites to propel the satellite up to the desired orbit, a second stage of the IUS firing several hours later to circularize the path 36,000 km above the Equator. The IUS is capable of delivering 2.5 tons to stationary orbit or it can be attached to a previously launched IUS for moving heavier payloads.

For the next several years the basic 2.5 ton capacity will be more than enough for military satellites adopting this station; DSCS-2 communication satellites weigh about 570 kg each and the Defense Support Program 647 early-warning satellites each weight less than 1 ton. Deposited in the correct path, the satellite will separate from the IUS and go about its business.

At the other end of the scale the Air Force wants to place in comparatively low polar orbit the next Big Bird development, a reconnaissance satellite scheduled to fly from 1985 or 1986 specially built for Shuttle operations. Because the winged transporter is capable of returning to Earth with sizeable load in the cargo bay, Air Force plans envisage one Big Bird successor placed on station while another previously sent up is retrieved and brought back to the ground. This replacement operation will significantly expand the role of the big reconsats and bring man-tended operations fully into the gamut of Air Force space activity; a man-tended activity is one where orbital hardware is visited by astronauts rather than being permanently manned like a space station.

In one typical mission, the Shuttle would fly into orbit from Vandenberg and rendezvous with the Big Bird successor, remaining several hundred meters from it while the replacement vehicle is slowly manipulated out of the cargo bay and deposited in space alongside the transporter. The Shuttle would then activate the systems on the new satellite and check its operation before moving across to the existing vehicle, linking up to it via the manipulator arm and gently maneuvering it down into the cargo bay.

It is this capacity to rendevous with other satellites and return to Earth with a load in the cargo bay which worries the Soviets, who see the Shuttle as a vehicle primarily designed to pluck Russian satellites out of space and bring them down to the United States. But such an operation would be very unwise for the Russians have already shown that some of their defense satellites carry explosive packages which could be detonated in the event of piracy. There would clearly be little gain in satellite snatching.

With the Shuttle, Air Force operations receive a new and expanded opportunity for space applications and without it the newly emerging generation of laser killersats would be impossible. The heavy lifting capacity plus the availability of on-site personnel to perform intricate tasks in orbit permits comparatively weighty laser packages to fly into space. Satellites built to return to Earth in the Shuttle's cargo bay are already designed, the Big Bird successor being just one example, but the winged transporter is also important for the timely launch of new systems. Throughout the coming decade the Shuttle will fly regularly into space with replacement satellites for existing defense missions or new satellites and vehicles designed to perform tasks impossible before.

One vital application serves to exemplify the transition from expendable rockets to the new era of manned reusable space flight: the family of navigation satellites launched now by Atlas rockets but soon to be lifted into orbit by the Shuttle. And it is a fitting example too, for navigation satellites now coming into use will enormously expand the way conventional or nuclear wars are fought, simultaneously opening completely new roles for large vehicles in space.

Position information is important in a modern conflict because the technology of today's weapon systems calls for precision and accurate emplacement, either of a warhead on the target or of a mobile field unit in its location with respect to the enemy. There is little time for consolidation, or for making lengthy observations to establish an exact map position. Navigation satellites have evolved through a 20-year period to provide military personnel and equipment with a ready-reckoner on location and altitude.

Without the wealth of valuable experience from the US Navy Ship Inertial Navigation System, the nuclear Polaris missile would probably have taken twice as long to develop and may never have been as efficient as it became; without the latest generation of navsats, several modern weapons and techniques about to be deployed would find little or no application in the real world of conflict. They are arguably the single most important military development of the 1980s. The origin of the navsat stems from the Navy Navigation Satellite System (NNSS), culminating in a program called Transit by the end of the 1950s. The purpose was to provide ships with means by which they could instantly gain access to accurate position information. In effect, the use of satellites for navigation extends the age-old principles by which maritime activity broadened the Old World.

Not until accurate chronometers could be constructed for use at sea did the seafaring Europeans colonize the globe. Combined with angular variations between the Earth's horizon and a specified star, the precise time gave the navigator all the information he needed to calculate the ship's position. Likewise, because stars are not always easy to observe, the availability of a radio signal from some known point in space can significantly broaden the reference sytem. Moreover, because the same radio signal which provides a position fix on the satellite will seem to rise in frequency as the satellite approaches, and lower in frequency as it recedes, this observed Doppler shift provides information on the relative speed of the satellite compared to the ship. Through all kinds of weather, the satellite signal beams its reference and, in theory at least, the navsat should be the simplest and most effective space application. But not so in practice, for there are several unknowns or, at best, uncertainties, which confuse the calculations. It is imperative to know the precise path of the satellite if the ship's relative position to a global grid is to make any sense at all. Because the Earth carries several major gravitational anomalies, a satellite's precise path is constantly changing with respect to its previous orbit. The navigators clock may not be as accurate as he thinks (and here accuracies in seconds are far too wide), radiation pressure on the satellite may push it slightly out of position, or the Earth's atmosphere may cause signal refraction because of particles in the ionosphere or "bending" of the path length due to the satellite's apparent motion. Many of these problems were examined and met by early navsats in the Transit series, first successfully sent up by Thor-Able rocket in 1960. By 1963 the program almost disappeared in the drive to veil public awareness of space projects then being developed for military use.

The Transit satellites had various configurations but most were in the form of a sphere 90 cm in diameter weighing 100 kg, placed in orbits between 220 km and 1,300 km at inclinations varying between 28 degrees and 90 degrees. In 1965 the basic system was declared operational with a claimed accuracy of 200 m. RCA got the contract to build 15 Transit navsats but the first three performed so well that the remaining 12 are still crated in storage and may never fly in space.

The system was initially activated to provide Navy ships, and particularly Polaris submarines, with position information but the equipment proved sufficiently versatile for it to embrace many civilian and commercial projects. Transit satellites regularly feed several thousand receivers around the globe not only to military users but also to merchant ships, cable-laying ships and off-shore oil rigs. The operational navsats are in polar orbits about 1,100 km above Earth. A second generation Transit called Nova is also being built by RCA Astro-Electronics, designed to fill US Navy requirements until the end of the decade. Weighing 167 kg, each Nova comprises a main octagonal body 52 cm in diameter, topped by a 27 cm diameter attitude control section, total length of the dual cylinder being 116 cm. Four solar cell panels are attached to the main body for electrical energy and a 7.9 m long scissors boom provides gravity gradient stabilization;

this technique allows the long axis of the satellite to point continuously at the Earth by aligning two masses, separated by a boom, with the center of the planet, thereby conserving attitude control gas otherwise expended for pointing control.

Three Nova satellites will begin operations in the early 1980s, but all will be sent aloft on Scout solid propellant rockets. Another navigation satellite of a very different type will move to Shuttle operations within the next three years. Where Transit and Nova class satellites provide the US Navy with the global reference system essential for submarine operations around the world, the expanded requirements of Air Force operations have made it necessary to look for a more sophisticated system. One through which fast moving aircraft can obtain immediate position fixes flying very low across hostile territory, one in which ballistic missiles can update their inertial guidance system, one in which cruise missiles can receive new guidance equations, and a system equally at home feeding navigation coordinates to a portable "man-pack" strapped to a soldier's back. The Navy Transit Program was supplemented by a few experimental Timation satellites, three of which were sent aloft between 1967 and 1974 to pioneer new and more accurate methods of operation. From this, and the pressing needs of the Air Force, it became apparent that a more precise system was indeed possible and that the combined needs of the four armed forces (Army, Navy, Air and Marine) should be met with a common program.

Through work in the Defense Navigation Satellite Development Program, systems requirements evolved for a unified capability and in 1974 the Navstar Global Positioning System (GPS) came into being. Through a constellation of 18 satellites in three equally spaced orbital rings inclined 63 degrees to the Equator, position information would be available in three axes with an accuracy of 16 m. It would also be possible to determine speed to within 0.2 km/hr. Each Navstar satellite—the entire constellaton is being built by Rockwell International—carries three extremely accurate rubidium atomic clocks for generating the evenly spaced binary pulses used during navigation. They are accurate to within one second every 36,000 years.

Four satellites are necessary for each navigational computation and because the user's receiver operates in a passive mode, reference to the continuously beamed Navstar signal will not disclose the position of the operator. The set will automatically select the four Navstar satellites most favorably positioned in the sky and lock on to their signals to compute the approximate range. Four equations will then be formed: the three axial coordinates of the user's position and the clock bias factor. A mini-computer will solve the equations for the operator's position and the time and determine his speed.

A shaped-beam helical antenna array on one end of the spaceframe transmits a signal to blanket the Earth. Electrical power is provided from two solar cell arrays designed to swivel and track the Sun as the satellite points Earthward. The main frame carries a solid propellant rocket motor for providing the final push necessary to get the satellite in its appropriate path and 18 hydrazine attitude control thrusters keep it pointing in the necessary direction.

Launched by an Atlas F rocket to an initial elliptical path, each Navstar weighs 759 kg when separated from its launcher, reduced to 455 kg when the solid motor finally fires to put it in a circular path nearly 20,200 km above Earth.

The first Navstar was launched on February 22, 1978, joined by four more over the next two years. The full complement of 18 satellites, ensuring that the requisite four are available at all times for any user anywhere on Earth, should be in full operational use by 1987, providing longitude, latitude and altitude information on demand; full availability of longitude and latitude information should be accessible two years before that, however.

From early 1985, Navstar satellites will fly into space aboard the Shuttle's cargo hold, attached to a simple solid-propellant boost stage to carry the satellite up to its circular orbit altitude. At apogee the on-board rocket motor will fire as normal to circularize the path. The boost stage selected will be cheaper and less complex than the Air Force's Inertial Upper Stage, probably comprising a commerical solid propellant booster like the one being developed by McDonnell Douglas for civilian satellites using the Shuttle. Called the Spinning Solid Upper Stage (SSUS), it will have the capacity to propel to stationary orbit satellites weighing more than 1 ton.

The world-wide service provided by Navstar will affect every branch of all four armed services. Between 1981 and 1987, when the system will be fully activated, many tests are planned both to flex the GPS constellation and demonstrate new applications. Tests really began in 1974 when a Navigation Technology Satellite, the first of several, ascended for a trial run of equipment then being considered for the

GPS program. A second NTS satellite went up three years later and helped solve several deficiencies in operating practice experienced with the first.

With a unit system life of at least five years, and satellites replaced by Shuttle when necessary, the GPS will carry responsibility for shaping applications only theoretically possible hitherto. Richard Schwartz, Rockwell's Navstar program manager, claims that "we are setting out to prove the largest operational satellite program ever undertaken." He bases this claim on the premise that Navstar will itself provide services unique to GPS users and that those users may not always be manned vehicles controlled by human hands and brain.

Colonel Bradford Parkinson is the Air Force Navstar manager and confidently expects "over 20,000 daily military users of the system." And on the question of what Navstar can support, Colonel Parkinson believes: "The applications of this system are limited only by our imaginations. Who can project the benefits of a system where anyone, at any time, can determine their exact location by just pushing a button?"

Some of those applications have already been tried out. In one test, the GPS satellites were used from Camp Pendleton, California, to guide a Marine Corps landing craft from an off-shore position across 2 km of water to within 25 m of the planned beach landing spot. Without sight or sound of shore, the landing craft was brought to the beach on instructions from the Navstar signal. In another demonstration, the Air Force brought a Phantom aircraft to rendezvous with a Lockheed C-141 simulating an aerial tanker, without either aircraft transmitting a signal. And in further applications, again involving a C-141, two parachute drops brought cargo down to the ground within 20 m of the target, on navigation release signals from Navstar.

In more complex simulations of combat activity, GPS receiver sets will be used aboard a massive B-52 bomber accurately to place bombs on target without any radar signal generated from the aircraft, two General Dynamics F-16 fighters will home in on mock intruders with the aid of GPS receivers, and a Grumman A-6 will rendezvous and land on an aircraft carrier using nothing but the Navstars in orbit to find the carrier's known position. In all examples, the ability of a manned device to move to where it is supposed to be at a specific time, without propagating a signal, is a unique demonstration of the expanded role for navigation satellites. It is the first project to see a phased transition from expendable launcher to reusable Shuttle.

Future operational roles embrace the use of Navstar for accurately guiding tactical battlefield missiles to their targets, placing MIRV warheads on planned coordinates, and positioning cruise missile trajectories around mobile anti-aircraft batteries sensed by the reconsats. In this way, Navstar is the first space application significantly to relieve the ground-based command structure from control of individual weapon systems. Within the next five years, aircraft will enter hostile airspace, submarines will slip into territorial waters of a foreign state, and missiles will be programmed to their targets on information available from Navstar.

In other applications now being energetically researched, Navstar will be used by other satellites for obtaining very accurate position information impossible to acquire from the Earth's surface. For instance, it is doubtful whether hot-kill anti-satellite weapons now planned for the 1990s would reach stationary orbit targets on direct ascent by Minuteman or Trident launchers if guidance commands steered the warhead from Earth.

Launched to a general target zone on stored commands placed aboard the rocket seconds prior to launch, Navstar would take over in space and talk to the final stage for terminal guidance accurately to bring the hot-kill head to the target's vicinity; from there the active radar seeker in the weapon itself would take over and home in. In this way, through a sequence of diminishing target gates, the hot-kill device could successfully hit a satellite only a few meters across along a flight path at least 36,000 km long.

In another application, defense satellites may in future carry a propulsion system for moving out of the path of a hostile device launched from the ground. The target satellite, perhaps an early-warning or communications satellite, would pick up information on the ascending vehicle from transmitters on the ground and receive from Navstar precise position information necessary to move away and then return to the same location.

The need for one satellite to know the exact position of another assumes major importance when, concurrent with the hot-kill stationary orbit device, medium-altitude battlesats patrol the space lanes with their deuterium-fluoride laser. There will emerge, at that time, an intra-space dialogue between highly sophisticated satellites and space vehicles not only communicating and controlling their own electronic command systems at the speed of light, but dealing a death burst from laser weapons killing at the speed of light also.

However, while navigation satellites in the GPS program promise to revolutionize combat operations on the ground and in space, Navstar is but one program now planned for flights aboard the Shuttle. For in the wake of killersats, battlesats, and anti-satellite weapons stored in space, the ordinary business which attracts such hostility goes on. And in an increasingly sophisticated manner. Most programs, if not all, reflect increasing concern for the implied hostility of Soviet killersats and for ground-based jamming or electronic-counter-measures aimed at low- and medium-orbit satellites. Several experiments on LES satellites planned and operated by the Air Force demonstrate the ability of systems and electronics to be effectively hardened against the attack. It may superficially seem a foregone conclusion that once hit by a laser gun the outcome is inevitable. But this is not so and several tests show the comparative ease of building a defense cover for sensitive satellites.

Tests carried out by the Russians point suspiciously toward projected capabilities for using a laser to knock down cruise missiles; the Soviet preoccupation with air defense of the Russian homeland has led defense staffs far up the road to countering mass intrusion. As an adjunct of that work it now seems feasible that the Russians can eliminate the eyes and ears of reconsats from ground-based laser sites. To protect US communicaton and early-warning satellites, systems engineers have adopted a variety of subtle tricks to evade the *coup de grâce* which may inevitably come in the opening minutes of an attack.

While it is not yet possible completely to hide the presence, or the identity, of an active satellite broadcasting information to the ground, it is possible to displace a decoy, or electronic shadow, of that satellite to one side or the other so that an offensive killersat would head for the mirage and not the actual hardware. But most defense measures now being taken for the satellites designed to fly in the remaining years of this decade adopt more conventional methods.

Frequency-switching is a capability designed to prevent jamming by programming a jump from one transmitted frequency to another at unannounced intervals on a schedule known only to the operators. In this way the opportunity for electronic ferreting is strictly limited and this provides an added advantage. Also, the physical design of future satellites takes account of possible hostilities aimed at the device although there is little that can be done to protect solar cells and other sensitive equipment. In fact, research into one natural phenomenon has stimulated proposals for another way of disabling a stationary orbit satellite. At an altitude of 36,000 km satellites collect an electrostatic charge due to asymmetric electron densities around Earth. Induced by solar activity, magnetic storms build up on the exterior of the spacecraft a charge of several thousand volts which can discharge through equipment carried as part of the sensor or communications payload. Several satellites, military and civilian, suffer these effects at stationary orbit altitude and considerable research has revealed a method of eliminating this charge by firing a beam of negative ions at the affected structure in much the same way a beam of ions can eliminate static on a commercial record disc. But tests have also shown that it is quite possible to build rather than dissipate a positive charge by firing an appropriate beam of cations at the satellite. Ion beams suitably adapted for the purpose are a branch development of tests on natural disturbances which could in the future lead to satellites equipped with their own de-energizing systems. By turning the negative beam into an ion gun, the system could be employed as an anti-killersat device capable of disabling the intruder before it reached its target. This would only apply to hot-kill devices designed to impact the target, for a laser-equipped battlesat would be expected to carry long-range capability outside the ion beam's range.

In other areas of attack monitoring, Navstar satellites are being equipped with radiation monitors to detect any attempt at using enhanced-radiation weapons to saturate the electronics; if a Navstar should fail, analysis of the dying telemetry would reveal if the systems malfunctioned because of a fault or because the satellite was hit by a wave of fast neutrons. Such discrimination could tip the balance in a time of crucial international stress.

Already, a new generation of hardware designed to replace existing or currently planned satellites carries one or other of the various hardening concepts developed by systems and design engineers. All of them will be sent into space by the reusable Shuttle.

North Atlantic Treaty Organization requirements project a need for NATO-4 satellites by the middle of the decade and specifications include a lifetime of at least ten years, a major increase in the capacity over the NATO-3 series, additional propellant and battery power for translating from one stationary orbit position to another on command, and the capacity to work with a greater number of ground stations. Interoperative communications with the new DSCS-3 series global strategic command network satellites will ensure continued survival in the event of a massive jamming exercise concurrent with a pre-emptive Warsaw Pact assault.

By using frequencies adopted on US communication satellites, NATO-4 will step into the global net at the flick of a switch. Improvements to the NATO system's ground segment will introduce ten new ground terminals plus two mobile stations for the Allied Command Europe, effectively following the example set by US defense communications where the vast majority of circuits go by satellite, lifting hardware from the vicinity of the battlefield into space.

NATO-4 series satellites will be designed exclusively for the Shuttle, taking advantage of its greatly relaxed launch environment compared with the extremes of a conventional rocket flight; the Shuttle will be limited to a maximum 3 g acceleration and the proud boast is that anyone or anything capable of surviving an airliner flight will safely ride out a Shuttle launch!

But the fourth generation NATO communication satellites are not the first to be built specifically with the Shuttle in mind. That pride of possession belongs to Hughes Communication Services Inc., a wholly-owned subsidiary of Hughes Aircraft Company, awarded in 1978 a contract from the US Government for satellites designed to replace the Fltsatcom series. Primarily built to carry US Navy communications, Fltsatcom (see Chapter Four) carries the majority of ultra- and super-high-frequency transmissions for ships and submarines at sea. But it also carries communication traffic for the Air Force's Afsatcom program, the Navy having granted channel capacity as and when available. This unofficial "leasing" to the Air Force is in contrast to the genuine, legalized, leasing where the Navy bought reserve capacity on several commercial satellites when funding cutbacks left its own services inadequate for the traffic load. The successor to Fltsatcom formalizes leasing policy in a unique project whereby HCS Inc. designs and builds several Leasat satellites which the US Government will use for an annual fixed fee.

HCS has arranged private financing for the venture and will only receive public money when the first satellite reaches orbit. The plan envisages Leasat satellites placed at four strategic stationary orbit longitudes beginning in the mid 1980s from where Defense Department requirements for UHF communications will be met; one each over the Atlantic and Indian Oceans and two over the Pacific at 90-degree intervals. Although aimed primarily at the Navy user, Leasat will also be employed for aircraft and ground forces of the Army, Air Force and Marine Corps. Satellite control stations are being set up in Guam, Hawaii, California and Virginia and a master Hughes Communication Services command post will operate in Los Angeles under the authority of the Naval Telecommunications Command Operations Center in Washington, DC.

Leasat is a big satellite taking full advantage of the Shuttle's cavernous cargo bay, another asset for satellite designers. The Atlas-Centaur employed for launching existing Fltsatcom satellites has a payload shroud allowing a 2.7 m diameter satellite to be carried inside while the Titan 3C, currently the Defense Department's most powerful launch vehicle, can accommodate 3 m wide payloads. But the Shuttle's 4.6 m diameter cargo bay affords optimum design opportunities and Hughes have designed Leasat to take almost all the available space.

With a diameter of 4.2 m, Leasat comprises a cylindrical hat-box structure 4.3 m tall, including large helical antennae on top which, when extended, give the satellite a height of nearly 6.2 m. Solar cells wrapped round the exterior ensure a minimum power level of 1,260 Watts after five years of use. Leasat incorporates several propulsion systems for pushing itself out to stationary orbit, circularizing its path at that altitude, and making minor adjustments to attitude and position. Spin-stabilized to maintain an Earth-pointing attitude, Leasat will be lifted to an initial parking orbit of 296 km by the Space Shuttle. Ejected by two springs, the satellite will be further spun up to about 30 rpm by small rocket thrusters operating on hydrazine propellant. Thus released, a solid propellant rocket motor will fire for 60 seconds to propel the satellite from low orbit to an elliptical path with an apogee of 36,000 km. This motor, buried within the cylindrical structure, is a modified third stage propulsion unit from a Minuteman 3 missile. When it burns out, a liquid propellant system takes over and provides the final push through two engines similar in design to rocket motors once used to control the attitude of Apollo spacecraft. At apogee, 36,000 km above Earth, the motors fire again to raise the perigee and circularize the path. An internal section of the satellite is spun in the opposite direction to the main body of the structure, effectively de-spinning the portion which carries the Earth-pointing antennae. The de-spun section also contains the telemetry, command, and communications equipment. At release from the Shuttle, Leasat would have weighed nearly 6.9 tons but after propelling itself to stationary orbit the satellite has a mass of only 1.3 tons. From that high position above Earth, the communications equipment will provide 13 separate UHF channels in the frequency range from 244 to 317 MHz. Like NATO-4 series satellites, Leasat will be required to operate for a design life of ten years, fast becoming the standard requirement now most of the teething troubles have dissipated from advanced satellite systems. Leasat is the first satellite which simply has to fly by Shuttle, for the very large diameter cannot be accommodated by any expendable launch vehicle available today or in the future.

Another program expected to benefit from the broader capabilities of the Shuttle would provide the Air Force with its own dedicated Afsatcom hardware rather than having transponders fly on other satellites like Fltsatcom; Afsatcom, readers will recall from Chapter Four, provides airborne communications primarily for polar routes flown by nuclear strike forces. Under a Strategic Satellite System (SSS) plan, special satellites in polar orbit would convey voice and data transmissions between the National Command Authority and aircraft, ICBM command posts, and nuclear submarines. About 25 channels would be available on each satellite and of this total, 15 would serve UHF needs while the other ten operated on SHF (super-high frequency) or EHF (extremely-high-frequency) bands.

Current UHF polar communications go via Satellite Data System spacecraft with a 12-channel capacity and existing Fltsatcom satellites in stationary orbit. SDS satellites carry the brunt of today's airborne communications on the exposed polar routes B-52 bombers would fly in the event of a major nuclear exchange. But these satellites are limited by the capabilities they possess already and SSS is projected as a network which would allow messages and information to be transferred from one side of the globe to the other without going via ground stations likely to be destroyed in the opening hours of war. Moreover, a completely autonomous spaceborne communications capability at UHF frequencies would play a major part in keeping channels open amid the massive electronic blockade expected from the Soviets in time of conflict; passed from one satellite to another, messages would only return to Earth when they arrived at the place of destination. Currently, Afsatcom needs are compromised by having to lease capacity from, or place transponders on, satellites designed for a completely different purpose. A Strategic Satellite System would do for the Air Force what Leasat should accomplish for Navy and Marine forces.

A truly novel aspect of the Strategic Satellite System is a plan to deploy a constellation of four satellites in the same polar-orbit plane but separated from each other by 90 degrees along the circumference of the orbital path, circling the Earth at a distance of more than 201,000 km. This is the most distant orbit ever used for military hardware, a path more than half-way to the Moon, and has been designed to safely place the satellites away from potential killersats. In this type of path, they would take 11 days to make one full orbit of the Earth, allowing prolonged use of each satellite over specific areas.

Tests carried out from LES satellites using EHF transmitters in Massachusetts show valuable capacity for countering the threatened jamming posed by Soviet systems deployed world wide for such tasks. In one example, an Earth antenna 3 m in diameter, radiating a 1,000-Watt signal, attempted to jam an 0.5-Watt signal from a 1.2 m diameter antenna broadcasting an EHF transmission to the satellite. It was unable to prevent the EHF signal getting through, demonstrating that a jammer operating at several thousand times the power of the terminal could not inhibit communications. This is a vital asset for Air Force needs. Moreover, the signals are not easily propagated down through the dense layers of the atmosphere. But for military users, that does not matter since the communicating aircraft would be high above the heavy moisture levels which attenuate the signals. It does, however, require an enemy jammer to penetrate what is in reality a very narrow spot beam.

The already burgeoning defense space budget is unable to contain all the new developments planned for the next few years and wherever possible the Pentagon is matching low priority civilian needs from outside agencies to its own high-priority requirements. In this way, a project gets the greatest support from the widest user community when it comes before Congress for money.

Currently, the submarine with its ballistic missile payload is the only strategic force against which there can be little opportunity of defense. If, however, a system capable of discriminating between water containing a large sub-surface boat and that devoid of anything more strategically relevant than a shoal of fish can be developed effectively, the under-sea deterrent can be eliminated. It would be a major breakthrough in naval warfare and expose almost every submarine in use to offensive attack at known locations.

The expanding Soviet commitment to undersea operations has been demonstrated by the Delta 3 submarine equipped with 16 SS-N-18 launch tubes, each missile capable of firing three MIRV warheads a distance of nearly 17,000 km. In 1980 the massive "Typhoon" Class submarine, with 20 SS-N-20 missiles, appeared on sea trials for the first time; it has a displacement nearly three times that of the Polaris- and Poseidon-equipped submarines operated by the US and British Navies and is half as big again as America's new "Ohio" Class carrying Trident missiles.

The return to earth of defense satellites in need of refurbishment or repair promises great savings, and before the end of the decade the Air Force hopes to have a special maneuvering unit designed to propel itself to a high orbit and bring down to the Shuttle's altitude satellites and space vehicles near the end of their useful lives. In this way many useful components could be recovered, or systems and sensors in need of repair could be replaced without bringing the complete satellite back to Earth; retrieved by the maneuvering unit and temporarily locked into the cargo bay, engineers could work on the offending hardware before returning the satellite to its original path.

In every way the issue is measured, future space defense needs can be met only with the reusable Shuttle. Without its copious payload capability none of the vital services planned for this decade would be possible. Without its capacity to carry men to the space environment, and without its ability to rendezvous with, inspect, service, or return to Earth, satellites already in space, there would be little practicality in research and development programs aimed at providing laser defense, killersats and the patrolling battlesats for space defense.

But the United States is not alone in expanding the inventory of roles for military space projects. The Soviet Union, aware of its own much bigger launch schedule which annually puts around 100 satellites into space, has worked to develop a Shuttle of its own for more than a decade. Observed in reconsat images and photographed by other sources, Russia's Raketoplan is likely to make its debut in space within the next two years. Smaller than the US Shuttle, probably no more than one-third its size, Raketoplan will be lifted into space on top of a conventional expendable boost rocket. It will probably carry a crew of two or three at most, compared to the Shuttle's maximum seven persons, and very little cargo.

The prime function of Raketoplan is to develop reusable systems for more advanced recoverable transporters planned for the early 1990s. As an interim vehicle, however, it will deliver limited quantities of cargo and supplies to orbiting space stations and provide a research tool for controlled descent through Earth's atmosphere. Delta-winged like the Shuttle, Raketoplan will have a limited maneuvering capability and is expected to land on a conventional runway. Already, full-scale models of Raketoplan have been drop-tested from large Soviet aircraft and the program seeks to gain contemporaneity with the Shuttle, thereby achieving a political advantage.

Unlike the Shuttle, however, Raketoplan has no chance of replacing existing rockets as satellite launchers, for it is too small to accommodate roles now pressed upon the Soviet Union by scientific developments in the field of nuclear and particle physics. Over the past decade, Russia has worked to develop the tool by which the nuclear stalemate could be smashed. Not by limiting, or descaling, offensive capability of strategic proportions but rather by the introduction of a weapon so unbelievably powerful that it could directly threaten all life on Earth.

7. The ultimate threat

Particle Beam Weapons and new military uses for space

"Any nation which deployed three dozen of these first-generation chemical laser stations would be able to permit or deny, to the rockets of any other nation, the privilege of entry into space." So opined Senator Malcom Wallop before the Institute for Foreign Policy Analysis, early in 1980, referring to results of studies carried out on the vulnerability of missile warheads streaking through space to their targets below. "If the system made a mistake in peacetime, the worst it could do would be to shoot down one of the Soviet Union's attempts to launch a weather satellite. We could apologize and pay for it. On the other hand, we could be confident that the system could keep clouds of missiles from descending on us."

It was the latest proposed application of a technology spurred by fears of Soviet supremacy in laser weapons and it opened the possibility of basing powerful lasers in space literally to vaporize the opposition, ascending over the horizon in the form of several thousand nuclear-tipped warheads. Yet for all the profound implications to the balance of power such a weapon would have on East-West attitudes, the space-based, anti-ballistic-missile (ABM) laser, was but a poor cousin to significantly more sinister developments already taking shape in the United States and the Soviet Union.

There is today, a race unlike anything yet witnessed on Earth before; the winner will have power over the ability of all other nations to wage war, in turn possessing control over military activity across the globe. There are but two contestants and both are shackled to the chase. A decade ago the probability of beam-weapons becoming a realistic proposition before the end of this century was low, in fact it was almost non-existent. But inevitably, in the development of a radical new form of conflict, fear that a potential adversary might get the weapon first excited scientific attention through defense projects

205

funded at government level. In a mood of suspicion and utter disbelief, the US Air Force intelligence machine assembled, in the early 1970s, information on the existence of a Soviet particle beam program. All but ridiculed by the CIA and the Defense Intelligence Agency, their conclusions were denied validity and interpretations were placed upon the evidence to convince analysts reluctant to agree on Soviet supremacy that the observed facilities were research establishments for nuclear power.

The United States had tried to develop a particle beam program under the code name See Saw, funded by the Defense Advanced Research Projects Agency a decade before. Following several years of limited success the effort was abandoned and in a manner typical of so many conclusions reached by US defense experts, if America found it difficult to develop this revolutionary concept then surely nobody else was any closer to success. It was a pitifully naïve excuse, for while America lacked the moral or political will to build super-weapons the Soviet Union had no such qualms and poured large sums of money into a vigorous beam program.

Because the charged-particle device is similar in application to the laser, these and microwave propagators are grouped under the general category of directed-energy weapons. With their macroscopic overview of related technologies peripheral to the central development, all three were studied by Russia's nuclear physicists under that common research heading.

A particle beam is a directed flow of high-energy particles. Electrons, protons or ions are given large quantities of energy by acceleration, usually in an electric field, provided through a linear or cyclotron device of immense size. If, however, the energy inducement is enhanced, perhaps by the injection of electrons as suggested by Soviet physicist Gersh I. Budker more than 20 years ago, the electromagnetic energy released from a proton accelerator within a weak magnetic field will crush the beam and allow the device to propel the particles at enormous energy levels.

Other methods are available, embedding a proton within an electron ring accelerated in a manner selected by Vladimir I. Veksler being one. The physics behind such ideas have been around for some time and fiction writers consistently adopted the beam-weapon, or the ray-gun, as an ultimate device for destruction. Travelling close to the speed of light, sub-atomic particles slamming into molecular structures produce effects varying from heat to vaporization. In this they are similar to laser devices, but possess better potential range limits and can work more effectively through the atmosphere.

Unfortunately, they can be deflected by magnetic fields, tend to be unstable, and require enormous quantities of electrical power. It is largely because of this latter need that physicists have been cautious about weapons application. A typical beam weapon would require an energy level of 1,000 billion joules per pulse (where a joule is a unit of work done in one second by a 1 amp current flowing through a resistance of 1 ohm) and particle energies of at least 1,000 million electron volts. But where such physics seemed to daunt defense scientists in the United States, the Soviet Union put its research facilities to work on several separate development packages each one of which would provide an important piece of the beam-weapon jigsaw.

Gradually, from the early 1970s, Air Force intelligence began picking up details of this program and because of its fragmented nature, pessimists in America preferred to believe that the assembled picture was being put together in the wrong way. A minority believed that Russia was assembling the tools for weapon tests expected to begin in the early 1980s and they kept up a campaign within the tightly controlled intelligence network to convince others of this possibility. The evidence was certainly ambiguous, although convinced of the advanced Soviet physics program—international conferences exposed the uncompromising lead attained by Russia in several beam-related fields—an observer could easily convince himself of the revolutionary new developments.

The most effective application of the beam weapon would be in the ABM role, neutralizing incoming warheads before they reached their targets and effectively screening the home country from ballistic missile attack. This would have the most profound significance for the concept of mutually-assured destruction, giving one country the power to blackmail all others. It was because of this that observers viewed with dismay the application of a test site at Azgir to beam weapons development.

Under the direct control of General P.F. Batitskiy, a Marshal of the Soviet Army, Azgir was operated by the PVO Strany national air defense force and any such application of a beam device to this center had obvious intent. But it was at the high-energy physics research establishment at Semipalatinsk that the real work was perceived.

Since the late 1960s, Soviet scientists had been working here to advance several technologies essential to realizing advanced physical possibilities. In fact, nearly 20 years earlier, atom spy Dr Klaus Fuchs had passed to the Russians details of work conducted on Britain's atomic research facilities that showed great promise with particle beam devices. Soviet physicist Andrei Sakharov used this work as the basis for his own research into explosive generation of electricity. Energy propagation, accelerator machines and electron injectors were central developments on the road to a breakthrough. Situated about 60 km south of Semipalatinsk, the facility had been built for a variety of related weapons developments, all exotic and every one dependent on advanced scientific fields. To the distant south-west lay the Sary Shagan facility where anti-ballistic-missile technology evolved throughout the '60s and '70s but at Semipalatinsk the evolution of new warheads was carried out underground, helping to mask the real intent of physicists employed on beam weapons. Several large buildings were observed by reconnaissance satellites and the regular movement of large vehicles and trucks, the establishment of work facilities and laboratories, and the transfer of equipment and supplies was steadily monitored by orbiting US satellites. Surrounding what was presumed to be a large particle accelerator, observers saw a building, 61 m wide and 213 m long, with reinforced concrete walls 3 m thick. The test area associated with the research facility, remote from other constructions at Semipalatinsk, was secured by additional wire fencing and extra guards. Not too far from the main building, the satellites began to observe unusual activity at the facility as four very large holes were dug into the ground. Boring through solid granite, engineers set up winch gear on towers over each hole and brought up material excavated from a bell-shaped void being gouged out below the surface. This underground chamber was occupied by two very large spheres, put together with several steel gores fabricated some distance away and brought to the winch heads separately over several weeks. Physicists examining the hardware in photographs returned to the United States believed this work to support magnetohydrodynamic or closed cycle gas core fission components essential to developing large beam weapons of the type which could be used for ABM screens. Then the satellites picked out long underground pipes laid down around the construction site, and several concentric rings were seen surrounding the single large building believed to contain the accelerator or the electron injector gun. On one routine observation of the site, reconsats picked out several large trucks and tank cars loaded with liquid hydrogen, interpreted by some as a cooling medium for drift tubes up to 1 km in length. There was immediate debate among the few privileged personnel investigating this intelligence as to how the Soviets could use such a dangerous gas for this purpose. But the Russians have for several years published scientifc papers outlining how they employ this technique already for several physics experiments.

Putting the evidence together into a coherent package, and receiving a breakdown of what each piece of hardware could be made to accomplish in the opinions of acknowledged experts, Air Force intelligence came up with a projected research plan believed to be under way at the facility. From what was thought to be a fission generator underground—electricity obtained from nuclear explosions—large cables would transfer the energy to nearby transformers, increasing the power for use in large capacitors at one end of the building. With the collective accelerator and the electron gun laying along one complete side of the 213 m long laboratory, power would be fed in to stimulate a beam of charged protons, bent through a system of mirrors along the pumped drift tubes operating in a vacuum to simulate space. There was debate among some analysts about the possibility of transferring such large quantities of power along cables, scientists at the Livermore Laboratory were openly sceptical about the methods, until it was learned the Russians acquired this technology from industrial processes developed in the United States for quite another purpose! Explosive generation of electricity had been pioneered by the dissident Andrei Sakharov and Soviet physicist Andrei Terletsky, once employed as a KGB agent in Sweden, and the methods were well researched by Russian scientists. In a tour of US nuclear research facilities, Soviet physicist Leonid I. Rudakov described several very advanced techniques of releasing energy by compressed fusion, capabilities then outside the scope of US facilities. It represented almost a quantum leap in the ability to generate massive quantities of electrical energy, stunned US scientists at Livermore and the governments's Energy Research and Development Administration (later the Energy Department), opened the very real possibility of charged beam weapons technology.

The ability to store enormous quantities of energy was considered another area where the Soviets would fail; evidence, said the pessimists, that Russia simply could not mount an operation of the type suggested by the Air Force intelligence network. But careful digging in files revealed methods employed by the Soviets for some time using very large water capacitors to contain under high pressure as much as 40 times the energy stored by other methods in use outside Russia. Using water as the dielectric, the Russians had solved the problem. Only then was the technology proved in a contract let by the Defense Department for use in America. But how could the Russians switch enormous power loads from the capacitors to the electron gun? Scientists revealed work already patented by a small US company proving the feasibility of power-switching techniques which, although not proof that the Russians have actually developed this ability, certainly removed theoretical obstacles. Having got the power in usable form this far along the chain, what of the formidable technologies embraced by the electron gun itstelf? US scientists refused to believe the Russians could conceivably evolve stable pulses of at least 100 million electron volts at the required energy level. But the High Energy Physics Institute at Novosibirsk has been operating small-scale equipment for many years and, if applied to the larger requirements at Semipalatinsk, scientists now believe the same principles would work well.

Then, in 1976, an early-warning satellite in stationary orbit over the Indian Ocean picked up tests with a very powerful fusion-pulsed magnetohydrodynamic generator at Azgir not far from the Caspian Sea, an experiment conducted in an underground chamber in the desert salt domes. Moreover, as predicted by Air Force intelligence, early-warning satellites detected large quantities of gaseous hydrogen with small amounts of tritium drifting through the upper atmosphere from Semipalatinsk on several separate occasions. If the facility did indeed use large quantities of hydrogen to evacuate the long drift tubes and to cushion the nuclear explosion generator, emissions would be an inevitable by-product. This was one area the Soviets could not conceal and it was seen repeatedly from November 1975. The signature of each emission was characteristic only of this type of release which would be made from tests like this, with xenon and krypton being present also.

In January 1978 a series 647 early-warning satellite detected thermal activity in the Semipalatinsk area and a US weather satellite backed this up several days later by sensing nuclear debris over the Aleutians. Plots of the airborne drift showed it to have come from the Semipalatinsk area and a search was immediately made of seismic records. Neither the conventional earthquake monitors nor defense sensors implanted in the ground to pick up nuclear explosions revealed any such detonations, although measured amounts of radioactivity would indicate a bomb five times the size of that dropped on Hiroshima. The only conclusion, based on other evidence of activity at the Semipalatinsk site, was that micro-explosions involving power generation had been carried out underground. And then from Sweden came similar evidence that the Russians were developing high-energy technology when, on five specific occasions, scientists measured levels of radiation uncharacteristic of any known nuclear detonation. Moreover, test facilities at Sarova near Gorki were observed to be working toward particle beam operations in support of the type of weapon suited to the anti-ballistic-missile defense role. Under the direction of Soviet physicist M.S. Rabinovich from Moscow's Lebedev Institute, a major particle beam development program emerged at Sarova in the late 1970s when an advanced electron beam accelerator came into operation. Where Semipalatinsk was the home of nuclear and particle physics to prove the concept, Sarova would perhaps become the headquarters of weapons applications. Under the tutelage of A.I. Pavlovskiy, a new accelerator came into use at Sarova designed to beam high-energy protons at 10 million electron volts with a 100 nanosecond pulse duration (a nanosecond equals one thousand millionth of one second).

In gathering together the abundant evidence pointing to Soviet beam-weapon developments, the Air Force intelligence personnel compiled a dossier of Russian achievements in physics and nuclear technology. With this and the reconnaissance data, Air Force intelligence personnel led by General Keegan presented their conclusions to the CIA and the Defense Intelligence Agency. The CIA's Nuclear Intelligence Board, when confronted with the prospect of having to admit the US deficiencies on such a wide scale, refused to accept the suggestion and interposed their own analysis that Semipalatinsk was an advanced nuclear energy research facility and nothing more. When confronted with "scientific" opinion that there were insurmountable barriers to the development of beam weapons, the Air Force intelligence group sought the judgement of specialists unconcerned with the complete package but who could proffer comment on the technical steps en route to such a capability. Keegan found agreement at every level that the Russians could, indeed probably had, passed all hurdles necessary to test such a device by the early 1980s. By systematically setting up review groups formed from small numbers of young scientists, the intelligence experts gathered evidence that more senior personnel were unwilling to admit. The young physicists were able to demonstrate how every step of the development process could be, and probably already had been, solved by the kind of work generally accepted as being under way in Russia. Nuclear physics was one area of scientific exchange where US scientists had had a good chance to observe research on civilian or energy-related projects. For a time after Rudakov announced major development strides on electron beam energy conversion, Western scientists were barred from Soviet facilities; the Russian physicist had clearly spoken out of turn and most of the research facilities, although nothing to do with directed-energy weapons development, were closed to US visitors. Gradually, having rearranged their work assignments and reviewed the specific areas of research involving peaceful versus military activity, the Russians opened the usual channels once more. But through it all, the nucleus of particle-beam advocates assembled to support the intelligence conclusions showed how Russian progress in so many nuclear and particle research fields would give them precisely the technology suggested by Keegan. Air Force intelligence dubbed the Semipalatinsk facility PNUT, for possible nuclear underground site, while the doubting CIA labelled it URDF-3, for unidentified research and development facility three.

General Keegan was openly opposed to down-scaling the magnitude of Soviet research in this field and has decided views about attitudes in the defense intelligence sector at large when considering Russia's military capabilities:

"Some years ago, I was the first, not to discover but to suggest, that certain extraordinary weapons development projects in the Soviet Union, far beyond anything ever undertaken in the Free World, might seriously inhibit or neutralize our strategic potential in the next decade . . . [My] experience with the US scientific community is that in its egocentricity it is functionally incapable of recognizing that the peasants behind the Potemkin facade are capable of doing something original, and originally creative, and beyond the ken and scope of our own technical capability. Persistently over the years, in our intelligence community in its tragic dependence on advice from our scientists, who tend to know very little about what's going on in the Soviet Union, there developed a propensity for these people to say 'no, they can't do it'."

Frustrated with a tradition for interpreting intelligence information to fit policies issued from the Pentagon, Air Force intelligence personnel approached CIA chief William Colby in 1975 to warn him about the impending availability of a Soviet anti-ballistic-missile screen. Colby set up special sessions with his own advisory panels and a year later, across an intense three-day period, Keegan presented fact after fact to the disbelieving group. When the secret report was issued to CIA staff members—nobody outside the Central Intelligence Agency was allowed copies—the deliberations of the advisory panels summarized that disbelief. While admitting the availability of every essential tech-nology needed to develop a particle beam weapon, they could not agree that those technologies had been assembled by Russia for just such a purpose. It was tantamount to saying that the CIA had deter-mined what the Soviets could do with their technology in the absence of Russia's awareness or interest in exploiting such a terrible device! It was fully in accord with the false, self-imposed image of a superiority in Western science which characterized so many conclusions regarding progress in the Soviet Union. Before Henry Kissinger flew to meet with the Soviets in talks leading toward SALT-2, Colby wrote him a letter advising him to be aware of "a facility [in the Soviet Union] related to nuclear functions that were unknown but that it might have high scientific application." *This was the only time a member of the White House staff, from the President to the members of the National Security Council, ever heard about suspected beam weapon develop-ment at Semipalatinsk.*

In 1977 the Air Force intelligence became a matter of public debate when General Keegan openly discussed the activity in Russia's re-search facilities. It caused a furor among scientists across the world, Russia closed its doors to reciprocal exchange of information, and the defense intelligence establishment was made to explain its scepticism about the Air Force findings. Views and opinion reflected entrenched attitudes: the majority of senior scientists doubted everything they were told about the intelligence reports; young rising physicists believed the conclusions were generally correct; the White House threw up its hands in disbelief. When approached by the influential US aerospace magazine *Aviation Week and Space Technology,* one official was re-ported to have said that: "One of the problems is that some US intelligence officials and scientists have difficulty in understanding the concepts involved. The technology is simply beyond their comprehen-sion." And of the Semipalatinsk facility concerned, he was quoted thus: "This is a case where the experimental hardware is identical to the equipment necessary to destroy an ICBM. If they can generate the charged-particle beam to test the device, the large amounts of hydrogen being burned there indicate they are, then they can generate for weapons use."

General Keegan was uncompromising about what he had gathered as evidence: "The Soviet Union . . . is 20 years ahead of the United States in its development of a technology which they believe will soon neutralize the ballistic missile weapon as a threat to the Soviet Union. It is my firm belief that they are now testing this technology."

Newly elected President Jimmy Carter, aware for the first time of suspected beam weapon technology, affirmed his own belief that "we do not see any likelihood at all, based on our constant monitoring of the Soviet Union as best we can, that they have any prospective breakthrough in the new weapons systems that would endanger the security of our country." That was on May 3, 1977. Within 18 months, the United States would put together a major five-year development plan for using particle beam weapons to defend aircraft carriers against Soviet missile attack, organize a working group of 36 senior scientists and engineers to monitor US developments in this field, and institute a broadly based development plan to get beam weapons operational as quickly as possible. Stimulus to this came in the form of tests actually carried out in space by Soviet scientists controlling unmanned and manned electron beam devices. Beginning with Cosmos 728 in 1975, and continuing with other satellites of this class as well as manned Soyuz spacecraft, Soviet physicists commenced a long-range test program of radiation experiments in space. Although on a much smaller scale than equipment under development at Semipalatinsk and Sarova, the orbital tests were a valuable part of proving the feasibility of every operational segment.

The time for vacillation and doubt was over and the US defense establishment, reluctant for so many years to accept the brunt of Soviet threats, moved quickly to set up a reciprocal development program. In 1978 the Navy sought and received funds for its Chair Heritage program designed to explore the technology of beam weapons and to plan accelerator development. While the Soviets had gone for big-power physics applications, as they had in rocket development, as they had also in nuclear bombs, the United States opted for miniaturized multi-purpose applications beams and were interested in using this development for protecting aircraft carriers at sea. Used as extensions of Continental US (CONUS) strike capability, carriers were becoming increasingly vulnerable to sea-launch cruise missiles. Not, it should be stressed, the super-sophisticated cruise weapons adopted by the United States for operational deployment in the 1980s but basically advanced versions of the old V-1 flying "buzz" bomb with guidance to carry them to a sea-borne target. With complements of up to 80 or 90 aircraft each, carriers were the fat targets of ocean warfare.

Released from Soviet cruisers, missiles of this type were being introduced with alarming speed. Where the United States' longest ranging shipboard missile could reach seaborne targets 100 km away, the new Soviet SS-N-12 could hit ships more than 470 km distant. To protect the carriers against this type of threat, particle beam weapons were soon chosen by the US Navy as a means of restoring the viability of large aircraft carriers. It was a threat worth deterring, for whereas the largest US shipboard missile carried a 225 kg warhead, six different types of Soviet cruise missile packed a punch between 1 and 2 tons. Moreover, with more than 230 Soviet ships armed with cruise missile the US Navy was outclassed ten-to-one.

Under the Navy plan, charged particle beams would be generated below decks and deflected by magnets through rotating carousels located at four or five positions on deck, drawing power from special units on board rather than tap the ship's existing generator supply. This was particle beam technology on the smallest practical scale, but implementation of the Chair Heritage program was a visible demonstration of how quickly the defense establishment responded to the exposed threat.

Propagation tests were scheduled to begin in 1980 so that high-priority development could begin to equip the fleet with anti-ship cruise missile defense weapons by the middle of the decade. Opting for a pulsed beam firing 10 nanosecond bursts every 15 microseconds, the program envisaged warhead interception out to a range of 10 km; pulsed beam propagation was necessary to cool the boundary between the flank of the pulse and the atmosphere because the beam itself would bore a hole through the air, reducing pressure along its path to just ten per cent of the normal atmospheric environment.

For its part, the Army watched with interest continued debate on the particle beam issue. Quick to exploit the technology, an Army/Los Alamos Laboratory team began work in 1978 on an anti-ballistic-missile project calling for the launch into Earth orbit of a neutral beam weapon named Sipapu, a word coined from the Indian phrase meaning sacred fire. Under physicist Edward A. Knapp, an Accelerator Technology Laboratory at Los Alamos was quickly brought into operation while the ground-based demonstrator was contracted to Austin Research Associates by the Army Ballistic Missile Defense Command.

During the second half of 1978, and at the direct behest of Congressional committees now busy monitoring rapid US beam weapon evolution, the Army shifted from a concept of intercepting ballistic missiles in the Earth's atmosphere with lasers, to space-based particle guns fired at the incoming re-entry vehicles. The response excited by Soviet development with killersat designs, whereby laser-equipped battlesats are planned for space patrol duties, was now repeated in the field of particle weapons. For just as the Soviets had moved toward a massive ground-based ABM beam, the US now selected, albeit provisionally, a preference for space-based anti-ballistic-missile particle weapons.

Studies performed for the Army mapped a preliminary schedule which envisaged development of a proton-beam weapon based on Earth but for ABM screening by 1990. There would be other duties for the orbital equivalent, of which more later. The basic Sipapu design relied upon a charge exchange cell neutralizing and accelerating a hydrogen beam. The negatively charged beam would then be collimated in a device designed to restrict its spread before being directed at the target. But technology development rather than application was very much the order of the day. The US had a lot of work to do just to reach the level of theoretical capability already possessed by the Soviets and they were early days to be definite on just what uses the new beam technology could be employed on.

There was no single statement which suddenly brought a wave of change to general scientific opinion in the United States, but between 1977 and 1979 a major transformation was completed where very few voices of dissent were heard. The great majority of senior, and junior, physicists were convinced, on close examination, that the Russians were in the final throes of putting together the elements of a big particle beam device capable of screening the Soviet Union. The US was a long way from that capability, but inertia was being acquired in the reciprocal system that would gain momentum by the early 1980s.

Central to the production of a working particle device was a means to generate large and intense beams. In a design concept known as the auto-resonant accelerator, Austin Associates came up with a device which could, theoretically, deliver the required ion beam in the 1,000 million electron volt range. It would form the basis for an intensive research effort over the next few years. But the neutral beam system preferred by the Army for Sipapu use evolved from work carried out by Soviet physicist V.G. Dudnikov of Novosibirsk's Institute of Nuclear Physics. To attempt fully to understand both the principle of operation and the potential applications of such a design, Los Alamos scientists put this meson medium-energy machine together from work conducted at the Soviet facility, widely published in the literature on nuclear and particle physics. As development work proceeded at the Army test center, scientists concentrated on the development of the charged particle device for use as a ground-based weapon and on the neutral beam weapon for space operations.

Sipapu was conceptually possible because the Shuttle provided the weight carrying capacity and the necessary internal volume to place the hardware in space. It would be impossible to contemplate launching sophisticated beam weapon hardware on top of an expendable booster where everything conducted in orbit would depend upon programmed timers or remote command. By providing a man-tended capability, the Sipapu hardware would be placed in space by several professional scientists and engineers alongside to operate it.

The ultimate, operational, Sipapu derivative would work without human attention but the preliminary test vehicles would need considerable handling in space. By 1980 development on both programs indicated the feasibility of a preliminary schedule where Sipapu would be ready, if necessary, to fly on demonstration in space by about 1985, followed five years later by the ground-based proton weapon, or charged particle device. Both would be designed to knock down incoming warheads, an objective identical to the very much larger Soviet system whose technology US scientists now believed may have been aimed too high for early deployment. If the Russians had opted for a less powerful system, albeit calling for several space-borne elements, they could easily have had such a system in orbit in 1980, some scientists believe.

During the sustained research efforts of the Navy and Army in particle beam developments, Air Force scientists looked on with interest, waiting for a technology fall-out which would point such weapons in the direction of anti-satellite plans. In 1980 the Army re-named

Sipapu to prevent offense to Indian tribes, calling its neutral, space-based ABM project White Horse. By now the Air Force was well advanced with its laser program designed to put up patrolling battlesats by the mid-1980s and decided on a cautionary line with particle beams. But where lasers were admirably suited for killing hostile vehicles aimed at the home country's defense satellites, or for knocking out military satellites owned by the opposing country, anti-ballistic-missile duties were most effectively conducted within seconds of the missile's engine being shut down en-route to the target. It is very difficult to track a ballistic missile from the time its engine stops because it no longer radiates thermal energy. By that time it has left Earth's atmosphere and is well on its way along the arched flight path which carries it far into space and back down through the atmosphere. Re-entering at speeds of about 24,000 km/hr, the warhead has only seconds to heat up through friction and reach the target zone. In those brief seconds it can be successfully located and destroyed by a fast ABM device, but the problem is compounded by the additional debris, electronic "chaff" and decoys scattered along the flight path to confuse enemy radar.

If the missile can be effectively tracked all the way through the boost phase, however, from firing off the pad or out of the silo until it exits the atmosphere, it is possible to determine with accuracy the precise target it is aimed at. If, at that time, a relatavistic weapon can zap the missile with a particle beam while the motor is still burning, and while it is still over foreign territory, chances are the hull will fall down on the land of the nation which launched it. This is because the missile will not have attained the necessary speed to fly all the way to its target. Consequently, the optimum method of eliminating an incoming missile is to cut its path short a minute or two after launch. The only conceivable way to do that is with a spaceborne particle beam weapon, for lasers have insufficient range and anti-ballistic-missiles, situated on home territory would be unable to fly round the globe before the warhead arrived on target. From space, however, looking down at the vicinity of the launch silos, a particle beam weapon could effectively knock out each missile as it ascended, not allowing a single round to exit the airspace of the country concerned. Any practical beam weapon placed in space for this purpose would be a comparatively small device, certainly a miniature equivalent of the big Soviet ground-based system, capable of delivering a blast measured in several equivalent kilograms of TNT. It would be quite sufficient, however, to neutralize the warhead and to generate harmful effects from neutrons or x-rays. It would not in itself comprise a weapon capable of waging war, merely constitute a defense screen against strategic missile attack from any other country. It would, however, significantly alter the balance of power, eliminating the opponent's short-range tactical and long-range strategic missile forces.

Yet because a particle beam weapon is unable to readily propagate radiation over great distances, there are limits placed upon the operational deployment of such a system. In weapon categories outlined by the Army for research in the technology of beam devices, scientists agreed that ranges of between 1 km and 10 km were easily achieved for ground or ship-based systems. But in space the beam range would need to be measured in several hundred kilometers at least and this calls for a more advanced form of the same technology. So in choosing to go along a road of miniaturization there may well be a price for ignoring the massive ground-based ABM device set up in Russia, that being the added time to get the necessary capability. Nevertheless, scientists are now convinced that it will be possible by the end of this decade to propagate beams 1,000 km in length from a space-based warsat designed to knock out missile heads soon after launch. But because a range of 1,000 km would require many such warsats to be in orbit around the Earth, so that they cover the complete surface from comparatively low altitude, the weight of the hardware necessary to propagate the beams and the fuel to operate them would place heavy demands on the launch system. Only the Shuttle is capable of lifting this type of equipment, needing the attention of astronauts several times before operations could begin, and a Lockheed study suggests that with a 1,000 km range per warsat the total amount of fuel necessary to ensure destruction of any missile from any area of the planet would not exceed 100 tons, assuming an efficiency of ten per cent. This is well within the lifting capacity of the re-usable transporter and should pose no logistical problems whatsoever, three flights being the most necessary to place this load in orbit.

The number of beam propagating warsats necessary to cover the entire surface of the globe, however, could reach an estimated 406 if each weapon had only a 1,000 km range, but an effective radius of five times that distance would reduce the number to a mere 21 warsats populating polar orbits spaced apart for global coverage. With an effective range of 10,000 km, only nine warsats would be needed.

Supporters of an early deployment plan for beam propagating warsats point out that even 406 satellites of this type should not daunt the operations planner; the Air Force regularly services and maintains 1,054 ICBM rounds in separate silos and about 400 manned stategic bombers, while the Navy operates more than 500 SLBMs in over 30 submarines. If the strategic importance of a particle beam warsat program, deployed as a space-borne anti-ballistic-missile screen, is such that it would completely neutralize the Soviet Union's interconti- nental strike force, such numbers are acceptable. Indeed, it could be said that this is to be preferred, for it would eliminate the need for three-quarters of the West's strategic capability. But such philosophies are the product of limited interpretation because any attempt to deploy an operational ABM system using warsats with beam technology would bring forth a swarm of Soviet anti-satellite devices designed to knock them down. In such a situation, however, the current attempt to evade annihilation by first eliminating the opponent's rocket forces would be mirrored in the warsat era by killersats designed to knock the beam weapons out of action before they could be triggered to stop the warheads ascending. Whereas at present the counterstrike weapons— ballistic ABM missiles and rocket-launched, hot-kill, anti-satellite weapons—respond at speeds of several thousands of kilometers per hour, an assemblage of battlesats and warsats would attempt to destroy each other by propagating death at the speed of light; should an anti- warsat device be launched it could be knocked out by the particle beam weapon before it reached orbit and if the device should be ground-based it would give away signs which could lead to its destruc- tion from the orbiting beam weapons before it fired its own death ray. Exchanges on this scale would be in addition to the major nuclear response for, while warsats were saturated with several hundred targets ascending at once, the killersats could get in and neutralize the beams by physically destroying the hardware in space. There is, therefore, little escape for the strategic weapons' race because nuclear and particle beam weapons would find application in respective areas of activity.

Peripheral applications of the beam weapon technology program now receiving major development funds in both super-power states would lead to anti-aircraft and anti-cruise missile weapons permanently in or- bit. Even large ships like aircraft carriers or cruisers would come under the universal threat, for beams directed at several hundred strategic warheads could equally well find targets of a more conventional type. There might, in fact, be advantage in using particle beams for this role, although they would be better located aboard ships at sea than in space because orbital weapons would threaten the ballistic missile force by implication. A space-based weapon designed to zap a cruise missile in flight through the atmosphere could also hit a ballistic warhead and would be seen as such by a potential enemy who would surely then seek a massive retaliation capability, thus politically neutralizing the effect of the beam weapon and effectively restoring the status quo at great cost for no strategic gain.

However, to return to the technology itself, what of the large power levels necessary for producing a particle beam? The Army's White Horse test project for ballistic missile defense calls for a nuclear reactor capable of providing up to 150 kW of electrical energy. Power production has traditionally been selected on weight and efficiency grounds to keep the satellite within the lifting capacity of the launcher.

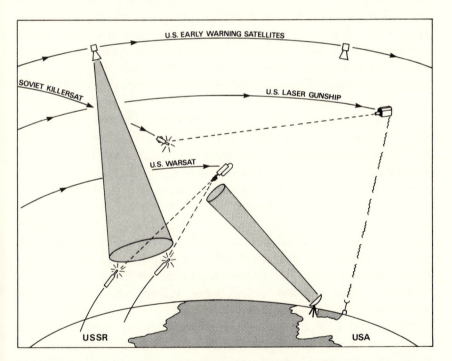

In this advanced space-warfare scenario, US early warning satellites detect the launch of Soviet strategic missiles and provide information with which a warsat can destroy them during ascent. Threatened by a Soviet killersat, the warsat is in turn protected by a US laser gunship acting on instructions from the ground with information processed from ground-based radars which have picked up the offensive killersat.

For power production over long periods at levels up to about 1 kW the solar cell is efficient. On a power/weight ratio they provide useful service lives and keep down systems costs. But solar cells are necessarily fragile and prone to contamination. Moreover, high power levels call for prohibitively large arrays on big frames spread over wide areas.

When it comes to power needs in the kilowatt range, the nuclear source becomes the most efficient. Ordinary batteries suffice for power levels up to approximately 5 kW and one-day mission life, or for low (50-Watt) power needs over a few days. But nuclear reactors for space use developed in the United States 20 years ago promised to generate up to 1,000 kW for periods exceeding two years. For various reasons, nuclear reactors were never adopted for operational satellites, although a 500-Watt reactor was sent into space experimentally in April 1965, from Vandenberg Air Force Base. Instead, the US concentrated on developing radioisotope thermoelectric generators which provide electrical energy via thermocouples attached to a radioactive core, usually of plutonium-dioxide. These two systems differ greatly; the former carries potentially very dangerous nuclear fuel while the latter can be adequately protected from distributing its dangerous products in the event of an accident.

Radioisotope generators were used to power all five scientific research stations placed on the Moon by Apollo astronauts and have been used in the past decade for electrical energy aboard Viking Mars landers and Voyager spacecraft now journeying in the outer planets. But they provide insufficient power for large military satellites using laser or beam weapon technology and the nuclear generator is the only answer. Political objection to the use of such power sources flared temporarily when Russia's Cosmos 954 plunged to Earth showering parts of Canada with radioactive debris in 1978. For a while President Carter pressed for a United Nations resolution banning nuclear reactors from space, then withdrew quietly when military advisers pointed out the repercussions of such a move.

Whereas an isotope generator produces electricity from the heat of radioactive decay, a nuclear generator uses a fuel, perhaps uranium-235, to control a fission process so that the thermal energy can be passed along to a set of thermocouples for conversion to electricity. A large amount of waste heat is produced which must be dispersed in space and an adequate radiator is essential for efficient operation. All elements of a long duration modular nuclear generator for various applications in space have been designed already by the Los Alamos Scientific Laboratory. With a potential output of at least 100 kW the device has been designed to fly into space aboard the Shuttle and, because of the potential danger should the reusable transporter fail to reach orbit, the generator will not be activated until it successfully gets on station above Earth. Uranium fuel will pose little or no hazard until the reactor begins to operate and stringent safety levels offer no obstacle to development. Adopting a basic design philosophy which requires the powerplant to account for no more than one-third the total weight of the satellite, Los Alamos has to keep the reactor down to 955 kg or less. This is determined by the lifting capacity of additional solid propellant boost stages used to send satellites from the low Shuttle orbit to stationary altitude 36,000 km above Earth. Several potential applications for this generator will call for its use on satellites in stationary orbit, for the continuing threat to satellite survivability by existing Soviet killersats has replaced sensitive solar cells with a design case for more resistant nuclear power sources. The Los Alamos reactor will find application, therefore, in passive early-warning, command and control, or communications satellites of the future, while more powerful developments are employed for directed-energy weapons.

But perhaps the most promising laser concept to solve the power problem originated when the Lawrence Livermore Laboratory conducted experimental work on the explosive generation of energy to pump excimer lasers using krypton fluoride. That led to the use of nuclear pumping sources for x-ray lasers capable of discharging a pulsed beam at 0.0014 microns. Under the code name Dauphin, Livermore set up a test program at the end of 1979 and within a year had successfully shown that a small nuclear charge detonated within a cavity would produce sufficient power through the x-ray laser to smash a target several thousand kilometers away. It was on the fringe of written science and a completely unexplored region of physics, but it would pose an almost insoluble problem for enemy missiles.

In operational satellite form, the device would comprise a small nuclear bomb placed at the center of a ring of lasing rods. When detonated, the nuclear fireball would expand and consume the satellite but not before propagating through each rod, at the speed of light, a bolt of energy, which, if directed at an ascending missile, would bore a hole right through the structure and come out the other side! It was a one-shot system because the satellite would be blown apart and vaporized, but each device could have several lasing rods, perhaps as many as fifty, which would be individually aligned with respective targets. A small force of x-ray laser warsats placed strategically in orbit could, theoretically, prevent enemy missiles from reaching their destination. Deployed with more conventional high-energy laser warsats, the nuclear-pumped x-ray satellites would present a formidable and almost impenetratable screen, leaving the former to knock out any missiles that leaked through the first layer of defense. But devices like this were for the future, and much work had to be done to bring feasibility to existing laser and particle beam technology.

By 1979 the US particle beam weapon program was a concentrated research and development effort aimed, through Chair Heritage and White Horse projects, at providing the technology for carrier defense against airborne cruise missiles and for space-based anti-ballistic-missile capability. In a recommendation to William Perry, Under-Secretary of Defense for Research and Engineering, the Defense Science Board strongly urged that a new directed energy technology office be set up to control the effort.

In the previous year, ominous signs of an even more expansive breakthrough were perceived in a move made by Soviet diplomats to halt future developments. For what the Russians had fallen upon during their massive research effort was potentially more devastating than lasers or ABM particle weapons. In applications for directed energy weapons the apparently small blast effect of the beam, while quite adequate for neutralizing metal warheads or the thin skin of an aircraft, was pitifully ineffective against large strategic targets on Earth. Facilities such as large docks or ports, factories producing large numbers of tanks or ammunition, and structures built to stand against nuclear blast were safe under the path of orbiting particle beams.

In fact, the inability to inflict widespread damage with such weapons made them suitable candidates for space operations where international agreement prevents the use of weapons capable of mass destruction. In this knowledge, US scientists were unconcerned with the high-energy effects a future generation of such weapons might have. During talks in Geneva aimed at resolving international arms issues, however, the Soviet delegation to the Committee on Disarmament drafted a proposal calling for a ban on weapons which could propagate, "charged and neutral particles to affect biological targets." The US delegation was confused about the language used because particle weapons were primarily useful in anti-ballistic-missile defense and had not been proposed for any other application, certainly nothing relating to "biological targets." Only when a group of advisory physicists examined the information did the implication come through. In their strenuous efforts to develop a massive ground-based shield against ICBM warheads, Soviet scientists had opened a chink of light on very distant applications which could lead to the orbiting in space of beam weapons capable of destroying all life on Earth. It was a horrendous possibility made plausible only by highly advanced physics at least a decade in the future, but the implication was there in Soviet scientific literature and the delegation endorsed the direction of Soviet thought by trying to use this clause to lever aside US work on all particle weapons. If the Soviets had been successful in moving ahead with this ban, US work on laser and particle beams would have been stalled on the agreement not to pursue development of systems likely to result in the ultimate weapon. The Russians would, meanwhile, have retained their own existing system intact. The United States refused to agree, the ploy was unsuccessful, but of greater importance was the illumination given to Russia's view about the ultimate use of beam weapons.

A particle weapon of immense power could, theoretically, propagate a beam of intense energy, forming a radioactive cone down to the surface of the Earth. While retaining, intact, all the physical and non-biological resources of the country against which the beam was directed, everyone in the beam's cone would die, every living thing would perish and mutants would emerge from lesser orders of life capable of surviving the irradiation. The use of such a terrifying weapon would be the ultimate application of enhanced radiation devices. The entire population of a nation could be destroyed in seconds and the limitations of use for such a device would not prevent the indiscriminate annihilation of all people everywhere.

There are very few who believe the enormous stockpiles of nuclear weapons available today could realistically be made to kill everyone on Earth; those weapons are targeted against each other's silos and major military and supply bases and estimates on the total dead from a complete nuclear exchange run to betweeen 20 per cent and 40 per cent of the population in the United States and Russia. But with an Earth-directed war station capable of directing massive energy levels at the ground, total annihilation is technically possible. Such weapons are at least several decades away, but the step from a basic anti-ballistic-missile beam satellite to the projected war station would be less than that which separated conventional high explosives from the Hiroshima bomb. Today, individual nuclear weapons sit atop Soviet missiles with a destructive capability equal to 1,250 Hiroshima bombs and the gap between the weapon dropped on Japan and today's arsenal is greater than that which now stands between battlesats and war stations. It is inconceivable that a single decision would ever be made to develop such a weapon but devices like this are not usually the product of single purpose commitment, coming instead in a series of separate development steps which culminate at the final product. The first steps have already been made with the tranformation of laser and particle weapons from research status to operational weapon systems and it will not be long before the vexed question of ABM screens reaches the international scene. When the Soviet Union can demonstrate the successful operation, and accurate emplacement, of a particle beam capable of knocking down incoming warheads the global strategy of nuclear stalemate will be over. It is not known for sure just how much more research the Russians have to do before deploying such a system but evidence shows that it cannot be very much.

In 1979 Soviet scientists successfully tested a charged-beam device against simulated military targets mounted on test stands. During research carried out in Leningrad, they successfully destroyed aluminum of the type used in missile nose cones, and in other activity the Russians have openly shown how to trigger the combustion of high explosives by penetrating it with a pulsed beam of charged particles. Experiments carried out by physicists V.D. Volovik and G.F. Popov demonstrate this to be a practical application already possible. With little extra work it could be fitted to weapons capable of hitting targets from space. Because most nuclear charges are triggered by high explosives, a beam directed at an ascending missile could initiate the nuclear reaction needed to detonate the bomb over the territory of the country which fired it. In this way, it would be suicide to launch nuclear-tipped missiles because their charges could be detonated just a few kilometers above ground.

In other work supporting the application to a ground-based ABM screen, successful tests in 1979 of a 500,000-volt ring switch would enable the Soviets quickly to lay a particle beam on any incoming target and to do so with great speed, enabling the same beam to hit several warheads in as many seconds. Toward the end of 1980, evidence emerged that the Soviets had successfully employed a flash-initiated, iodine-pulsed laser in a series of tests aimed at knocking out incoming warheads. An intense study by US physicists concluded that the Soviets achieved a high success rate in simulated attacks against their own, dummy, warheads launched down the rocket firing range. In nuclear terminology, Sary Shagan, it seems, had gone critical. Using similar concepts, scientists from the Los Alamos laboratory accurately duplicated the observed tests, using an iodine laser to explore the technology. Official US opinion now endorses the belief expressed secretly in 1975 by Air Force intelligence experts that the Soviet Union is very far ahead of the United States in directed energy weapon technology. Their basic physics is at a significantly higher level in areas that relate to magnetohydrodynamics, particle science and subatomic beam tests.

If any of that work aims to place beam weapons in space, the Russians will need a lifting capability as generous as the US Shuttle and that may take longer to achieve than the weapons themselves. For the interim, period, Russian plans undoubtedly include the operational use of a ground-based ABM screen. But laser battlesats will not appear before the mid- to late- 1980s, and space-based particle beam weapons of significant size may well await the turn of the century. In the meantime, the revolutionary new Shuttle transportation system will open new possibilities in other fields also.

So far, we have seen how the ability to reduce the severity of the launch environment by cutting down acceleration, reducing vibration and increasing the payload volume, makes possible completely new missions for the military man of space. Payloads and satellites can be returned to Earth after use, and the Shuttle can itself serve as the first stage of a delivery system capable of sending spacecraft to any desired orbit. But these are really just peripheral advantages swept up in the general technology of a completely new system. The ability for Air Force, Army or Navy personnel, including non-astronaut scientists from research or laboratory establishments, to accompany their experiments on test flights in the Shuttle is a *fundamental* shift in the development of new weapon or sensor hardware. Several technical developments the Defense Department would like to try before buying will ride into orbit during the 1980s. Most reflect the changes to strategic conflict induced by a new generation of ground-based systems.

First, the early warning segment will need to be increasingly alert for a pre-emptive strike against the continental United States. There is little time to vacillate. Series 647 early-warning satellites are expected to report a Soviet missile launch within the first minute of its emerging from an underground silo. It would take another 1½ minutes to get that information to the National Command Authority. Simultaneously, from somewhere appreciably closer, submarine-launched ballistic missiles would break surface en route to an air burst over Washington. Within 12 minutes the SLBM warheads would detonate over the US capital, followed about 15 minutes later by the first ICBM warhead striking a Minuteman silo. There would be considerable ballistic traffic coming from the Soviet Union by that time but the important element here is the time it would take the target to be computed by ground radars. Moreover, the 2-5 micron band used by the 647 series to scan for an attack is particularly sensitive to ground-based lasers because of the electromagnetic window open for such beams at that wavelength. It would be easy for the Russians to blind the infra-red sensor in the closing second of an attack launch, creating ambiguous readouts and confusion to the National Command Authority.

As outlined in Chapter Five, series 647 satellites operate detectors positioned within a Schmidt telescope offset from the satellite's long axis, the complete assembly made to spin at 5-7 rpm for circular scans of the Earth below. Because the scanner rotates 360 degrees between observations of a specifc target against the Earth's surface, accurate tracking of the missile's path is analagous to tracing the footsteps of an actor across the celluloid image of a motion film when only one frame in 360 can be seen. He ends up across the other side of the stage but his route is unknown or, at best, contains too few "inputs" to determine the path. So it is with missiles which can now, at best, generate warning as their engines release heat, yet can be seen intermittently by the early-warning satellite.

Invented by John Carson of Carson-Alexiou, Inc., a mosaic starting infra-red sensor was put together by Grumman Aerospace in the early 1970s. It was a revolutionary new type of warning device in that it provided an infra-red view of the Earth below through several hundred thousand separate detectors positioned at the focal plane of a telescope pointing straight down. Each detector would "stare" at the circular zone on Earth covered by its angular spread, at most a few tens of kilometers square, picking up a single register of a missile launch in the region. When the missile moved across to the space observed by the adjacent detector its track would begin a sequential set of registers in much the same way individual elements of a television picture present a flow of information across the screen.

Added advantage is obtained through a five-fold increase in sensitivity to radiation sources so that dimmer infra-red targets can be observed and tracked. The response time, too, is enhanced because the system is continuously looking at very many different segments of the Earth without blinking, as existing series 647 satellites seem to do by spinning slowly.

By the end of the 1970s, Air Force interest in the focal-plane mosaic starer increased to a level where test operations aboard a Shuttle-launched satellite were planned. If the system could be made operational later in the 1980s, sensitive to infra-red emissions in the 8-12 micron band where ground-based lasers would be unlikely to operate, system vulnerability would be reduced and responsiveness increased dramatically.

The focal-plane array is now expected to make its test debut in space aboard the Teal Ruby satellite, as part of a Shuttle payload, aimed at proving the use of the infra-red detector for tracking individual aircraft from orbit. If such a mission is possible, detector arrays could be placed in stationary orbit to locate and observe aircraft moving across the globe without the need for large, exposed, ground-based radar units scanning the horizon. A significant application for this type of device would be in the air defense of Europe and Great Britain. At present, radar installations along Britain's north-east coast would be easy targets in a major war and yet, without the radar eye watching and tracking incoming aircraft, interceptors would be unable to engage the enemy with anything like the effectiveness needed to counter an already ominous 3:1 Warsaw Pact advantage.

Teamed with Lockheed, Grumman competed with Rockwell International for a contract to develop the Teal Ruby payload but lost out when Rockwell got the work in 1977. Several problems with subcontractors deferred plans for the Teal Ruby launch date and, when the Shuttle, too, was delayed beyond the original flight date defense officials programmed the mission for 1982.

The Teal Ruby project is but one in an integrated set of experiments called the high-altitude large optics program, or HALO for short. Under the auspices of the Defense Advanced Research Projects

Agency, HALO will provide several unique opportunities to test promising technology in the space environment before building definitive
operational hardware. Its objective is to assemble by the middle of the
decade an inventory of equipment designed to observe in various
windows of the electromagnetic spectrum small areas of the ground for
tracking aircraft and cruise missiles. In this way, space capability is
helping to build a completely new overview of military activity on the
ground, in the air and across the oceans. While massive ground-based
radars look for incoming ballistic missile heads, satellites will, within
a decade, monitor more conventional operations conducted by both
East and West.

Of peripheral interest, it should be said that improvements to the
Ballistic Missile Early Warning radars (looking east from Fylingdales,
north-east from Thule, and north from Clear) included from 1977 the
addition of a very powerful phased-array radar antenna looking north-
west and west from Shemya close to the Kamchatka Penninsula.
Called Cobra Dane, its search and tracking coverage extends over a
120 degrees azimuth and the system is designed to detect an object the
size of a basketball 3,200 km away and simultaneously track 100
separate targets. The giant 29-meter diameter antenna is enclosed
within a massive fixed structure housing steering units, signal proc-
essors and control equipment. With a sloping face angle of 20 degrees
to the vertical, Cobra Dane can cover space up to 80 degrees from
horizontal. As described in Chapter Six, the Vought hot-kill, F-15
launched, anti-satellite device will be operational by 1985 and the
Space Defense Operations Center deep within Cheyenne Mountain, to
which all early-warning radars are responsible, will use the tracking
facilities for monitoring interceptions of hostile satellites.

Designed to examine the feasibility of observing and tracking objects already in space, the Air Force plans to launch a Shuttle mission
in 1983 to test Satellite Infra-Red Experiment (SIRE) sensors developed by Hughes Aircraft Company's Electro-Optical and Data Systems
Group. It may lead to satellites specifically designed to serve a
monitoring role by watching for hostile spacecraft in higher orbits or
for detecting shadow satellites placed in space to step in and replace
critical functions knocked out by killersats. This is one method of
averting a complete loss of capability and the placement of passive
satellites to be switched on only in the event of war has already been
made possible by using the Shuttle to launch several objects at the

same time. Not every object can necessarily be tracked and one or two satellites could be placed in a holding mode ready for duty in time of war. If the Soviets place similar satellites in orbit it would be good to know of their existence beforehand and scientists believe the minute temperature changes across the surface of the satellite when compared to the cold of space would lead to their detection. SIRE is designed to extend the scientist's optimism and prove the case in space.

Another application of advanced technology now promising very great benefit to military space operations will be demonstrated in 1982 aboard the same Space Test Program satellite which carries the Teal Ruby mosaic infra-red array. Called the Lasercom system, the device aims to prove the feasibility of using lasers to carry communications and data much the same as a more conventional radio signal. Lasers are not only useful for burning holes in light metals or for projecting holograms into the night sky. They are potentially the most effective means of sending information across great distances. The Defense Department wants to see if it can project large quantities of information to satellite data banks in space, rendering it less vulnerable to interception or destruction, and to determine if it can transfer data from one satellite to another, from ground sites to the National Command Authority, or from ships and aircraft to communication satellites in space. The main difference between radio and laser communication is that the latter can handle significantly more data because the carrier frequency on to which the information would be impressed is orders of magnitude higher than available radio frequencies. Both use propagated electromagnetic radiation, however, and both require modulation and demodulation equipment.

The senior Defense Department scientist for laser communication, James D. Barry, believes the equipment is theoretically capable of transferring in one second data equivalent to the information in an entire set of *Encyclopaedia Britannica*. Moreover, laser communication would be immune to jamming and would be totally secure for military operations. Prototype testing of an early experimental device began in 1978 at White Sands Missile Range, New Mexico, prior to incorporating hardware in the satellite. The Defense Department will spend six months studying the experiment and is expected to make a decision about full-scale production by 1983.

If developed, laser communication between satellites and ground users will precede the evolution of a fully autonomous space-based data handling facility. It is in the enormous quantities of data which can be transmitted quickly that the prime attraction lies and, if such technology is proved operationally sound, many of the functions now conducted in ground facilities will be delegated to automatic data banks stored in space. Large switching facilities in orbit, with communication and command dialogue from strategic systems around the world, could within the next few years provide a direct link to the Boeing E-4B Advanced Airborne National Command Post. Essentially a converted Boeing Jumbo Jet, the AANCP would convey the President, the head of Strategic Air Command and about 50 top military personnel high above the nuclear holocaust for co-ordination of strike forces against the attacker. If connected to a space-based communication and data storage/handling station, the AANCP would be completely separated from vulnerable Earth-based systems and would probably maintain more efficient contact with strategic forces.

The Lasercom experiment module to be flown aboard the Space Test Program satellite will be comparatively small, occupying a cylinder 96 cm long and 51 cm in diameter, but the practical demonstration of laser communication between a point in space and a station on the ground would be just the sort of proof scientists need to convince defense officials that such equipment is essential to the needs of the 1980s.

Future requirements, which stem from an urgent need to improve communication between shore-based command stations and the fleet ballistic missile submarines, from which would come the seaborne nuclear strike, would link satellites and lasers in a more advanced application which the Defense Department is keen to pursue. In theory, signals modulated to a blue-green laser would penetrate the oceans and provide a means of talking directly to submerged boats. At present, EC-130 Tacamo aircraft are employed for submarine communication through surface antennae deployed by the submarine. By the end of the 1980s, all that could change if plans now formulated are allowed to go ahead.

There are two ways of using satellites to reach submarines. In one method a laser whose wavelength would allow it to penetrate deep water would be aimed at a satellite reflector positioned in stationary orbit high above the Equator. Bounced from the reflector back down to the ocean, a large area of the surface would be illuminated by the beam. The entire North Atlantic could be covered by a single reflector.

There would be sufficient energy, however, for a sensitive receiver on board a submerged nuclear submarine to pick up the signal and demodulate the information from the carrier wave. A variation on this technique would have communication sent to a stationary orbit satellite by conventional radio waves and re-broadcast from the satellite to the ocean at blue-green laser wavelengths. There would be significantly less beam spread with this method, however, and the space-based laser would have to scan the surface back and forth to ensure reception below the surface.

Laser reflection is not a new idea. Apollo astronauts left on the surface of the Moon flat packs of retro-reflectors designed to mirror lasers broadcast from Earth. By measuring the precise time delay between the signal broadcast from Earth and the reflected signal back at the same site, scientists are able to measure the distance between Earth and Moon to within a few centimeters. The problems inherent in the laser communications idea are less formidable than those successfully met by Apollo scientists a decade ago. Several reflector satellites would be necessary completely to cover the world's oceans and this approach would reach operational use before the more advanced alternative where laser propagating satellites were placed in space. It is worth pondering, however, the dilemma of an orbiting laser beam viewed by the Russians as an anti-ballistic-missile weapon; in the interests of security it would be impossible to allow inspection to prove the satellite's communication role.

The idea for under-sea laser communication, either by reflection or direct propagation, originated with Lawrence Livermore Laboratory scientist Lowell Wood when an earlier plan to deploy a land-based, extremely-low-frequency antenna was successfully overturned by environmentalists protesting the project's impact on local communities. The laser system is now actively under way by the Defense Advanced Research Projects Agency and is expected to become operational by the turn of the decade.

The importance placed on maintaining communication with the undersea fleet stems from a reliance inevitably placed upon boats' captains to make unilateral decisions about firing their Poseidon or Trident ballistic missiles. If communication fails, and if the captains perceive the war to have moved beyond containment, it is their responsibility to push the button without waiting for a resumption of communication, if that ever came. Beneath the ocean surface lurk more than 30 US submarines with a capacity to hit a total of 4,800 targets; each new "Ohio" Class submarine with its 24 Trident missiles could devastate nearly 200 cities. The Defense Department is concerned that this force be at all times under the authority of the National Command and the spaceborne segment is the only means to achieve that.

Throughout the 1980s, military equipment destined for unique tasks like some of those mentioned here will be accompanied into space and operated by scientific and defense personnel flying the Space Shuttle. But there is a fourth capability, added to benefits of a more benign launch environment, the ability to launch big satellites like laser and particle weapons, and orbital tests with new and revolutionary systems: the ability to construct and assemble large orbiting facilities, providing completely new uses for space.

In the past, manned space flight required specially-built vehicles for carrying astronauts from one place to another. Only Skylab, or Russia's Salyut space station, allowed men to live and work in space on an almost routine basis. Now, with the Shuttle, military operations will carry men into the orbital void to erect and put together large antennae, modular space stations and giant reflectors. Along with the increasing use of micro-processors, or silicon chips, space systems will allow battle management to enter a wholly new realm of information and data transfer.

At a tactical level, Air Force studies have revealed future needs and a considerable effort is now being applied to developing large space structures. For instance, a multi-beam, phased-array antenna in stationary orbit, 67 m across and weighing 11 tons, would provide 100,000 separate voice channels to millions of users on the ground across a battle zone nearly 2,000 km across. In this "theater-wide" communications concept nobody could ever lose contact with his local command authority and the channels could be made readily secure against enemy jammers.

For accurate emplacement of tactical weapons, and the precise delivery of shells, bombs and rockets, an x-shaped antenna 3.8 km wide would provide, from stationary orbit, a capacity for individual units to locate their positions to within 45 m through information displayed on a wrist-watch sized monitor. Every soldier could receive a monitor as standard issue. Also, a suitably equipped antenna 70 m in diameter and similarly placed in stationary orbit could provide 100 beams to control up to 3,000 remote-piloted-vehicles, or RPVs, equipped to send back to the satellite images of the battle zone or enemy positions. As presently conceived, antenna platforms of this type would weight about 9 tons and control their robots across a 1,800 km wide battle front. At a more developed level, a 300 m diameter multi-beam antenna could lay down 1,000 beams for troop communications via wrist-watch radios while a similar sized antenna, appropriately equipped, could serve as a reflector for laser channels. Optical lenses capable of filtering selected wavelengths could also be asembled in space, structures combining many smaller elements which together would provide a telescope 300 m across. A positive move to procure such a system has already been made with the HALO program. Similarly, a 30 m diameter stationary orbit antenna would pick up thermal patterns on the ground from tanks, trucks or other tracked vehicles. In this way, infra-red detectors used today are just the beginning of a new generation of intelligence apparatus through which the inability to move without detection becomes an accepted price for mobility on and off the battle zone. In an ambitious plan developed by the Air Force, a very large antenna 9 km across would pick up and track objects moving in any one of three dimensions; nothing larger than a bullet would get by.

Such schemes may seem beyond the abilities of present-day space systems. But not so. For the means to build such large structures in space already exist. Because large antennae or girder assemblies which characterize this type of construction present a very low weight to size ratio, the Shuttle's lifting capacity plus its generous cargo space is best employed for carrying rolls of aluminum which can be fabricated into beams and truss-like structures in orbit. If pre-formed beams and girders were placed aboard the Shuttle they could fill the available volume but leave considerable weight-lifting capacity unexploited. It would take many Shuttle flights just to lift the necessary material into space.

The complex problems associated with space construction have already been avoided by a unique machine appropriately called the Beam Builder. Designed and built by Grumman Aerospace to a government contract issued in 1977, the machine measures 4.3 m in length and 2.4 m across. The ground demonstration model weighs less than 10 tons but a space-qualified prototype, now in development, will weigh only 7.7 tons. When the Beam Builder is mounted in the rear of the Shuttle's cargo bay it will be ready to manufacture construction beams

1 m across from thin sheets of aluminum. By loading three rolls of raw aluminum stock in from separate positions 120 degrees apart, the integral rolling mills pre-shape the sections and cut vertical braces supplied from dispensers already in the machine. The braces are spot-welded to the ends of the caps to start the beam off and 1.5 m of cap-members are formed for a second set of cross braces. Each beam has a triangular cross-section and includes 1.5 m long bays which continue to be disgorged from the machine as long as the aluminum drums last. Specific lengths can be automatically cut off by shears which sever the three caps. The Beam Builder can automatically machine and fabricate the girders at a rate of 0.7 m per minute and has demonstrated a capacity to fabricate a continuous 300 m length beam with an axial compression load of up to 620 kg. In the weightlessness of space there would be few stresses to design for and the assembly of large structures to support antennae platforms, work stations or test rigs would be much simpler than on Earth. NASA is interested in the Beam Builder, too, and teams with the Defense Department in plans for demonstrations in orbit by 1985. If the machine works, and through the experience of countless ground demonstrations there is little reason it should not, the industrialization of space will be a reality within the next few years. Set in operation by a few orbital spidermen, the Beam Builder will fabricate up to 42 m of truss per hour. In the event a large antenna was needed, several Beam Builder machines would be attached to a stable platform like rolling mills in a steel factory, disgorging several kilometers of girder per day.

Once produced, a Manned Remote Work Station (MRWS) comprising a transparent pressurized cabin 3 m high by 2 m in diameter would provide habitation for a single operator to work, from the inside, manipulator arms designed to grasp the pre-formed girders and move them to the construction site. There, teams of suited astronauts would fix the beams together in the appropriate order. The MRWS and associated hardware would have been lifted to the low orbit site by Shuttles and manned work teams would probably occupy a temporary, pressurized, cabin, stablized in orbit as a rest center and living area for off-duty crews.

Very large antennae, similar to those already designed by Air Force engineers, could be assembled within a few weeks by a work force of no more than 20 men working three shifts. This is well within the capability of a launch system which already anticipates carrying more than 1,000 people into space over the next ten years. Because the Shuttle is expected to fly more than 400 missions over the coming decade, and because each vehicle can carry up to seven people, this total would be easily met and probably exceeded. Where previous launch systems and manned spacecraft had to carry the entire complement of equipment necessary to complete a designated mission, future operations based on the Shuttle will "transport materials to space and do the actual fabrication up there," according to Don Ingram, head of the Grumman Space Program team that successfully designed the Beam Builder.

There is literally no theoretical limit to the size such structures could be built and very large antennae, such as the proposed space-based radar defense network, would lift the entire Ballistic Missile Early Warning System into orbit, increasing its effectiveness because it would look down from stationary orbit over one complete hemisphere. Such projects are not for the immediate future, but they do belong to the same era as the particle beam weapons placed in space to disable ballistic missiles launched in anger.

Technically, the consensus of a broad range of scientists, technologists and engineers is that such systems could be in operational use by 1990. In reality, they may more properly belong to the end of this century. Their antecedents are here today, however, in the form of prototypes built to demonstrate the feasibility of concepts beyond the imagination of the men who began the space programs of today. It is a true, but sobering, thought that the men who first landed on the Moon would not then have understood the technology which now exists.

Dr. Edward Teller, the man who worked closely with Oppenheimer to produce the atom bomb and who contributed more than any other to the development of the hydrogen bomb, has reached conclusions about the formidable role automated systems will have in a future battle scenario. Called the S-1, Teller's space-based software would take over many operations now carried out on the ground or in the air. The ultimate aim is to produce a system of modules that could perform all the functions, most integrated, to prosecute strategic nuclear war in the absence of human control. This would effectively render impotent all attempts to halt aggression by destroying the enemy, a transformation in the concept of war that has prevailed for thousands of years. If the S-1 is ever built and put into orbit it would be the most advanced computer brought to operational status and would probably have a greater effect on strategy than the nuclear-tipped missiles it would assume to control. In an era of x-ray laser ABM satellites and S-1 space-based control systems, strategic war would be unwinnable and unstoppable—with human beings uncomfortably in the middle.

If there is one area where the United States promises to hold supremacy for some time to come it is in the revolutionary world of space industrialization, which will arrive at the beginning of regular Shuttle flights. The opportunity to fabricate, erect, construct and assemble the hardware necessary for transferring major defense functions to the space environment is here already. The Soviet Union has no such capacity and is unlikely to achieve any before the next decade; having limited itself to a mini-shuttle which affords little opportunity for lifting heavy loads to space, Russia is dependent upon the ground-based systems which may become intolerably vulnerable ten years from now.

Already, projections from US defense scientists include the use of orbital data platforms which, by the turn of the century, will perform 100 million operations each second, a capability achieved by marrying sophisticated space technology to the fully developed micro-processor. Yet the technology which makes this possible will be only a start.

Even as science and defense interests are united in the vanguard of advanced technology, new ground is being prepared for extraordinary applications that today seem as far off as controlled fusion reactions would have seemed to Isaac Newton—had he known at all about their inevitable application. From the study of far-off energy sources and the science of astro-physics, a new awareness of matter and gravity has emerged since the 1960s. Black holes—collapsed stars—are no longer figments of scientific extremism. And today, theoreticians at certain institutions are juggling figures and equations because there is just a possibility that controlled gravitational collapse could one day, in another century, become reality.

These scientists are not the astronomers who search daily for evidence of new black holes but defense scientists who simply do not believe, as most would like to assume, that the second half of the 20th century will see the end of man's expanding command over nature and the forces of universal law. Controlled gravitational collapsars are miniature black holes held in a state of equilibrium until allowed to implode, at which point they would consume a measured quantity of mass before reaching balance with the environment. If developed as a weapon, devices like this would consume a significant fraction of the earth's crust before reaching the stability essential to preserving the balance of the planet. There is general agreement among astrophysicists that black holes may reach this level of equilibrium in nature, and serious doubts now exist that collapsars go on consuming irrespective of their size. If that is so, and if controlled collapsars are ever expressed mathematically, their application as mega-weapons would be a matter for technology, which is traditionally within the bounds of theoretical physics.

Nobody today can sensibly propose the eventual development of controlled collapsars, but the physics is unfolding with each passing year, and man may yet find himself faced with the destruction of his own planet. Physicists working to perfect the first atomic bomb had a trace of doubt that their calculations were as profound as they had to be to stop a chain reaction enveloping the earth. It would be ironic if in another century the physicists of that day were on the wrong side of their calculations.

8. Star Raker

New weapons, new shuttles and future prospects

The scenario at the beginning of this book will probably never happen, but the hardware it adopts is already on the drawing board. Particle beams capable of eliminating a nuclear strike force are theoretically sound and, as discussed in the previous chapter, are being developed with great haste. As for the freighter, that too has been designed and its construction proposed by Rockwell International's Space Division— the people who build the Shuttle. It is even called Star Raker, and it could be operational by 1995.

The only difference here is that no one has yet given the go-ahead to build it. But they soon must, or give permission for full-scale development with a vehicle much like the freighter described. The Shuttle is expected to commence full operational service before the end of 1982, an event preceded by several test flights designed to explore every fold of the performance envelope. Each Shuttle will make at least 100 flights into space and is expected to have a service life of ten years. A replacement for this reusable transporter, or a vehicle designed to provide even better economy, must match the mission traffic projected for the closing decade of this century.

Because the Shuttle will replace all existing, expendable, launch vehicles it cannot simply slip out of service without some other form of launcher ready to take its place. For that reason, and because development is expected to take at least ten years for a vehicle of this type, design concepts for a Shuttle successor are now being examined with interest by NASA and Air Force personnel.

Star Raker is one answer among several proposed designs and, unlike the existing Shuttle, would re-use all its hardware; the Shuttle's main propellant tank is jettisoned on each flight and the big solid rocket boosters have a life of 20 missions at most. In attempting to find a more lasting solution to re-usable space transportation needs,

Rockwell has put together a Star Raker design which would lift about three times the load of the present Shuttle, take off and land on a conventional runway and operate from any airport capable of handling liquid oxygen and liquid hydrogen.

Propellant for the three main rocket engines and the ten turbofans would be carried in large tanks throughout the airframe, the latter using hydrogen as fuel. Those same turbofan engines would re-start during the descent, providing Star Raker with a "go-around" capability denied to the present Shuttle which, being a glider on the way down, must land on the first try. Star Raker would be capable of flying long distances through the atmosphere before igniting its rocket engines to reach space, as demonstrated by the scenario at the beginning of this book where an equatorial orbit was planned.

With a cargo capacity three times the size and weight of the Shuttle, Star Raker is sized for a larger traffic load than current systems. But as you will have perceived already, there is every likelihood that by 1990 the Shuttle itself will be far too small for planned operations. It is reasonable, therefore, to marry a modestly expanded payload capability and a more efficient use of modern technology to a second generation Shuttle. The several unique technologies pioneered by the Shuttle, such as thermal insulation and new high-pressure rocket motors, call for second-generation developments on a vehicle like Star Raker. Already, considerable progress has been made in developing new and improved thermal tiles to protect the spaceframe during descent. Moreover, because of a lower wing loading for Star Raker, temperatures on the undersurface would be several hundred degrees lower than equivalent areas on the Shuttle, easing the problems experienced by this first reusable launcher.

During the 1980s, increasing use of stationary orbit high above the Shuttle's maximum operating altitude for defense satellites and test vehicles now in the design state calls for a special tug to ply between respective space lanes with traffic delivered and retrieved at that position. The solid propellant, expendable, boost stages like the Inertial Upper Stage are an acceptable start but, with a payload limit of about 2.7 tons, more advanced cargo requirements will call for a better means of lifting loads from the Shuttle to stationary orbit.

To send loads from a low orbit to any desired path around Earth, a liquid propellant system would be better than the current solids because it can be refuelled and left in orbit for use when necessary. Solid rocket motors cannot easily be shut down and reignited and several separate firings would be necessary when shifting cargo from one orbit to another. Liquid propellant systems are inherently more expensive because of the complex plumbing and control systems necessary with this type of rocket stage, but their use as orbital tugs will pay back development costs and provide a significant return in the better and more efficient use of space operations they afford.

By the end of the 1980s, development of in-orbit liquid propellant tugs should dramatically increase the opportunities for reaching stationary paths and by then the expanding use of space construction projects for building large antennae and erecting orbital facilities will justify the more expensive transfer system. But freighters like the Shuttle and Star Raker are peacetime solutions to the problem of lifting comparatively large loads into space. In time of hostility they would be useless, hampered by the several large ground facilities they require and exposure on the open launch pads from where they ascend. It would take at least a day to get a Shuttle spaceborne, and probably not much less for the second generation freighter. The Air Force will need to replace satellites knocked out by Soviet killersats or disabled by high-energy, ground-based, lasers. For that reason some kind of protected launch capability is vital if basic spaceborne functions are to be preserved in a hostile environment. There has been little opportunity to provide an all-conflict launch capability. The technical problems are enormous and the rockets have simply not been available. Launch vehicles like the current, expendable, types (Atlas, Titan, Delta) are all adapted versions of ballistic missiles developed more than 25 years ago, all employ significant quantities of liquid propellant and all would be exceptionally vulnerable in the opening minutes of war. Unlike the solid-propellant Minuteman ICBM and Trident SLBM, they require considerable time to make ready for flight and cannot be housed in any form of underground silo. The Shuttle is no better in this regard because it uses liquid cryogenic (super-cold) propellants needing considerable ground equipment to prepare and deliver. Fuels and oxidizers of this type cannot be kept in the launcher more than a few hours at most, and so the Shuttle cannot be held ready for flight but must be prepared uniquely for a particular mission. Because missiles like Minuteman and Trident are already carried in protected environments, with propellants which remain intact for long periods, it would be logical to choose these for lifting essential satellites into space; ascending from inside their vertical silos or submarine tubes, they would be ideal boosters for replacement satellites while the surface of the Earth all around blazed with nuclear fire. But these missiles, although the most powerful weapons available to the United States, are simply not big enough, nor do they have enough thrust, to lift the kind of weights which characterizes most defense satellites. Although capable of delivering a 680 kg warhead across intercontinental distances, the additional speed necessary to get a satellite in orbit would offload so much potential payload that no significant weight capability would remain. As you will recall, from the information contained in Chapter Four, the Russians use their SS-9 Scarp to put FOBS warheads and the current generation of killersats in orbit. But although dating back 20 years, the SS-9 is significantly more powerful than any ballistic missile yet developed in the West. Capable of sending a warload exceeding 5.4 tons nearly half way round the globe, when used as a satellite launcher the missile can still lift in excess of 3,000 kg to space. The only comparable system available to the West lies perhaps in the 53 silos where the only Titan 2 missiles to be deployed still reside awaiting the call to action. These missiles are essentially the same as Titan 2s used to send two-man Gemini spacecraft into space in the mid-'60s. Suitably adapted, they could be relieved of an operational strike role for one capable of replacing vital satellites.

Titan is protected from area blast by silo doors which open only seonds prior to launch, contains storable propellant ensuring a preparation time measured only in minutes, and would be capable of orbiting satellites weighing in excess of 1,000 kg. First deployed in 1963, the 53 Titan missiles now in separate silos across Arizona, Arkansas and Kansas could be modified for this type of role and serve a useful term as satellite launchers. Titan and Minuteman silos are becoming increasingly vulnerable to heavy-weight missiles fielded by the Soviet Union and the enormous 6.8-ton throw weight of the SS-18, deployed from 1974 (as of 1981, more than 300 were available for use), threatens the silos which would be used to launch replacement satellites. Ultimately, some form of insurance against destruction would be necessary to validate the space-dependent defense forces. That may come through development of a Minuteman replacement, similarly designed to evade destruction from a preemptive first strike. Called M-X, the missile represents America's first effort to replace the land-based ballistic strike force; operational from 1963, along with Titan 2, technical improvements to Minuteman have been the only answer to a massive and unparalleled escalation in Soviet strike power. Now, after a quarter-century of duty, part of the Minuteman force will be replaced from 1986 by a new and more powerful deterrent to stiffen the land-based leg of the CONUS defense triad. With a capacity to deliver a maximum ten nuclear warheads, each M-X will lift the same weight as a Titan 2 but contain advanced technology making it a completely new device. Although pitifully small compared to the SS-18—which can deliver a nuclear punch equal to 20 existing Minutemen—the M-X's greatest asset was to be its basing mode. Instead of lying trapped in a fixed silo, each M-X would move between 23 launch positions on a random basis. With many more positions than missiles, the Soviet ICBM force would have to knock out all 23 positions to be sure of getting the missile which could fire back at Soviet silos or cities—and with each M-X capable of hitting ten separate targets that would be a credible deterrent.

Two hundred M-Xs were planned by the Carter administration, with a total 4,600 launch positions sufficiently far apart to require individual warheads to destroy them. The logic of the Carter administration in selecting this basing mode was as follows. Because, under the terms of the SALT agreements, the Soviets are limited to a maximum 8,000 separate MIRV warheads, and because it would take two warheads to destroy each protected launch position, the Soviets could knock out a maximum 4,000 positions, leaving 600 intact; it could just be that the 200 M-Xs were in some of those 600 remaining positions. Against that kind of second-strike capability, the Russians would be exposed to the full fury of the M-X force with its total 2,000 potential targets.

When President Reagan came to power, his defense secretary, Caspar Weinberger, was unconvinced that an expensive construction program of this sort was in the best defense interests of the United States. Additional studies were carried out, and in mid-1981 a new plan emerged—one that took account of the need for impending ABM developments. The Carter plan for M-X produced a costly and exaggerated work project that locked out anti-missile or space-based technology. Reagan and Weinberger, eager to preserve options, decided to deploy just 100 M-X and to defer until mid-1983 a decision on the ultimate basing mode, when full scale research into laser and particle beam technology would define a major program of ABM applications. In the meantime, because the missile would be ready long before a final basing option could be undertaken, the first 40 M-X would be put in vacated Minuteman silos, replacing on a one-for-one basis 40 of the older, smaller, missiles.

The arguments employed to support the original M-X basing mode can be used for building a protected satellite launch system, but they stand the test of scrutiny better than the Carter administration's deployment plan. M-X is capable of lifting into space many of the satellites and payloads essential to battle management in any future war. Modifications to the missile would fit it well for the role envisaged here, but release of ten percent of the total M-X force to satellite launch duty would provide only ten poential delivery missions to orbit. In a radio and electronically hostile environment, M-X launched satellites would get through and place their payloads in space, preserving the vital functions they perform. But there are better ways of sending satellites to space in the adverse environment of a running nuclear war than with expensive missiles primarily built to destroy enemy targets (which may comprise weapon systems more overtly disastrous than the satellites, which would serve only to support defensive systems). It would be like buying a tank to run supplies behind the front line.

By the mid-1980s, when both US and Soviet anti-satellite systems will be fully operational, the need to quickly replace orbital sensors will no longer be avoidable. There will be no possibility of retaining the services of Shuttles or their successors in a future war because the technical job of building an underground facility for these heavy launchers would be daunting and far too expensive. Yet just about the time M-X missiles are deployed, a third need will emerge in addition to heavy lift transporters and hot-war satellite boosters: the airborne segment of the anti-satellite weapon.

Launched now by F-15 Eagle aircraft, the Vought impact device, propelled on its way by two solid rockets in tandem, will need a more capable platform than this converted air superiority fighter could provide. That need will be concurrent with the next generation of air fighters and revolutionary new designs like the forward-swept wing and high-zoom attack capability, now proposed by designers in the United States, could play a part in shaping the anti-satellite weapons of the 1990s. By then, low altitude satellites will be within range of ground-based lasers while the stationary orbit satellites, 36,000 km above, will be within the operating range of modified air-launched impact devices. It is for those that a new generation of carriers would be built, aircraft to improve upon the job now done by Eagles. With uncertainty surrounding the actual performance of the anti-satellite weapon built to knock out stationary orbit satellites, the requirements for an air-carrier are similarly vague just now. There is, however, general agreement that performance greatly in excess of that possessed by the F-15 would be an asset for rapid dispersal in the opening minutes of attack. An initial climb rate of about 25 km/min would place the anti-satellite device above the atmosphere within five minutes of an attack warning. Current F-15s would take twice that time.

In funded studies on the vexing problem of how to sustain a satellite replacement service during wartime, Rockwell International and General Dynamics have each conducted separate analyses of competing concepts. Much of this work is highly classified, and it is possible to discuss their findings only in general terms, but principles of operation are common to all contenders. During a major nuclear exchange, where each side would be trying to knock out the satellites vital for operating stategic weapons, tiny space cruisers could ascend from vertical silos to place single satellites in space. The cruiser would perhaps be delta-shaped, be no longer than 8 meters and weigh a maximum 3 tons. Strap-on propellant tanks would fuel rocket motors in the tail, and the vehicle could be flown by a single pilot in a small one-man cockpit halfway along the cone shaped nose. Reentering like miniature Shuttle vehicles to land at Air Force bases, the space cruisers could be used in peacetime to routinely replace military satellites as older vehicles wore out or needed updating. Instead of using a heavy lifting system like the NASA Shuttle, the Air Force may develop its own space cruiser for the 1990s based on its civilian partner and on experimental lifting-body test vehicles flow by NASA in the 1960s.

But the Air Force space cruiser could be lifted on its way by Shuttle, up to three such vehicles being carried in the orbiter's cargo bay and released in low orbit from where they could fly to stationary orbit high above earth. In time of war, when the Shuttle would be vulnerable, the space cruisers could strap on their external, barrel-shaped tanks and hide in silos until launched on satellite replacement missions. And if studies now being carried out prove the idea has more merit than for mere satellite flights, diminutive space cruisers could assume the role of manned interceptors chasing Soviet satellites in orbit. Combined with remotely controlled laser gun-ships, manned space interceptors could stimulate the development of hypersonic fighters twisting through the orbital space lanes at Mach 25 to gun down the watchdogs of enemy action.

The ability rapidly to knock out satellites in comparatively low orbit would be a vital concern also because ocean surveillance satellites are now used increasingly by the Soviets for accurately plotting US and NATO surface ships, against which the large numbers of airborne cruise missiles deployed by the Russians would be targeted. Also, terminal guidance updates for missiles flying beyond the range of radar equipment would depend upon the satellites. To deny their use would be to save from attack a large segment of the Atlantic traffic which, in time of war, would carry massive stocks of weapons and personnel. But the United States would similarly depend on orbiting eyes for guidance equations passed to M-X missiles.

In the wake of MIRV technology, advanced maneuverable warheads are now planned which will attempt to evade anti-missile missiles by twisting and turning along a circuitous path down through the atmosphere. Active tests were under way during 1980 from Vandenberg Air Force Base and the system will play an important part in advancing the M-X concept. A similar capability for Navy Trident missiles has produced the Mk 500 warhead which could be operational this decade.

In other developments aimed at using the maximum capacity of M-X, the SALT-1 agreement, which permits both sides to deploy up to 100 anti-missile missiles, is expected to be taken up by the United States. The Russians have always had an ABM force, albeit with only 64 missiles, but the United States dismantled the start it made in the late 1960s to provide Sprint and Spartan ABM defense systems. Now, with increasingly vulnerable Minuteman silos, the additional cost of an ABM force, within the limits of SALT-1, seems an attractive idea.

In a program called Talon Gold, defense scientists are studying the use of space-based laser weapons for knocking out incoming warheads but an interim plan already proposed would make use of some redundant M-X launch positions to house ABM missiles. In this type of mission, satellites would provide the initial tracking, and control the interception by taking charge of combined activity below through secure radio or laser data links.

Then there is the problem of the third component in the equation. Predictions about the shape of future military space needs so far take no account of the Chinese contribution. It is more than ten years since the People's Republic of China first launched their own satellite, an 173 kg vehicle sent aloft in April 1970. Since then, satellites weighing up to 3.5 tons have been placed in orbit with recoverable capsules sent back down through the atmosphere. China's first attempt at space activity came to an abrupt end when relations ran sour with the Soviet Union early in the 1960s and cooperation in technical projects ceased. But concerted efforts sustained through the Cultural Revolution brought their own reward and China emerged as a space-faring nation, launching, on average, one satellite each year for the duration of the 1970s. China places considerable importance on reconnaissance over the Sino-Soviet border, sensitivity toward increasing Soviet military power being particularly acute in the wake of the Afghanistan invasion of 1979. For several years China has professed interest in manned space flight but, such are the technical requirements of even a modest program, that the country is unlikely to achieve this before the mid-1990s. The main Chinese launch site is located at Shuang Ch'eng-tzu, south-west of the Gobi Desert, and the rockets used to launch satellites into space have evolved from ballistic missiles developed independent of the Soviet Union; what little cooperation there was vanished long before the present technological era. China itself has enormous problems in the decades ahead and would be unlikely to join Soviet, American and European levels of space activity. In September 1981 China launched three satellites into orbit with a single rocket, giving evidence that the PRC's strategic rocket program is more developed than most experts had believed. As for Europe, the unified efforts of 11 countries formed in 1975 into the European Space Agency (ESA) center on the development and application of the Ariane launch vehicle and the Spacelab manned laboratory. No country in Europe is anywhere near proposing the beginning of a military space project, although France has consistently shown interest in a reconnaissance satellite for its own domestic use. Severed from the military alliance in NATO, France feels especially vulnerable to external pressures from both East and US power blocks.

Ariane is a commercial competitor of outstanding merit and, from its Guiana launch site on the coast of South America, promises to service many launch needs for foreign customers. But it is the Shuttle's low-cost payload capability which should attract the most foreign traffic and the next decade may see increasing numbers of Third World states book space aboard the civil flights for lifting satellites with a dual capability: Earth resources satellites or weather satellites which double as reconnaissance platforms high above the Earth.

NASA openly asserts its concern about this and protests at any suggestion that it should be used to launch military satellites. But roles are becoming increasingly ambiguous, and it would be difficult to refuse a payload slot for a customer prepared to pay for a geological satellite also capable of spying on an enemy. The proliferation of military space capabilities will assuredly follow as inevitably as the space age followed the first ballistic missiles. For the present, killersats and particle beam weapons promise significantly to re-shape the profile of future conflict.

It is unlikely the world will maintain peace for the remainder of this decade: what has happened already in Afghanistan set the pace for laser and particle beam weapon development; sustained Soviet aggression throughout the orbit of its imperialistic domain excites a major arms race for fear the Bear will break through its Asian gate; violation and abrogation of SALT agreements gave us little faith in paper sentiments; consistent development of killersats opens the very real possibility of conflict in space; a monstrous imbalance in strategic weapons provides incentive for Russian adventure throughout the world.

Perhaps the most damaging disparity is that both sides perceive the threat from different positions. Flouting the conventions of military doctrine, the Soviets have evolved a formula using strategic equipment to secure a major objective ahead of tactical solutions. Conversely, the United States has demonstrated an inability to secure tactical problems ahead of strategic needs, using the latter to solve the former. It is the US preoccupation with strategic conflict which may be the undoing of Western-style freedom, for while America sits behind a shield of strategic capability, the Soviets push and shove to gain a tactical foothold. Where the West perceives a SALT agreement to be a demonstration of conciliation, the Russians regard it instead as an affirmation that major threats exist. For this reason, the Soviets are inclined to escalate their arms capability during and after a SALT agreement. The West is unable to see the reason for this, preferring to believe that the Russians are exploiting loopholes, which indeed they are. But the fact that Soviet Russia understands the way it feels about detente, and recognizes that interpretation to be different from the US view, compromises any benevolent feeling of pity for the Soviet leaders. For in the wake of behaving the way it wishes to, irrespective of the view taken by America, Russia reveals an intractability close to aggression.

In the Soviet view, the West must accept the way Russians view the world, and not expect them to change because that view is different to other nations'. In the American view, the Soviets become entrenched and unbending, reluctant to give ground at a political or military level. So, with a conflict of interpretations, how will the remaining years of this century change the nature of East-West dialog? Clearly, natural resources dominate the picture and will probably play the deciding role in moving East and West to direct nuclear confrontation over Middle East oil. By 1985, the Soviets may have to import oil to meet internal demand while in the world as a whole the shortfall will probably equal the current oil output from the Saudi Arabian fields. Former Air Force Secretary Thomas C. Reed is convinced of imminent confrontation over the depleted reserves in reminding the West that "Brezhnev said detente was a stratagem to allow the Soviets to build up their military and economic power so that by 1985 a decisive shift in the balance of world power would enable the Russians to exert their will whenever they wished."

Sometime between 1985 and 1989, depending on how successful the West is at conserving oil, an imbalance between supply and demand will emerge where no amount of new production capacity will save the day. For the Russians, cold winter will have a new meaning. Thomas Reed believes that the Soviets will "be at their energy deadline and will try to solve their problems by means of the Mid-East at the expense of the free world . . . They will hope to avoid nuclear confrontation, but if it comes they will not blink." Events have already begun in that grim scenario. In April 1978 Afghanistan's President Daoud and his impartial republican government were overthrown by Marxist Nur Mohammad Taraki and, within weeks the Soviets moved to influence the policy of their neighbor state. For a year they tried to balance the forces of dissent and bring stable administration to the country from the capital, Kabul. To the many Afghan people who upheld Islamic traditions and religious dogma, the pro-communist regime was anathema. In mid-1979, the Kremlin debated whether to use force and, against his inclinations, Brezhnev succumbed to persuasion from military advisers who were seen with increasing frequency driving through the gates of Moscow's citadel. As preparations got under way and motorized infantry divisions began a massed build-up along the border, a gunfight in Kabul, instigated by the Soviets in an attempt to kill the then Prime Minister Hafizullah Amin, backfired and Taraki was murdered instead. Amin took over control and promised his Moscow bosses that order would prevail. Three months later the country was in worse turmoil than ever and the Soviets knew they had to move quickly. On December 27, 1979, airborne troops landed in Kabul, motorized divisions, bringing with them armored personnel carriers and tanks, rolled fast across the border to secure villages and towns en route to the southern mountains. In the ensuing confusion, several government leaders were quickly executed by KGB assassination squads and, in the early hours of the morning, Amin fell dead during a Soviet attack on his palace. From deep within the Soviet Union, Russian engineers broadcast a message, ostensibly transmitted from the Kabul radio station, acclaiming with relief the cheerful sight of Russian troops quelling disorder and uniting the country. Brought from Eastern Europe, Babrak Karmal, a hard-line communist hated by Islamic adherents, was set up as Afghanistan's leader.

All three Marxist regimes had a bloody record. At Pol-I-Charki prison outside Kabul, executions averaged 50 each night and in mass sweeps of the city, thousands were brought to prison. Throughout the countryside, Soviet advisers presided over mass executions, and in the mountain areas napalm forced thousands of people from their homes while chemical weapons flushed out the hidden guerrillas. In the following months, KGB officers took control of all vital functions, news reporters were expelled, more than 5,000 political advisers were brought in and over 100,000 troops took up position. In and around Kabul, military fortifications began to grow, permanent barracks were set up and heavy artillery backed up the mobile armored columns. Within six months nearly one million Afghans had taken refuge in neighboring Pakistan and Soviet casualties reached 10,000. And all the while, heavy troop concentrations were reported just across the border in Soviet Russia. During January, Red Army units began to reinforce their strength along positions inside Russia east and west of the Caspian Sea immediately north of Iran, wracked by this time with several competing religious factions which sought control of the country. The strategy was emerging, the threat had been defined.

With an interest in controlling the oil economy of the Middle East, Russia was poised to execute a classic pincer movement across the border with Iran. From each side of the Caspian, fast-moving Soviet

Armies could, if they wished, quickly join forces south of Tehran, completely encircling the capital city and cutting off Iranian forces to the south. On Iran's eastern border, Russian troops from Afghanistan could then move rapidly for the Straits of Hormuz, sealing the entrance to the Persian Gulf, in an unchallenged thrust at lightning speed. Within 12 hours, estimates said, the Red Army would have control of the southern ports.

To Iran's west, Iraq deepened its political hostility toward the revolutionary state while Soviet infiltrators stirred trouble between the two countries. The advance into Iran did not come immediately and today Russian forces stand poised for the right political time to conduct that move. Time is on the Soviet side, for having gained Iran they would be in a good position to command the entire Middle East region.

The break in relations with the United States, and an increasing need for technical assistance to get the oil fields back in production, places Iran in an especially vulnerable position for Soviet persuasion, and the Russian occupation may not call for the use of arms. If not, if the Russians are invited to support Iran's future development, it would be almost impossible for the US to honor former President Carter's pledge made less than one month after the invasion of Afghanistan: "An attempt by an outside force to gain control of the Persian Gulf region will be regarded as an assault on the vital interests of the United States. It will be repelled by use of any means necessary, including military force."

In this, the United States judged the possible intrusion of Soviet forces to be a strategic military threat and rather than settle the issue at a tactical level is prepared to use "any means necessary" to keep the Soviets out. In fact, if the Russians gain Iran by peaceful means, there would be no excusable reason in international law for America to move in. Nevertheless, whether over the acquisition of Iran or the possession of other Middle East states which will undoubtedly follow, conflict is inevitable, for both sides seek the diminishing reserves which keep the respective societies alive.

On April 24, 1980, CIA Director Stansfield Turner told a US Senate committee that, "oil production is probably at or near its peak and will decline throughout the 1980s." Moreover, said Turner, to maintain the same kind of economic growth in the United States the rate of fuel consumption must drop by one-third in the decade ahead. That is probably an unattainable goal and must lead to increasing domestic unrest and public discontent. For the Soviet Union the position is probably worse. Turner reported that, "oil production is already declining in all of the major oil-producing regions except West Siberia, and further gains even there are uncertain . . . Meanwhile, the decline already underway in older major production regions probably will accelerate as reserves are depleted." But, continues Turner "the prospective decline in Soviet oil production is only part of the problem. Coal output [in Russia] is nearly stagnant, and natural gas production, although growing, is limited. Soviet leaders will probably try to weather the crunch with a combination of belt-tightening, slower economic growth, cutbacks in oil exports and increased oil imports on the best terms they can get . . . The big loser inevitably will be the Soviet consumer . . . The Soviets have been averaging one bad crop year in three during the last two decades." And in seeking the low-cost oil reserves needed to bolster an already flagging Soviet economy, the CIA Director concluded that, "military action cannot be ruled out."

Yet even these, albeit subjective, assessments seem modest when the undisputable facts are examined. The Soviet economy is in decline, not only because of world trade recession but also because Russian-style socialism is unable to match the needs of its own people and of the client states it has set up around the globe. Countries in the Eastern Bloc, as well as Cuba, Libya and Vietnam, drain Soviet resources to an alarming extent. Without Soviet aid they would be unable to survive and yet they are dragging Russia to the brink of extremism as it wrestles with diminishing trade gaps.

In the four years between 1977 and 1981, Russian grain imports increased 250 percent, increasing from 10 million tons to 35 million tons. Between 1979 and 1981, food imports went up by 140 percent, from an equivalent $5,000 million to $12,000 million. And throughout the decade of the 1970s, economic aid to client states rose from $2,000 million to a staggering $24,000 million, an increase of 1,200 percent in ten years. Extended credit, stagnant trade figures and a diminishing gold reserve are prime movers in Soviet foreign policy which now must seek to influence world oil prices or go bankrupt.

With more than $35 billion in gold slowly draining to pay for services and aid, the economy is unable to sustain through trade with the West, the largest asset lies largely unused—oil. With little prospect of an increase in demand for some time to come, Russia is unable to turn its oil into currency and unless it influences the West's market price this situation is unlikely to change. For that reason many are suspicious about the creeping involvement of Soviet agents in Middle East states from Iran to Egypt. If prices stay at their current levels, and if demand changes only slowly throughout this decade, the Soviets will be unable to switch from using their reserves to pay the bills. It is ironic that Russia desperately needs the free market forces it is prevented from adopting because of dogmatism and political ideology in a socialism that has created a millstone for the Russian people.

In addition to these indigenous troubles, America's restriction of grain sales to the Soviet Union above minimal levels agreed several years ago is expected to cause large reductions in the livestock quota available for food. The US Department of Agriculture believes that a single bad winter now "would necessitate massive herd liquidation." By 1985 the situation will be more critical for Russia than at any time since the beginning of the Soviet Republic, and the need to show force to gain territorial assets without conflict will be a vital ingredient of Soviet foreign policy. The Russians have nothing to gain by attacking Europe; they have everything to gain by maintaining their pressure on the Middle East. In building to an unprecedented peak the Warsaw Pact forces which face limited NATO units, Russia has the psychological tool to get its way in the Middle East without a major nuclear exchange. This policy has worked already, for when President Carter chose to blockade the Persian Gulf he was reminded of the Soviet base at Umm Qasr on Iraqi land at the extreme north of that waterway. By cutting off foreign shipping access, the US resistance would face Russian determination to use that facility for whatever purpose it deemed fit. Knowing that US and NATO forces in Europe would be unacceptably depleted if a conflict broke out in the Gulf, Carter acquiesced and turned instead to more direct attempts at freeing US hostages held in Iran. The only solution will be for NATO to seek an ever-widening front along which to deter aggression. But inevitably a show of force will ensue because the rich oil reserves are the ultimate objective of both East and West. And it is within that scenario for the coming years in this decade that a new form of conflict may emerge, one in which the proxy use of devastating weapons may save the world from direct nuclear confrontation. In much the same way that satellites were seen at first as a very obvious means of demonstrating rocket power, so might a space war be the only way of visibly demonstrating nuclear and strategic might. It is now accepted philosophy in the Pentagon that a war begun during the coming decade will start in space, and it is toward that objective that the laser and particle beam weapons are so eagerly sought today. Lieutenant General Thomas Stafford, the ex-astronaut who left NASA to head the military space development program, believes that, "Under certain circumstances, space may be viewed as an attractive arena for a show of force," and justifies this by reminding Senate commitee members that, "Conflict in space does not violate national boundaries, does not kill people and can provide a very visible show of determination at relatively modest cost."

It is not difficult to imagine how such a proxy conflict could begin. Increasingly, space systems supporting military objectives intrude further and further upon national rights. Reconnaissance is accepted as a viable means of verifying treaties and agreements on arms and force posture; the several more intrusive methods used for controlling weapons over hostile airspace are causing deep concern already among major world powers. If the world manages to avoid such a confrontation for another decade, a second generation of space weapons like those discussed in the previous chapter will be available for the proxy war. But by the end of this century developed versions of such weaponry would, if turned upon the planet itself, cause more destruction and loss of life than any assemblage of nuclear missiles. It may be that public outrage at increasingly complex nuclear delivery systems is already out of date. It may be that public debate on the new space weapons should begin now, for within a decade it will be too late to stop the momentum of development and deployment. Perhaps, in that context, there is no better plea than words from Alexander Solzhenitsyn in his Letter to Soviet Leaders concerning the spread of nuclear forces: "This calamitous future, which is just around the corner at the current rate of development, weighs heavily on us creatures of the present—on those who wield power, on those who have the power of influence, and on those who have only a voice to cry: there must never be such a war. This war must not happen, ever. Our task must be not to win the war, for no one can possibly win it, but to avoid it."

When President Reagan assumed office in January 1981 it signalled a new mood throughout America. Gone were the cautious policy statements aimed at smoothing the worst fears of Soviet power politics; gone were the guarantees of negotiation at any price; gone, the resolve to slowly erode Western arms as an example of benevolent intent and international communion. In the first year of the administration's term, signals went out with a clear and unambiguous message: that the Soviet Union either becomes an international companion of nations large and small, regulating its internal as well as external behavior according to the letter of UN language, or it invokes the full force of America's technical resources in a concerted drive to maintain a lead in defense systems across the full spectrum of weapons technology. The new mood was articulated by preparation for a major expansion of space-based activity for military use.

In 1981, the US Air Force set up a Directorate of Space to assemble and coordinate the many revolutionary new concepts and projects emerging from advanced technology, and the Air Force Space Division established a Space Laser Program Office to administer initiatives with ABM and anti-satellite directed energy weapons. The Defense Advanced Research Projects Agency increased by 45 percent the projected funds for 1982 on laser and particle beam research, and new study contracts went out to industry for a concerted effort at presenting a strategic policy plan to the President by 1983. In that year the selection of emphasis on strategic rocket, ABM and directed-energy weapons will fuse US defense policy into a cohesive assembly of present and future technology applications.

The intent of the new administration, to leave no stone unturned in efforts to lead with laser and particle beam research, was articulated by President Reagan's science advisor, George A. Keyworth. In testimony before a Senate committee he said: "I believe laser and directed energy weapons represent an enormous possibility. . . . I believe they represent the only truly credible antiballistic missile alternative for. the future. . . . I believe the Administration must take some initiative to bring the parties and various perspectives together to address this issue. I would consider it definitely on the forefront of my docket."

Some say all talk of nuclear disarmament is too late. That there are simply too many weapons, too many countries frantically seeking possession of the atomic bomb to turn back the clock. The genie, they say, is already out of the bottle. But there is another genie emerging, if not released already, that is infinitely more threatening for the future peace of all men on earth. And it is just as unstoppable.

Appendix

Annual military satellite totals

	Reconnais-sance		Communi-cations		Weather		Ocean surveillance		Early warning*		Navigation		Killersats		Totals	
	US	USSR	US	USSR	US	USSR	US	USSR	US	USSR	US	USSR	US	USSR	US	USSR
1958			1												1	
1959	6										1				7	
1960	6		2		2				2		2				14	
1961	13		2		1				3		3				22	
1962	30	5	3		4				1		1				39	5
1963	24	7	4	1	3	2			4		3				38	9
1964	32	12	3	3	3	2			4		3				45	17
1965	26	17	7	8	6	4			2		4				45	29
1966	33	21	11	2	6	2		1	1		4		2		57	25
1967	26	27	17	5	6	4			2	2	3		9	1	63	40
1968	23	36	11	4	4	2			1	1	1		2	4	42	48
1969	18	43	5	2	3	2		3			1				27	52
1970	16	39	3	14	5	6		1	5		1	1		2	32	64
1971	10	43	5	21	2	4		2	1		1	2	1	3	19	78
1972	11	37	3	24	4	5		1	2	1	1	3	2		21	71
1973	7	47	4	33	2	3		1	2	1	1	3	1		16	88
1974	8	38	3	24	4	6		2	2	1	1	4			16	75
1975	6	41	5	37	3	6		3	1	2	1	4		6	17	93
1976	5	43	11	29	3	5	4	2	2	1	4	8		7	25	95
1977	2	50	2	8	1	4	4	2	2	3	2	7		4	12	78
1978	4	76	5	20	1	5			2	2		8		1	16	112
1979	2	56	3	25	1	3		2		2		6			8	94
1980	3	40	2	30		2	1	3		5		6		1	8	87
Totals:	311	678	112	289	64	67	9	24	39	21	38	52	17	29	590	1,160

*Includes nuclear detection satellites

Index

Index

Advanced Airborne National Command Post (AANCP) 232
Advanced Research Projects Agency (ARPA) 125, 178, 180, 206, 229, 233
Aerospace Applications Unit, 4000th 117
Afghanistan 20, 21
Afsatcom (program) 132, 133, 135, 198, 200
Agena A (Rocket Stage) 32, 33, 40, 42, 47-50, 55, 144, 145
Agena B (Rocket Stage) 54, 58, 77, 155
Agena D (Rocket Stage) 59-63, 66, 68, 111, 147
Air Force Ballistic Missile Division (AFBMD) 44, 182, 183
Air Force, US *Throughout*
Air Research and Development Command (ARDC) 24, 182
Aldrin, Edwin 92, 155
Anti-Ballistic Missile (ABM) 84, 87, 171-176, 205, 207, 211-227, 248
Anti-Satellite Systems 154, 156, 162-181, 196, 218, 220, 230, 243-248
Apogee, Point of (definition) 37-39
Apollo project 64, 90-92, 99, 106, 107, 184, 185, 194, 222, 233
Arms Control and Disarmament Agency, US 164
Armstrong, Neil 92, 155
Army Ballistic Missile Agency (ABMA) 24, 25, 44
Army, US 21-25, 31, 41-44, 117, 125-127, 147, 157, 192, 199, 216-217, 227
Atlantis Shuttle 177
Atlas (missile and launcher) 24, 28-32, 39, 48, 55, 58, 59, 125, 145-148, 190, 193, 243
Atlas-Centaur (launcher) 132, 183, 199
Austen Research Associates 216, 217
Azgir, Soviet beam station at 207, 210

Backfire (bomber) 93-95, 171
Ballistic Missile Early Warning System (BMEWS) 140, 144, 150, 230, 237
Barry, James D. 6
Battlesat 179-182, 195, 202, 216, 218, 219
Bell Telephone Laboratories 156, 177

B-52 (aircraft) 136, 173, 194, 200
Big Bird 66, 68, 76, 77, 88, 94, 103, 106, 189
Block IVA weather satellite 116, 124
Block IVB weather satellite 116, 124
Block 5A weather satellite 116
Block 5B/C weather satellite 116
Block 5D weather satellite 117-123, 130
Boeing Aerospace 173, 179
Braun, Wernher von 21-31, 41, 42, 43

C-119 (recovery aircraft) 50, 54
C-130 (recovery aircraft) 50, 69
Cape Canaveral 11, 48, 91, 99, 129, 132
Carter, President Jimmy 20, 21, 71, 93, 97, 164, 165, 171, 222, 253, 255
Chair Heritage (project) 214, 215, 224
Challenger, Shuttle 187
CIA (Central Intelligence Agency) 46, 47, 69, 73, 83, 96, 97, 103, 104, 206, 211, 212, 213, 253, 254
Cobra Dane (radar) 230
Columbia, Shuttle 187
Consolidated Space Operations Center 183, 188
Cosmos (satellites) 59, 66, 103, 112-114, 146, 152, 153
Cosmos *Throughout*
Cruise missile 78, 94, 95, 175, 179, 195, 215, 220, 230, 248
C-series (rocket) 103, 161

Defense Communications Agency (DCA) 127, 129, 131
Defense Intelligence Agency (DIA) 206, 211
Defense Navigation Satellite Development Program 192
Defense Satellite Communications System (DSCS) 127-134, 135, 137, 188
Defense Support Program (DSP) 149, 197
Delta (launcher) 135, 183
Department of Defense (DOD) 50, 55, 83, 105, 106, 107, 115, 125, 129, 132, 147, 171, 175-180, 198, 210-236
Discoverer (program) 47-55, 59, 65, 76, 144, 146

Discoverer 1-13 (satellites) 53
Discoverer 13-38 (satellites) 54-55
Discovery, shuttle 187
Dornberger, Major Walter 24
Dudnikov, V.G. 217
Dyna-Soar (space glider) 43, 63, 185

Eastman Kodak 51,55
EC-130 Tacamo (aircraft) 232
Edwards Air Force Base 172
Eisenhower, President Dwight D. 30, 31,
    44, 71, 75, 106, 125
Energy Research and Development Admin-
    istration (ERDA) 209
Enterprise, Shuttle 186
European Space Agency (ESA) 249

F-15 (aircraft) 173, 179, 230, 246
F-16 (aircraft) 194
F-111 (aircraft) 94
FB-111 (aircraft) 173
FBI (Federal Bureau of Investigation) 97
Ferret satellites 59, 77, 87, 95, 98, 103,
    105, 106, 144
Fltsatcom (satellite) 132, 133, 198, 200
Ford, President Gerald 93
Fractional Orbit Bombardment Systems
    (FOBS) 139-143, 150-154, 151, 244
F-series launcher 113, 157, 160
Fuchs, Dr. Klaus 208
Funk, Major General Ben I. 148

Gagarin, Yuri 47, 58
Gapfiller (program) 132
Gemini (program) 63, 91, 107, 155, 244
General Dynamics 171, 194
General Electric 59, 130
GEODSS 180, 181
Global Positioning System (GPS) Navstar,
    193-196
Global Weather Central 117-119, 121
Gorizont (program) 138
Gorshkov, Sergei 108, 110
Grumman Aerospace 228, 229, 235, 237
Grumman A-6 (aircraft) 194

HALO (High Altitude Large Optics) 229,
    230, 235
Helms, Richard 83
High Altitude Test Vehicle, (HATV) 27
High Energy Physics Institute (at
    Novosibirsk) 210
Hughes Aircraft Company 121, 134, 177,
    198, 230
Hughes Electro-Optical and Data Systems
    Group 230
Hydrogen bomb 22, 30, 41

Inclination, orbital 36-39
Inertial Upper Stage (IUS) 188, 193, 242
Initial Defense Satellite Communications
    System (IDSCS) 126-128

Intercontinental Ballistic Missile (ICBM)
    Throughout
Interferometry, principle of 112
International Telephone and Telegraph (ITT)
    145

Jackson, Senator Henry 83
Johnson, President Lyndon B. 42, 63, 71,
    106, 147, 156
Jupiter (missile) 24, 25, 28, 30
Jupiter C (rocket) 31, 42

Kamchatka Peninsula 87
Keegan, General George E. 79, 80, 167,
    211-212
Kennedy, President John F. 20, 44, 55,
    58, 60, 71, 90, 106, 156
Kennedy Space Center (KSC) 187
KGB 97
KH-11 (reconnaissance satellite) 69-70,
    96-97, 106
Killersats 21, 159-167, 169-174, 180, 182,
    189, 196, 197, 201, 216, 220, 223, 230,
    243, 244, 250
Killersat limitation talks 164-167, 171
Kissinger, Henry 82-88, 213
Kodiak, Alaska (tracking station) 49
Knapp, Edward A. 216
Kremlin 21, 72, 238
Krushchev, Premier Nikita 31, 41, 45, 71,
    73

Landsat (satellite) 130
Laser applications 162, 170, 175, 176, 177,
    179, 180, 189, 195, 196, 206, 208,
    215-220, 223-229, 246, 248, 256
Laser, continuous beam 177, 182
Laser, deuterium flouride 182, 195
Laser, excimer 177, 178
Laser, gas 177
Laser gunship 182
Laser, hydrogen flouride 151, 178
Laser, krypton flouride 223
Laser, solid state 177
Laser, x-ray 223, 237
Lasers, pulsed 177
Leasat (satellite) 199-200
Lightning (aircraft) 94
Lincoln Experimental Satellite (LES) 126,
    135, 196, 201
Livermore Laboratory 210, 223, 233
Lockhead Missiles and Space Co. 32, 45,
    47, 68, 69, 144, 219, 229
Los Alamos Laboratory 215, 217, 223
Lunar Orbiter (program) 51

Manned Orbital Laboratory (MOL) 63-64,
    68, 89, 90
Manned Remote Work Station (MRWS) 236
Marines, US 127, 192, 199, 200
Marisat (satellite) 132, 133, 134
Martin Marietta 110-112

McDonnell Douglas 63, 173, 193
Mercury (manned project) 43, 107
Meteor (satellite) 123, 124
Midas (program) 48-51, 54, 144-146
Middendorf, J. William, 170
Ministry of Aviation Signal Research and Development Establishment 134
Ministry of Defence, UK 134
Ministry of Supply, UK 25
Ministry of Technology, UK 134
Minuteman (missile) 60, 74, 78, 80, 81, 136, 141, 173, 181, 183, 195, 199, 228, 243, 244, 248
MIRV (Multiple Independently targeted Re-entry Vehicle) 74, 76, 82, 143, 195, 245, 248
Mosaic starter 229
Maser, development of 176, 177
Molniya (satellite) 136, 137, 152
MRV (Multiple Re-entry Vehicle) 74, 76, 80, 82, 143
Mutually Assured Destruction (MAD) 23
MX (missile) 183, 244-248

National Advisory Committee for Aeronautics (NACA) 29-32, 44
National Aeronautics and Space Administration (NASA) *Throughout*
National Command Authority 132, 133, 136, 228, 231, 234
National Oceanic and Atmospheric Administration (NOAA) 123
National Photograhic Interpretation Center 69
National Security Council 171, 213
NATO 41, 46, 80, 110, 129, 134-135, 140, 151, 153, 159, 172, 176, 198, 248, 249
NATO (Satellite) 134-135, 198-199
Naval Research Laboratory, US 110, 111
Navigation Technology Satellite (NTS) 184
Navsats 190-192
Navstar (satellite) 192-197
Navy Bureau of Aeronautics 26
Navy, US 25, 27, 30, 32, 54, 73, 112, 127, 132, 190, 192, 198, 200, 214-217, 220, 227, 248
Nike-X 156, 170
Nike Zeus 156, 170
Nimbus (satellite) 122, 130
Nixon, President Richard M. 55, 64, 75, 82, 106, 184
NORAD 140, 144, 162, 183

Office of Scientific Research and Development 26
Orbital designations 35-39
Orbital flight, principles of 33-39

Particle beam weapon, development of 206-218, 219-227, 236
Particle beam weapon, principle of the 206, 207

Pentagon 43, 44, 64, 73, 83, 87, 105, 130, 131, 166, 172, 175, 201, 213, 256
Perigee, argument of 37-38
Perigee, point of 37-38
Phantom (aircraft) 94, 194
Plesetsk 61, 100, 103, 152, 160, 161
Polar Orbit, constraints of 52, 124, 187, 191
Polaris (missile) 25, 72, 74, 78, 79, 111, 190, 191
Poseidon (missile) 79, 111, 181, 233
Powers, Francis Gary 44-47, 55
Progress (supply ship) 89
Project 266 147
Project 417 116
Project 437 156
Project 461 146
Project 467 64, 66
Project 505 156
Project 612 64
Project 647 147-150, 182, 188, 210, 228, 229
Project 706 155
Project 749 110
Project 922 156
Project 949 147, 151
Project 1010 69

Radio Corporation of America (RCA) 115, 116, 121, 191
Reagan, President Ronald 166
Redstone Arsenal 23, 42
Redstone (missile) 24-30, 41
Resolution (of camera systems) 66-67
Rockwell International 170, 186, 192, 194, 229, 241
RPV (remotely piloted vehicle) 234
Rudakov, Leonid I. 209, 212

S-1 System 226
Sadat, President Anwar 100, 101, 102, 103
Sakharov, Andrei 208, 209
SALT (Strategic Arms Limitation Talks) 75, 76, 78-88, 93, 94, 95, 96, 143, 161, 166, 171, 213, 245, 248, 250
Salyut (space station) 88-92, 98, 159, 167, 234
Samos (program) 48-53, 58, 59, 67, 144
Sapwood (*see* SS-6) 39, 136
Satellite Data System (SDS) 135, 200
Satellite flight, principles of 33-39
Saturn (rocket) 42, 43
Sary Shagan 87, 208
Schmidt (telescope) 150, 228
Schriever, General Bernard A. 64, 175
Scout (rocket) 116, 173, 192
Semipalatinsk 208-214
Ship Inertial Navigation System (SINS) 190
Sipapu, (*see also* White Horse) 216, 217, 218
Skylab (space station) 64, 184, 234
Skynet (satellite) 134-136

Soviet Navy, expansion of the 108-110, 157
Soyuz (spacecraft) 88, 89-93, 99, 159, 214
Space and Missile Systems Organization
   (SAMSO) 183
Space Division, Rockwell International 241
Spaceship (Moon landing) 29
Space Shuttle 29, 107, 132, 164, 183-189,
   191-200, 217, 219, 220-231, 235-243,
   249
Space station (proposed by von Braun) 28,
   42
Spinning Solid Upper Stage (SSUS) 193
Sprint (missile) 87, 248
Sputnik 1 31, 32, 41, 42, 91, 92, 103, 145
Sputnik 2 41
Sputnik 3 41
Sputnik 4 41
SRAM (Short Range Attack Missile) 173
SS-5 Skean (rocket) 160, 166
SS-6 Sapwood (rocket) 41, 45, 47, 136
SS-7 (rocket) 79
SS-9 (missile) 113, 143, 157, 166, 244
SS-10 Scrag (missile) 142
SS-16 (rocket) 80, 81
SS-17 (rocket) 81, 82
SS-18 (rocket) 81, 82, 98, 113, 245
SS-19 (rocket) 81, 82, 83
SS-20 (rocket) 81, 93
SS-N-8 (missile) 111
SS-N-12 (missile) 215
Stafford, Thomas P. 256
Standing Consultative Commission 84, 96
State Department, US 83, 87
Stationary orbit, concept of 39, 126,
   128-137, 145, 149-152, 174, 175, 180,
   181, 188, 192-197, 199, 222, 229,
   233-237, 243, 246
Statsionar (satellite) 137
Strategic Air Command (SAC) 72, 117,
   119, 135
Strategic Rocket forces 81, 88
Submarine Launched Ballistic Missile
   (SLBM) 57, 72, 73, 78, 108, 111, 149,
   152, 181, 220, 243
Sun-synchronous orbit 67, 116, 119, 187

Talon Gold (program) 248
Teal Ruby (project) 229-231
Thor (missile) 24, 32, 33, 40, 42, 59, 61,
   116, 156
Thor-Agena (launcher) 33, 41, 49, 53, 63,
   66, 68
Tiros (satellite) 115, 122
Titan (missile) 24, 30, 40, 41, 60, 63, 78,
   146, 181, 183, 243, 244
Titan 3C 63, 64, 133, 147, 148, 151, 199
Titan 3C-Transtage 126, 133
Titan 3D 64, 66, 70, 77
Transit 190-192
Trident (missile) 181, 195, 233, 243, 248
TRW 69, 127, 132, 147-149, 179, 181
Tyuratam 46, 61, 96, 97, 99, 123, 143,
   160, 165

United Nations 21, 58, 102, 140
Univac computer 117, 118
U-2 (spy-plane) 45, 46, 76, 97, 98

V-2 (rocket) 21, 25, 26, 30, 173
Vance, Cyrus 20, 98, 165
Vandenberg Air Force Base 48, 53, 54,
   66, 69, 111, 116, 121, 187, 189, 222, 248
Vanguard (rocket) 30, 40
Vela (satellite) 148-150
Voskhod (spacecraft) 89, 91
Vostok (spacecraft) 47, 58, 59, 61, 66, 88,
   89, 91, 99
Vought Corporation 156, 172, 173, 174,
   179, 181, 246

Weapon System 117L 32, 47, 144, 146
Western Development Division 24, 182
White Cloud (surveillance system) 111, 114
White Horse 221, 224

X-1 (project) 30
X-2 (project) 30
X-15 (project) 30, 32, 44

Zond (program) 91, 92
Zumwalt, Admiral Elmo R. 82, 87, 88